P9-DNB-353

***Irrational Exuberance***

# *Irrational Exuberance*

**Robert J. Shiller**



*Princeton University Press*
*Princeton, New Jersey*

Published by Princeton University Press, 41 William Street, Princeton, New Jersey 08540
In the United Kingdom: Princeton University Press, Chichester, West Sussex



*Library of Congress Cataloging-in-Publication Data*
Shiller, Robert J.
Irrational exuberance / Robert J. Shiller.
p. cm.
Includes bibliographical references and index.
ISBN 0-691-05062-7 (cloth : alk. paper)
1. Stocks—United States. 2. Stock exchanges—United States. 3. Stocks—Prices—United States. 4. Risk. 5. Dow Jones industrial average. I. Title.
HG4910.S457 2000
332.63'222'0973—dc21 99-088869

This book has been composed in Adobe Palatino and Berkeley Old Style Book and Black by Princeton Editorial Associates, Inc., Scottsdale, Arizona, and Roosevelt, New Jersey

The paper used in this publication meets the requirements of ANSI/NISO Z39.48-1992 (R1997) (*Permanence of Paper*)

http://pup.princeton.edu

Printed in the United States of America

10 9 8 7 6 5 4 3

*To Ben and Derek*

# *Contents*

# *Figures and Tables*

## *Figures*



## *Tables*

# *Preface*

This book is a broad study, drawing on a wide range of published research and historical evidence, of the enormous recent stock market boom. Although it takes as its specific starting point the current situation, it places that situation in the context of stock market booms generally, and it also makes concrete suggestions regarding policy changes that should be initiated in response to this and other booms.

The need for such a book is particularly urgent today, in view of the widespread and quite fundamental disagreement about the stock market. When people disagree at such a basic level, it is usually because they possess only pieces of the overall picture. Yet meaningful consensus can only be achieved by laying out all the available facts. I have therefore tried in this book to present a much broader range of information than is usually considered in writings on the market, and I have tried to synthesize this information into a detailed picture of the market today.

Why did the U.S. stock market reach such high levels by the turn of the millennium? What changed to cause the market to become so highly priced? What do these changes mean for the market outlook in the opening decades of the new millennium? Are powerful fundamental factors at work to keep the market as high as it is now or to push it even higher, even if there is a downward correction? Or is the market high only because of some *irrational exuberance*—wishful thinking on the part of investors that blinds us to the truth of our situation?

The answers to these questions are critically important to private and public interests alike. How we value the stock market now and in the future influences major economic and social policy decisions that affect not only investors but also society at large, even the world. If we exaggerate the present and future value of the stock market, then as a society we may invest too much in business start-ups and expansions, and too little in infrastructure, education, and other forms of human capital. If we think the market is worth more than it really is, we may become complacent in funding our pension plans, in maintaining our savings rate, in legislating an improved Social Security system, and in providing other forms of social insurance. We might also lose the opportunity to use our expanding financial technology to devise new solutions to the genuine risks—to our homes, cities, and livelihoods—that we face.

To answer these questions about today's stock market, I harvest relevant information from diverse and, some would say, remote fields of inquiry. Insights from these fields too often go unnoticed by market analysts, but they have proved critical in defining similar market episodes throughout history, as well as in other markets around the world. These fields include economics, psychology, demography, sociology, and history. In addition to more conventional modes of financial analysis, they bring potent insights to bear on the issues at hand. Much of the evidence is drawn from the emerging field of behavioral finance, which, as the years go by, is looking less and less like a minor subfield of finance and more and more like a central pillar of serious finance theory.

I marshal the most important insights offered by researchers in these fields. Taken as a whole, they suggest that the present stock market displays the classic features of a *speculative bubble:* a situation in which temporarily high prices are sustained largely by investors' enthusiasm rather than by consistent estimation of real value. Under these conditions, even though the market could possibly maintain or even substantially increase its price level, the outlook for the stock market into the next ten or twenty years is likely to be rather poor—and perhaps even dangerous.

I do not purport to present a wholly new conception of financial market behavior. This book is a work neither of economic theory nor of econometrics, although it partakes in both. Rather, it is an attempt to characterize the complex nature of our real markets today, considering whether they conform or do not conform to our expectations and models. By assembling the most relevant evidence, economic and otherwise, on the state of the market, I hope to correct what I consider to be the perilous policy paths now being followed by legislators and economic leaders. I also hope to challenge financial thinkers to improve their theories by testing them against the impressive evidence that suggests that the price level is more than merely the sum of the available economic information, as is now generally thought to be the case.

Within the past generation the branch of financial theory that is derived from the assumption that all people are thoroughly rational and calculating has become the most influential analytical device to inform our mastery of the market. Those financial theorists who consider the market price to be a cunningly efficient processor of financial information have had a profound effect on the systematic management of the world's wealth, from the corner stockbroker right up to the Federal Reserve. But most of these scholars of finance and economics shrink from public statements about the level of the stock market (although they are often more loose-lipped in expressing their opinions at lunch and over beers) because they do not want to be caught saying things in public that they cannot prove. Assuming the mantle of scientific detachment, these financial economists tend to fall back on the simple but elegant model of market efficiency to justify their professional position.

However, there are serious risks inherent in relying too heavily on such pristine models as the basis for policy discussion, for these models deal only with problems that can be answered with scientific precision. If one tries too hard to be precise, one runs the risk of being so narrow as to be irrelevant. The evidence I present in the following chapters suggests that the reality of today's stock market is anything but test-tube clinical. If the theory of finance is to grow in its usefulness, all economists eventually will have to grapple with these messier aspects of market reality. Meanwhile, participants in public debate and economic policy formation must sort out this tangle of market factors now, before it is too late.

Among the unanticipated consequences of today's investment culture is that many of the tens of millions of adults now invested in the stock market act as if the price level is simply going to keep rising at its current rate. Even though the stock market appears based on some measures to be higher than it has ever been, investors behave as though it can never be too high, and that it can never go down for long. Why would they behave this way? Their logic is apparently consistent with the free-rider argument. That is, if millions of researchers and investors are studying stock prices and confirming their apparent value, why waste one's time in trying to figure out reasonable prices? One might as well take the free ride at the expense of these other diligent investors who have investigated stock prices and do what they're doing—buy stocks!

But unknown to most investors is the troubling lack of credibility in the quality of research being done on the stock market, to say nothing of the clarity and accuracy with which it is communicated to the public. Some of this so-called research often seems no more rigorous than the reading of tea leaves. Arguments that the Dow is going to 36,000 or 40,000 or 100,000 hardly inspire trust. Certainly *some* researchers are thinking more realistically about the market's prospects and reaching better-informed positions on its future, but these are not the names that grab the headlines and thus influence public attitudes.

Instead the headlines reflect the news media's constant attention to trivial factoids and "celebrity" opinion about the market's price level. Driven as their authors are by competition for readers, listeners, and viewers, media accounts tend to be superficial and thus to encourage basic misconceptions about the market. A conventional wisdom of sorts, stressing the seemingly eternal durability of stocks, has emerged from these media accounts. The public has learned to accept this conventional—but in my view shallow—wisdom. To be fair to the Wall Street professionals whose views appear in the media, it is difficult for them to correct the conventional wisdom because they are limited by the blurbs and sound bites afforded them. One would need to write books to straighten these things out. This is such a book.

As noted earlier, the conventional wisdom holds that the stock market as a whole has always been the best investment, and always will be, even when the market is overpriced by historical standards. Small investors, in their retirement funds, are increasingly shifting their investments toward stocks, and the investment policy of 100% stocks in retirement funds is increasingly popular. They put their money where their mantra is. This attitude invites exploitation by companies who have an unlimited supply of equities to sell. "You want stocks? We'll give you stocks."

Most investors also seem to view the stock market as a force of nature unto itself. They do not fully realize that they themselves, as a group, determine the level of the market. And they underestimate how similar to their own thinking is that of other investors. Many individual investors think that institutional investors dominate the market and that these "smart money" investors have sophisticated models to understand prices—superior knowledge. Little do they know that most institutional investors are, by and large, equally clueless about the level of the market. In short, the price level is driven to a certain extent by a self-fulfilling prophecy based on similar hunches held by a vast cross section of large and small investors and reinforced by news media that are often content to ratify this investor-induced conventional wisdom.

When the Dow Jones Industrial Average first surpassed 10,000 in March 1999, Merrill Lynch took out a full-page newspaper ad with a headline saying, "Even those with a disciplined long-term approach like ours have to sit back and say 'wow.'" In the bottom left corner of the page, next to a stock plot ending up at 10,000, appeared the words "HUMAN ACHIEVEMENT." If this is an achievement worth congratulating, then we should congratulate employees whenever they submit glowing self-evaluation reports.

At present there is a whiff of extravagant expectation, if not irrational exuberance, in the air. People are optimistic about the stock market. There is a lack of sobriety about its downside and the consequences that would ensue as a result. If the Dow were to drop to 6,000, the loss would represent something like the equivalent value of the entire housing stock of the United States. There would be harmful and uneven effects on individuals, pension funds, college endowments, and charitable organizations.

We need to know if the price level of the stock market today, tomorrow, or on any other day is a sensible reflection of economic reality, just as we need to know as individuals what we have in our bank accounts. This valuation is the future food on our tables and clothes on our backs, and nearly every decision to spend money today ought to be influenced by it. We need a better understanding of the forces that shape the long-run outlook for the market—and it is such an understanding that this book is intended to provide.

### *Outline of This Book*

After an introductory chapter placing the current stock market into historical context, Part I discusses precipitating events: factors outside the stock market, such as technology and demography, that nevertheless shape the market's behavior. It also covers amplifying mechanisms that cause these precipitating factors to have such an outsized effect on the market. These mechanisms can reinforce confidence in the market despite its already high price by creating situations in which price changes cause further price changes, thus beginning the speculative bubble.

Part II introduces cultural factors that further reinforce the structure of the speculative bubble. These factors include accounts of the economy that contend that it has moved into a "new era" that makes it impervious to downside forces, accounts that are amplified by the news media. Examples of similar "new era" thinking at each of the previous market peaks in the twentieth century are recounted, as are numerous examples from other countries.

Part III discusses the evidence we have collected about the psychological anchors and herd behavior that further define the speculative bubble.

Part IV investigates attempts on the part of academic and popular thinkers to rationalize the recent market levels through, for example, the efficient markets theory and the "learning" of certain "facts" about the behavior of the market.

Part V analyzes the implications of the current speculative bubble for individual investors, institutions, and governments. Several prescriptions for urgently needed policy changes are offered, as are suggestions for ways in which individual investors can lower their exposure to the consequences of a "burst" bubble.

# *Acknowledgments*

Jeremy Siegel, while clearly not agreeing with me on all points, urged me to set down my ideas in this book. He is its real instigator. Jeremy has been a lifelong friend. Our families regularly vacation together, and I learned a distinctive approach to finance from him while strolling the beach together or watching our children fish.

John Campbell, my former student, then co-author on a dozen scholarly papers on financial markets, and for years a close friend, has been my intellectual other half in formulating many of the ideas that led to this book. My original work on volatility in financial markets was refined and significantly advanced with his collaboration. He has also offered many helpful suggestions for this book and comments on the manuscript.

Peter Dougherty, my editor at Princeton University Press, has been an extremely important formative influence on the book, helping to define the fundamental aspects of its structure. He has been a great colleague and more—really almost a collaborator. Peter Strupp of Princeton Editorial Associates was an unusually helpful copy editor.

I was fortunate to have several excellent research assistants to help me during the writing. Peter Fabrizio unearthed the truth about many of the historical events discussed. Yuanfeng Hou performed careful data analysis. Luis Mancilla was a skillful fact finder. Steven Pawliczek was the source of many important ideas.

I am also blessed with a number of friends and colleagues who read drafts of the manuscript and provided extensive comments: Stefano Athanasoulis, John Geanakoplos, William Konigsberg, Stephen Morris, Sharon Oster, Jay Ritter, Martin Shubik, and James Tobin.

My colleagues at the Cowles Foundation for Research in Economics at Yale University—Donald Brown, Stefan Krieger, and William Nordhaus—have been a great help. I must also take this occasion to express gratitude to our late founder, Alfred Cowles III, an investment manager in the early part of this century and patron of mathematical economics, who tabulated the pre-1926 dividend and earnings data used in this book.

Help from my colleagues at the new Yale International Center for Finance—its director, William Goetzmann, as well as Zhiwu Chen, Roger Ibbotson, Ivo Welch, and Jeffrey Wurgler—is also acknowledged. Roger, who is currently giving talks entitled "Dow 100,000" and predicting a brilliant future for the stock market, has been a willing foil for my ideas.

Support from my colleagues at Case Shiller Weiss, Inc.—its president, Allan Weiss, as well as Karl Case, Neel Krishnaswami, and Terry Loebs—is much appreciated. As a team, they are attempting to put into practice some of the improvements to our society's risk management institutions that I describe at the end of this book.

I am grateful to the Russell Sage Foundation for sponsoring the behavioral finance workshops that Richard Thaler and I have been organizing for the past ten years at the National Bureau of Economic Research. The term *behavioral finance* refers to research on financial markets that takes into account the details of human behavior, including human psychology and sociology. This book benefits immeasurably from the work of the many scholars in the emerging field of behavioral finance, which is now beginning to take a solid place in university finance departments.

The U.S. National Science Foundation has supported much of my basic research on financial markets. Their continuing support of my work for over twenty years now has enabled me to focus attention on issues independent of financial pressures.

I am also grateful to Brad Barber, Scott Boorman, David Colander, Ray Fair, Peter Garber, Jeffrey Garten, Trevor Greetham, Stefan Krieger, Ricky Lam, Benoit Mercereau, Stephen Morris, William Nordhaus, John Rey, Colin Robertson, and Mark Warshawsky for helpful discussions, and to my assistant Carol Copeland and typist Glena Ames for much help. Yoshiro Tsutsui of Osaka University and Fumiko Kon-Ya of the Japanese Securities Research Institute have collaborated with me for the last dozen years on questionnaire survey research exploring investor attitudes in Japan as well as the United States. Help from Josephine Rinaldi and Walt Smietana at CompuMail has been much appreciated. I should certainly also thank the numerous investors who have taken the time to fill out questionnaires for me.

To my wife, Virginia Shiller, who is a clinical psychologist, I owe fundamental gratitude for getting me really interested in psychology and convincing me of its importance in economics. She has given the most careful reading and criticism to the entire book and has helped me greatly in articulating my ideas. She also kept the home fires burning while I spent long days and nights working.

# *Irrational Exuberance*

# One

# *The Stock Market Level in Historical Perspective*

When Alan Greenspan, chairman of the Federal Reserve Board in Washington, used the term *irrational exuberance* to describe the behavior of stock market investors in an otherwise staid speech on December 5, 1996, the world fixated on those words. Stock markets dropped precipitously. In Japan, the Nikkei index dropped 3.2%; in Hong Kong, the Hang Seng dropped 2.9%; and in Germany, the DAX dropped 4%. In London, the FT-SE 100 index was down 4% at one point during the day, and in the United States, the Dow Jones Industrial Average was down 2.3% near the beginning of trading. The words *irrational exuberance* quickly became Greenspan's most famous quote—a catch phrase for everyone who follows the market.

Why did the world react so strongly to these words? One view is that they were considered simply as evidence that the Federal Reserve would soon tighten monetary policy, and the world was merely reacting to revised forecasts of the Board's likely actions. But that cannot explain why the public still remembers *irrational exuberance* so well years later. I believe that the reaction to these words reflects the public's concern that the markets may indeed have been bid up to unusually high and unsustainable levels under the influence of market psychology. Greenspan's words suggest the possibility that the stock market will drop—or at least become a less promising investment.

History certainly gives credence to this concern. In the balance of this chapter, we study the historical record. Although the discussion in this chapter gets pretty detailed, I urge you to follow its thread, for the details place today's situation in a useful, and quite revealing, context.

### *Market Heights*

By historical standards, the U.S. stock market has soared to extremely high levels in recent years. These results have created a sense among the investing public that such high valuations, and even higher ones, will be maintained in the foreseeable future. Yet if the history of high market valuations is any guide, the public may be very disappointed with the performance of the stock market in coming years.

An unprecedented increase just before the start of the new millennium has brought the market to this great height. The Dow Jones Industrial Average (from here on, the Dow for short) stood at around 3,600 in early 1994. By 1999, it had passed 11,000, more than tripling in five years, a total increase in stock market prices of over 200%. At the start of 2000, the Dow passed 11,700.

However, over the same period, basic economic indicators did not come close to tripling. U.S. personal income and gross domestic product rose less than 30%, and almost half of this increase was due to inflation. Corporate profits rose less than 60%, and that from a temporary recession-depressed base. Viewed in the light of these figures, the stock price increase appears unwarranted and, certainly by historical standards, unlikely to persist.

Large stock price increases have occurred in many other countries at the same time. In Europe, between 1994 and 1999 the stock market valuations of France, Germany, Italy, Spain, and the United Kingdom roughly doubled. The stock market valuations of Canada, too, just about doubled, and those of Australia increased by half.

In the course of 1999, stock markets in Asia (Hong Kong, Indonesia, Japan, Malaysia, Singapore, and South Korea) and Latin America (Brazil, Chile, and Mexico) have made spectacular gains. But no other country of comparable size has had so large an increase since 1994 as that seen in the United States.

Price increases in single-family homes have also occurred over the same time, but significant increases have occurred in only a few cities. Between 1994 and 1999 the total average real price increase of homes in ten major U.S. cities was only 9%. These price increases are tiny relative to the increase in the U.S. stock market.[1]

The extraordinary recent levels of U.S. stock prices, and associated expectations that these levels will be sustained or surpassed in the near future, present some important questions. We need to know whether the current period of high stock market pricing is like the other historical periods of high pricing, that is, whether it will be followed by poor or negative performance in coming years. We need to know confidently whether the increase that brought us here is indeed a *speculative bubble*—an unsustainable increase in prices brought on by investors' buying behavior rather than by genuine, fundamental information about value. In short, we need to know if the value investors have imputed to the market is not really there, so that we can readjust our planning and thinking.

### *A Look at the Data*

Figure 1.1 shows, for the United States, the monthly real (corrected for inflation using the Consumer Price Index) Standard and Poor's (S&P) Composite Stock Price Index from January 1871 through January 2000 (upper curve), along with the corresponding series of real S&P Composite earnings (lower curve) for the same years.[2] This figure allows us to get a truly long-term perspective on the U.S. stock market's recent levels. We can see how differently the market has behaved recently as compared with the past. We see that the market has been heading up fairly uniformly ever since it bottomed out in July 1982. It is clearly the most dramatic bull market in U.S. history. The spiking of prices in the years 1992 through 2000 has been most remarkable: the price index looks like a rocket

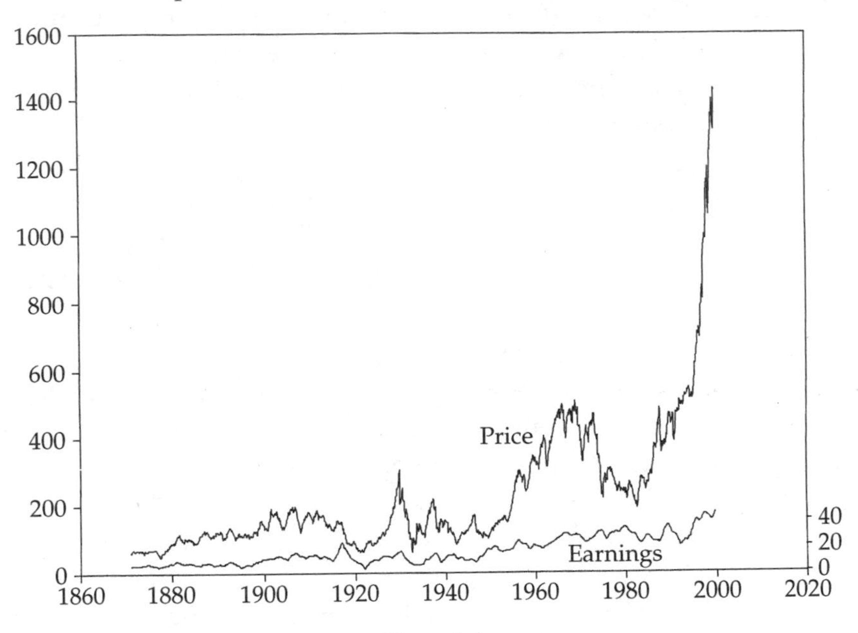


*Figure 1.1*

***Stock Prices and Earnings, 1871–2000***

Real (inflation-corrected) S&P Composite Stock Price Index, monthly, January 1871 through January 2000 (upper series), and real S&P Composite earnings (lower series), January 1871 to September 1999. *Source:* Author's calculations using data from S&P Statistical Service; U.S. Bureau of Labor Statistics; Cowles and associates, *Common Stock Indexes;* and Warren and Pearson, *Gold and Prices.* See also note 2.

taking off through the top of the chart! This largest stock market boom ever may be referred to as the *millennium boom.*[3]

Yet this dramatic increase in prices since 1982 is not matched in real earnings growth. Looking at the figure, no such spike in earnings growth occurs in recent years. Earnings in fact seem to be oscillating around a slow, steady growth path that has persisted for over a century.

No price action quite like this has ever happened before in U.S. stock market history. There was of course the famous stock run-up of the 1920s, culminating in the 1929 crash. Figure 1.1 reveals this boom as a cusp-shaped price pattern for those years. If one corrects for the market's smaller scale then, one recognizes that this episode in the 1920s does resemble somewhat the recent stock market increase, but it is the only historical episode that comes even close to being comparable to the present boom.

There was also a dramatic run-up in the late 1950s and early 1960s, culminating in a flat period for half a decade that was followed by the 1973–74 stock market debacle. But the price increase during this boom was certainly less dramatic than today's.

### *Price Relative to Earnings*

Part of the explanation for the remarkable price behavior between 1990 and 2000 may have to do with somewhat unusual earnings. Many observers have remarked that earnings growth in the five-year period ending in 1997 was extraordinary: real S&P Composite earnings more than doubled over this interval, and such a rapid five-year growth of real earnings has not occurred for nearly half a century. But 1992 marked the end of a recession during which earnings were temporarily depressed. Similar increases in earnings growth have happened before following periods of depressed earnings from recession or depression. In fact, there was more than a quadrupling of real earnings from 1921 to 1926 as the economy emerged from the severe recession of 1921 into the prosperous Roaring Twenties. Real earnings doubled during five-year periods following the depression of the 1890s, the Great Depression of the 1930s, and World War II.

Figure 1.2 shows the price-earnings ratio, that is, the real (inflation-corrected) S&P Composite Index divided by the ten-year moving average real earnings on the index. The dates shown are monthly, January 1881 to January 2000. The price-earnings ratio is a measure of how expensive the market is relative to an objective measure of the ability of corporations to earn profits. I use the ten-year average of real earnings for the denominator, along lines proposed by Benjamin Graham and David Dodd in 1934. The ten-year average smooths out such events as the temporary burst of earnings during World War I, the temporary decline in earnings during World War II, or the frequent boosts and declines that we see due to the business cycle.[4] Note again that there is an enormous spike after

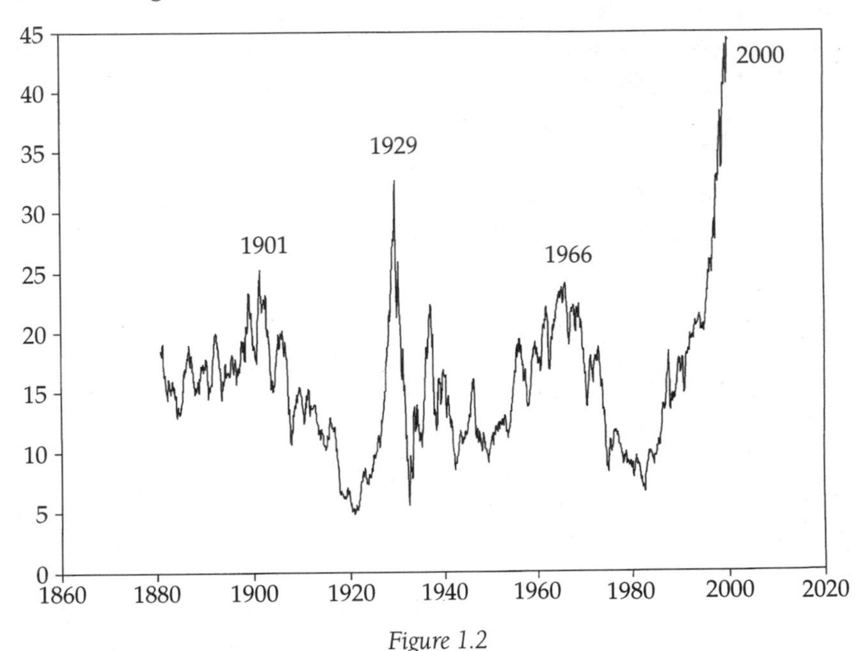


*Figure 1.2*
***Price-Earnings Ratio, 1881–2000***

Price-earnings ratio, monthly, January 1881 to January 2000. Numerator: real (inflation-corrected) S&P Composite Stock Price Index, January. Denominator: moving average over preceding ten years of real S&P Composite earnings. Years of peaks are indicated. *Source:* Author's calculations using data from sources given in Figure 1.1. See also note 2.

1997, when the ratio rises until it hits 44.3 by January 2000. Price-earnings ratios by this measure have never been so high. The closest parallel is September 1929, when the ratio hit 32.6.

In the latest data on earnings, earnings are quite high in comparison with the Graham and Dodd measure of long-run earnings, but nothing here is startlingly out of the ordinary. What is extraordinary today is the behavior of price (as also seen in Figure 1.1), not earnings.

### *Other Periods of High Price Relative to Earnings*

There have been three other times when the price-earnings ratio as shown in Figure 1.2 attained high values, though never as high as the 2000 value. The first time was in June 1901, when the price-earnings ratio reached a high of 25.2 (see Figure 1.2). This might be called the "Twentieth Century Peak," since it came around the time of the celebration of this century. (The advent of the twentieth century was celebrated on January 1, 1901, not January 1, 1900.)[5] This peak occurred as the aftermath of a doubling of real earnings within five years, following the U.S. economy's emergence from the depression of the 1890s.[6] The 1901 peak in the price-earnings ratio occurred after a sudden spike in the price-earnings ratio, which took place between July 1900 and June 1901, an increase of 43% within eleven months. A turn-of-the-century optimism, associated with expansion talk about a prosperous and high-tech future, appeared.

After 1901, there was no pronounced immediate downtrend in real prices, but for the next decade prices bounced around or just below the 1901 level and then fell. By June 1920, the stock market had lost 67% of its June 1901 real value. The average real return in the stock market (including dividends) was 3.4% a year in the five years following June 1901, barely above the real interest rate. The average real return (including dividends) was 4.4% a year in the ten years following June 1901, 3.1% a year in the fifteen years following June 1901, and –0.2% a year in the twenty years following June 1901.[7] These are lower returns than we generally expect from the stock market, though had one held on into the 1920s, returns would have improved dramatically.

The second instance of a high price-earnings ratio occurred in September 1929, the high point of the market in the 1920s and the second-highest ratio of all time. After the spectacular bull market of the 1920s, the ratio attained a value of 32.6. As we all know, the market tumbled from this high, with a real drop in the S&P Index of 80.6% by June 1932. The decline in real value was profound and long-lasting. The real S&P Composite Index did not return to its September 1929 value until December 1958. The average real return in the stock market (including dividends) was –13.1% a year for the five years following September 1929, –1.4% a year for the next ten years, –0.5% a year for the next fifteen years, and 0.4% a year for the next twenty years.[8]

The third instance of a high price-earnings ratio occurred in January 1966, when the price-earnings ratio as shown in Figure 1.2 reached a local maximum of 24.1. We might call this the "Kennedy-Johnson Peak," drawing as it did on the prestige and charisma of President John Kennedy and the help of his vice-president and successor Lyndon Johnson. This peak came after a dramatic bull market and after a five-year price surge, from May 1960, of 46%. This surge, which took the price-earnings ratio to its local maximum, corresponded to a surge in earnings of 53%. The market reacted to this earnings growth as if it expected the growth to continue, but of course it did not. Real earnings increased little in the next decade. Real prices bounced around near their January 1966 peak, surpassing it somewhat in 1968 but then falling back, and real stock prices were down 56% from their January 1966 value by December 1974. Real stock prices would not be back up to the January 1966 level until May 1992. The average real return in the stock market (including dividends) was –2.6% a year for the five years following January 1966, –1.8% a year for the next ten years, –0.5% a year for the next fifteen years, and 1.9% a year for the next twenty years.

### *A Historical Relation between Price-Earnings Ratios and Subsequent Long-Term Returns*

Figure 1.3 is a scatter diagram showing, for January of each year 1881 to 1989, on the horizontal axis, the price-earnings ratio for that month, and, on the vertical axis, the annualized real (inflation-corrected) stock market return over the ten years following that month. This scatter diagram allows us to see visually how well the price-earnings ratio forecasts subsequent long-term (ten-year) returns. Only January data are shown: if all twelve months of each year were shown there would be so many points that the scatter would be unreadable. The downside of this plotting method, of course, is that by showing only January data we miss most of the peaks and troughs of the market. For example, we miss the peak of the market in 1929 and also miss the negative returns that followed it. The price-earnings ratio shown in Figure 1.3 is the same as that plotted in Figure 1.2. Each year is indicated by the last two

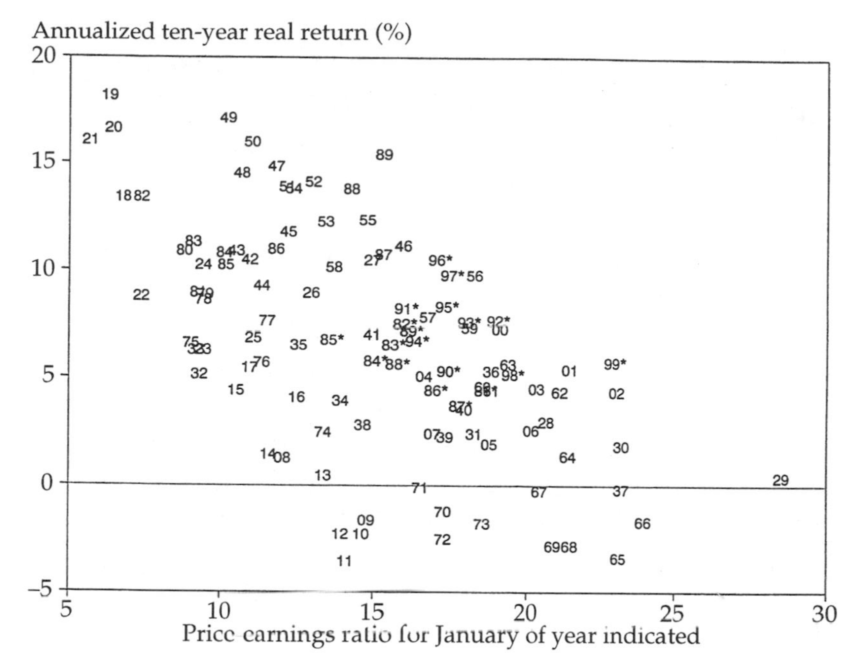


*Figure 1.3*

***Price-Earnings Ratio as Predictor of Ten-Year Returns***

Scatter diagram of annualized ten-year returns against price-earnings ratios. Horizontal axis shows the price-earnings ratio (as plotted in Figure 1.2) for January of the year indicated, dropping the 19 from twentieth-century years and dropping the 18 from nineteenth-century years and adding an asterisk (*). Vertical axis shows the geometric average real annual return per year on investing in the S&P Composite Index in January of the year shown, reinvesting dividends, and selling ten years later. *Source:* Author's calculations using data from sources given in Figure 1.1. See also note 2.

digits of the year number; years from the nineteenth century are indicated by an asterisk (*).

Figure 1.3 shows how the price-earnings ratio has forecast returns, since each price-earnings ratio shown on the horizontal axis was known at the beginning of the ten-year period. This scatter diagram was developed by fellow economist John Campbell and me. Plots like it, for various countries, were the centerpiece of our testimony before the board of governors of the Federal Reserve on December 3, 1996.[9]

The swarm of points in the scatter shows a definite tilt, sloping down from the upper left to the lower right. The scatter shows that in some years near the left of the scatter (such as January 1920, January 1949, or January 1982) subsequent long-term returns have been very high. In some years near the right of the scatter (such as January 1929, January 1937, or January 1966) subsequent returns have been very low. There are also some important exceptions, such as January 1899, which still managed to have subsequent ten-year returns as high as 5.5% a year despite a high price-earnings ratio of 22.9, and January 1922, which managed to have subsequent ten-year returns of only 8.7% a year despite a low price-earnings ratio of 7.4. But the point of this scatter diagram is that, as a rule and on average, years with low price-earnings ratios have been followed by high returns, and years with high price-earnings ratios have been followed by low or negative returns.

The relation between price-earnings ratios and subsequent returns appears to be moderately strong, though there are questions about its statistical significance, since there are only about twelve nonoverlapping ten-year intervals in the 119 years' worth of data. There has been substantial academic debate about the statistical significance of relationships like this one, and some difficult questions of statistical methodology are still being addressed. We believe, however, that the relation should be regarded as statistically significant.[10] Our confidence in the relation derives partly from the fact that analogous relations appear to hold for other countries and for individual stocks. Figure 1.3 confirms that long-term investors—investors who can commit their money to an investment for ten full years—do well when prices were low relative to earnings at the beginning of the ten years and do poorly when prices were high at the beginning of the ten years. Long-term investors would be well advised, individually, to stay mostly out of the market when it is high, as it is today, and get into the market when it is low.[11]

The recent values of the price-earnings ratio, well over 40, are far outside the historical range of price-earnings ratios. If one were to locate such a price-earnings ratio on the horizontal axis, it would be off the chart altogether. It is a matter of judgment to say, from the data shown in Figure 1.3, what predicted return the relationship suggests over the succeeding ten years; the answer depends on whether one fits a straight line or a curve to the scatter, and since the 2000 price-earnings ratio is outside the historical range, the shape of the curve can matter a lot. Suffice it to say that the diagram suggests substantially negative returns, on average, for the next ten years.

Part of the reason to suspect that the relation shown in Figure 1.3 is real is that, historically, when price was high relative to earnings as computed here (using a ten-year moving average of earnings), the return in terms of dividends has been low, and when price was low relative to earnings, the return in terms of dividends has been high.[12] The recent record-high price-earnings ratios have been matched by record-low dividend yields. In January 2000, S&P dividends were 1.2% of price, far below the 4.7% that is the historical average. It is natural to suppose that when one is getting so much lower dividends from the shares one owns, one ought to expect to earn lower investing returns overall. The dividend is, after all, part of the total return one gets from holding stocks (the other part being the capital gain), and dividends historically represent the dominant part of the average return on stocks. The reliable return attributable to dividends, not the less predictable portion arising from capital gains, is the main reason why stocks have on average been such good investments historically.

Returns from holding stocks must therefore be low when dividends are low—unless low dividends themselves are somehow predictors of stock market price increases, so that one can at times of low dividends actually expect stock price to rise more than usual to offset the effects of the low dividends on returns. As a matter of historical fact, times when dividends have been low relative to stock prices have *not* tended to be followed by higher stock price increases in the subsequent five or ten years. Quite to the contrary: times of low dividends relative to stock price in the stock market as a whole tend to be followed by price *decreases* (or smaller than usual increases) over long horizons, and so returns tend to take a *double* hit at such times, from both low dividend yields and price decreases. Thus the simple wisdom—that when one is not getting much in dividends relative to the price one pays for stocks it is not a good time to buy stocks—turns out to have been right historically.

### *Worries about Irrational Exuberance*

The news media have tired of describing the high levels of the market, and discussion of it is usually omitted from considerations of market outlook. And yet, deep down, people know that the market is highly priced, and they are uncomfortable about this fact.

Most people I meet, from all walks of life, are puzzled over the apparently high levels of the stock market. We are unsure whether the market levels make any sense, or whether they are indeed the result of some human tendency that might be called irrational exuberance. We are unsure whether the high levels of the stock market might reflect unjustified optimism, an optimism that might pervade our thinking and affect many of our life decisions. We are unsure what to make of any sudden market correction, wondering if the previous market psychology will return.

Even Alan Greenspan seems unsure. He made his "irrational exuberance" speech two days after I had testified before him and the Federal Reserve Board that market levels were irrational, but a mere seven months later he reportedly took an optimistic "new era" position on the economy and the stock market. In fact, Greenspan has always been very cautious in his public statements, and he has not committed himself to either view. A modern version of the prophets who spoke in riddles, Greenspan likes to pose questions rather than make pronouncements. In the public exegesis of his remarks, it is often forgotten that, when it comes to such questions, even he does not know the answers.

*Part One*

# ***Structural Factors***

## *Two*

# *Precipitating Factors: The Internet, the Baby Boom, and Other Events*

If the growth of the economy does not in itself justify the increase in the value of the stock market since 1982, then what has changed since 1982 to cause the market to climb? What precipitating factors started this remarkable surge? What, in particular, has happened since July 1997, when the price-earnings ratio passed above its former record high, set in September 1929, and then proceeded to move up by yet another third by the start of 2000? To answer these questions, it is not enough to say that the markets in general are vulnerable to *irrational exuberance*. We must specify what has changed to cause the market to behave so differently from other times.

Most historical events, from wars through revolutions, do not have simple causes. When these events move in extreme directions, as price-earnings ratios have in the recent stock market, it is usually because of a confluence of factors, none of which is by itself large enough to explain these events.

Rome wasn't built in a day, nor was it destroyed by one sudden bolt of bad fortune. More likely, it owed its fall to a plurality of factors—some large and some small, some remote and some immediate—that conspired together. This ambiguity is unsatisfying to those of us seeking scientific certitude, especially given that it is so hard to identify and isolate the precipitating factors to begin with. But that is the nature of history, and such ambiguity justifies the constant search for new and better information to expose at least the overall contours of causation.

Recognizing these limitations, let us look at a list of factors—twelve of them—that may help explain the present speculative market. These factors make up the *skin* of the bubble, if you will. I concentrate here mostly on *factors that have had an effect on the market that is not warranted by rational analysis of economic fundamentals.* The list omits consideration of all the small variations in fundamental factors (e.g., the growth in earnings, the change in real interest rates) that *should* rationally have an impact on financial markets. In more normal times or in markets for individual stocks, such rational factors would assume relatively greater prominence in any discussion of changes in prices. Indeed it is thanks to a market's ability to respond appropriately to such factors, for a variety of investments, that well-functioning financial markets generally promote, rather than hinder, economic efficiency.[1] The list of factors here was constructed specifically to help us understand the extraordinary recent situation in the stock market, and so it concentrates on less rational influences.

In detailing these twelve factors, I describe the reaction of the general public, not just of professional investment managers. Some observers believe that professional investment managers are more sensible and work to offset the *irrational exuberance* of the nonprofessional investing public. Therefore these observers might argue that a sharp distinction should be drawn between the behavior of the professionals and the nonprofessionals.[2] Professional investors, however, are not immune from the effects of the popular investing culture that we observe in individual investors, and many of the factors described here no doubt influence their thinking as well. There is in fact no clear distinction between professional institutional investors and individual investors, since the professionals routinely give advice to the individual investors.

Some of these factors exist in the background of the market, including the revolution in information technology, a linking of patriotic feeling with supposed "victory" over foreign economic rivals, increased emphasis on business success, the political shift in support of business, the demographics of the Baby Boom, the decline of inflation and the economics of money illusion, and the rise of gambling and pleasure in risk taking in general. Others operate in the foreground and shape the changing culture of investment. These include greatly increased media coverage of business, the aggressively optimistic forecasts of stock analysts, the rise of 401(k) plans, the mutual funds explosion, and the expanding volume of trade.

Despite their varied origins, these twelve factors have something in common: they have contributed to the self-fulfilling psychology of a roaring stock market. It is this self-fulfilling psychology that—at least for now—binds the bubble.

### *The Arrival of the Internet at a Time of Solid Earnings Growth*

The Internet and the World Wide Web have invaded our homes during the second half of the 1990s, making us intimately conscious of the pace of technological change. The World Wide Web first appeared in the news in November 1993. The Mosaic Web browser first became available to the public in February 1994. These dates mark the very beginning of the World Wide Web, when only a few people had access to it. Large numbers of users did not discover the Web until 1997 and later, marking the very years when the NASDAQ stock price index (which is heavily weighted toward high-tech stocks) soared, tripling to the beginning of 2000, and price-earnings ratios took off into unprecedented territory.

Internet technology is unusual in that it is a source of entertainment and preoccupation for us all, indeed for the whole family. In this sense, it is comparable in importance to the personal computer or, before that, to television. In fact, the impression it conveys of a changed future is even more vivid than that produced when televisions or personal computers entered the home. Using the Internet gives people a sense of mastery of the world. They can electronically roam the world and accomplish tasks that would have been impossible before. They can even put up a Web site and become a factor in the world economy themselves in previously unimaginable ways. In contrast, the advent of television made them passive receivers of entertainment, and personal computers were used by most people before the Internet mainly as typewriters and high-tech pinball machines.

Because of the vivid and immediate personal impression the Internet makes, people find it plausible to assume that it also has great economic importance. It is much easier to imagine the consequences of advances in this technology than the consequences of, say, improved shipbuilding technology or new developments in materials science. Most of us simply do not hear much about research in those areas.

Spectacular U.S. corporate earnings growth in 1994, up 36% in real terms as measured by the S&P Composite real earnings, followed by real earnings growth of 8% in 1995 and 10% in 1996, coincided roughly with the Internet's birth but in fact had little to do with the Internet. Instead the earnings growth was attributed by analysts to a continuation of the slow recovery from the 1990–91 recession, coupled with a weak dollar and strong foreign demand for U.S. capital and technology exports, as well as cost-cutting initiatives by U.S. companies. It could not have been the Internet that caused the growth in profits: the fledgling Internet companies were not making much of a profit yet, and indeed they still are not. But the occurrence of profit growth coincident with the appearance of a new technology as dramatic as the Internet can easily create an impression among the general public that the two events are somehow connected. Publicity linking these twin factors was especially strong with the advent of the new millennium—a time of much optimistic discussion of the future.

The Internet is, of course, an important technological advance in its own right, and it, as well as other developments in computer technology and robotics, does promise to have an unpredictable and powerful impact on our future. But we may question what impact the Internet and the computer revolution should have on the valuation of existing corporations. New technology will always have an impact on the market, but should it really raise the value of existing companies, given that those existing companies do not have a monopoly on the new technology?[3] Should the advent of the Internet raise the valuation of the Dow Jones Industrial Average—which until very recently contained no Internet stocks?[4]

The notion that existing companies will benefit from the Internet revolution is belied by the stories of E*Trade.com, Amazon.com, and other upstarts, who did not even exist just a few years ago. Still more new companies will appear in the future, in the United States and abroad, and these will compete with the companies in which we invest today. Simply put, the effect of new technology on existing companies could go either way: it could boost or depress their profits.

What matters for a stock market boom is not, however, the reality of the Internet revolution, which is hard to discern, but rather the *public impressions* that the revolution creates. Public reaction is influenced by the intuitive plausibility of Internet lore, and this plausibility is ultimately influenced by the ease with which examples or arguments come to mind. If we are regularly spending time on the Internet, then these examples will come to mind very easily.

### *Triumphalism and the Decline of Foreign Economic Rivals*

Since the end of the cold war most other countries have seemed to be imitating the Western economic system. Communist China has been embracing market forces since the late 1970s. Increasing tolerance of free markets within the Soviet Union culminated with the breakup of that nation in 1991 into smaller, market-oriented states. The world seems to be swinging our way, and therefore it starts to seem only natural that confidence in the premier capitalist system would translate into confidence in the market, and that the U.S. stock market should be the most highly valued in the world.

These political events have unfolded gradually since the bull market began in 1982. The intervening years have also seen the decline in the Japanese market after 1989, the prolonged economic slump in Japan, and the Asian financial crisis of 1997–98, which coincided roughly with the dramatic burst of the U.S. stock market into uncharted territory at the end of the millennium. These foreign events might have been viewed as ominous developments for the U.S. stock market, as the harbinger of what bad things could happen here, but instead they were seen by many as the weakening of major rivals. The relation between the United States and its economic rivals is often described in the media as a competition in which there can only be one winner, as in a sports event. The weakening of a rival is thus viewed simplistically, as good news.

The triumphalism is associated with patriotic feeling. Of course, patriotic self-congratulation has long been in evidence in discussions of the stock market. In the 1990s Merrill Lynch used the slogan "We're Bullish on America." In the 1950s, the New York Stock Exchange used the slogan "Take Stock in America." Popular slogans during the bull market of the 1920s were "Be a Bull on America" and "Never Sell the United States Short." But while such patriotic associations have long been with us, the associations assume more prominence after a perceived economic victory. Extensive public discussion of perennial economic problems, which we may hear after the country feels humbled by failures, seems out of bounds after a triumph.

## *Cultural Changes Favoring Business Success or the Appearance Thereof*

The bull market has been accompanied by a significant rise in materialistic values. A Roper-Starch questionnaire survey in both 1975 and 1994 asked, "When you think of the good life—the life you'd like to have, which of the things on this list, if any, are part of that good life, as far as you personally are concerned?" In 1975, 38% picked "a lot of money," whereas in 1994 fully 63% did.[5]

Materialistic values do not by themselves have any logical bearing on the level of the stock market. Whether or not people are materialistic, it is still reasonable to expect them to save for the future and to seek out the best vehicles for their savings. But it is plausible that such feelings would influence their demand for stocks, which have long held out at least the possibility of amassing substantial and quick riches. Such feelings have transformed our culture into one that reveres the successful businessperson as much as or even more than the accomplished scientist, artist, or revolutionary. The idea that investing in stocks is a road to quick riches has a certain appeal to born-again materialists.

In the late 1980s and early 1990s, downsizing (the movement to release surplus staff and the consequent decline in job security) led to a change in the way people viewed their lives. The experience of being laid off, or at least of knowing others who had been, was often viewed as a violation of an implicit pact of loyalty between employee and employer. Such an experience encouraged workers to take control of their own lives and to rely less on employers, to become in effect economic entities unto themselves, rather than parts of a larger economic organization.

Labor unions have long been in decline: the fraction of wage and salary workers who were union members fell to 13.9% in 1998, down from 20.1% in 1983.[6] The reasons for the decline are controversial, but a key factor appears to be an erosion of solidarity and loyalty among workers, an attitude that has come to be replaced by an individual business-success ethic. By pursuing speculative investments, people in effect create for themselves a second job—one where they are, at last, their own boss. And in many cases it is a job that seems to provide a source of income—income derived from one's direct interaction with the world at large, not as part of an organization.

Firms have tilted their compensation packages for management away from fixed salaries toward participation, as investors, in the firm. By 1998, employee stock options had reached 6.2% of the outstanding shares in a sample of 144 of the largest S&P 500 firms.[7] With such options—which hold out the promise of substantial wealth if the stock price rises above the exercise price of the options—management has an incentive to do everything they can to boost share prices. They have an incentive to maintain an appearance of corporate success, an image of the company as working toward a brilliant future. They have an incentive to undertake corporate initiatives whenever they think the market will respond to them, even if they themselves are doubtful of the value of these initiatives. For example, managers the world over have of late been scratching their heads to figure out how they can redefine their firms as Internet companies because of the high market valuation such companies currently enjoy. This headlong rush to achieve dot-com status may lead them to undertake new and costly Internet-related investments with little concern for their long-run consequences.

Managers holding incentive options also have an unusual incentive to substitute share repurchases for a portion of the dividend payout, since the direct effect of such a substitution is to increase the value of the managers' options. Between 1994 and 1998, the 144 firms mentioned earlier repurchased on average 1.9% of their outstanding shares each year, more than offsetting the 0.9% of shares issued per year, largely to meet the exercise of employee options.[8] This level of substituting share repurchasing for dividends alone should have boosted share prices by a few percentage points.[9]

### *A Republican Congress and Capital Gains Tax Cuts*

When Ronald Reagan was elected in 1980, so too was a Republican Senate, the first since 1948. In 1994, the House went to the Republicans as well. Sensing the changed public attitudes that had elected them, these lawmakers were much more pro-business than their Democratic predecessors. This change in Congress has boosted public confidence in the stock market, because of a variety of controls that the legislature can exert over corporate profits and investor returns.

Consider taxation. No sooner had the Republican Congress been seated in 1995 than proposals to cut the capital gains tax became prominent. In 1997, the top capital gains tax rate was cut from 28% to 20%. After this cut had been enacted, Congress talked of cutting rates further. A 1999 tax bill would have cut capital gains taxes still further, had President Clinton not vetoed it.

Anticipation of possible future capital gains tax cuts can have a favorable impact on the stock market, even when tax rates actually remain unchanged. From 1994 to 1997, investors were widely advised to hold on to their long-term capital gains, not to realize them, until after the capital gains tax cut. This had a strengthening effect on the market. At the time of the 1997 capital gains tax cut, there was fear that investors who had been waiting to sell would do so and bring the market down, as had apparently happened after capital gains tax cuts in 1978 and 1980. But this did not happen in 1997. Of course, many investors must have thought there could be an even more favorable capital gains tax rate in their future, and if so there would have been no reason to sell right after the 1997 cut took effect.

It is likely that the general atmosphere of public talk of future capital gains tax cuts, of possible indexing of capital gains taxes to inflation, and of analogous tax cuts such as estate tax cuts has created among investors a reluctance to sell their appreciated stocks. If capital gains tax rates may be cut sharply in the future, why sell when the rates are as high as 20%? Having been advised by experts to wait and see about capital gains tax cuts, many investors could be expected to defer sales of appreciated assets until we are more clearly at a historic low in capital gains tax rates. Such an atmosphere of holding, not folding, naturally places upward pressure on stock prices.

### *The Baby Boom and Its Perceived Effects on the Market*

Following World War II, there was a substantial increase in the birth rate in the United States. Peacetime prosperity encouraged those who had postponed families because of the depression and the war to have children. There were also postwar birth rate increases in the United Kingdom, France, and Japan, but they were not as protracted or strong as that in the United States, no doubt at least in part because the economies of those nations were in such disarray after the war. Then, around 1966, the growth of U.S. and world population showed a dramatic decline, one that continues to this day. This decline was unusual, if not unique, by historical standards: it did not occur because of famine or war, but rather because of an endogenous decline in the fertility rate.[10]

Advances in birth control technology (the pill was invented in 1959 and became widely available by the mid-1960s in the United

States and many other countries) and social changes that accepted the legality of contraception and abortion were instrumental in lowering the rate of population growth, as were growing urbanization and advances in education and economic aspiration levels. Now the Baby Boom and the subsequent Baby Bust have created a looming social security crisis in many countries of the world: when the Boomers grow old and finally retire, the number of young working people available to support the elderly population will decline worldwide.[11]

The Baby Boom in the United States was marked by very high birth rates during the years 1946–66, and so there are in the year 2000 (and will be for some time) an unusually large number of people between the ages of 35 and 55. Two theories suggest that the presence of so many middle-aged people ought to boost today's stock market. One theory justifies the high price-earnings ratios we see today as the result of those Boomers' competing against each other to buy stocks to save for their eventual retirement and bidding share prices up relative to the earnings they generate. According to the other theory, it is spending on current goods and services that boosts stocks, through a generalized positive effect on the economy: high expenditures mean high profits for companies.

These simple Baby Boom stories are just a bit too simple. For one thing, they neglect to consider *when* the Baby Boom should affect the stock market. Maybe the effect of the Baby Boom has already been factored into stock prices by investors. They also neglect such factors as the emergence of new capitalist economies worldwide and their demand, in another twenty years, for U.S. stocks. The theory that the Baby Boom drives the market up owing to Boomers' demand for goods would seem to imply that the market is high because earnings are high; it would not explain today's high price-earnings ratios.

If life-cycle savings patterns (the first effect) alone were to be the dominant force in the markets for savings vehicles, there would tend to be strong correlations in price behavior across alternative asset classes, and strong correlations over time between asset prices and demographics. When the most numerous generation feels they need to save, they would tend to bid up *all* savings vehicles: stocks, bonds, and real estate. When the most numerous generation feels they need to draw down their savings, their selling would tend to force down the prices of *all* these vehicles. But when one looks at long-term data on stocks, bonds, and real estate, one finds that there has in fact been very little relation between their real values.[12] Possibly these differences across asset classes could still be reconciled with a Baby Boom theory, by postulating that people in different age groups have different attitudes toward risk because of age-related differences in risk tolerance, that the stock market is relatively high now because the numerous people in their forties today are naturally less risk averse than older people. But such a theory has never been carefully worked out or shown to explain relative price movements. It is also noteworthy that the personal savings rate in the United States has recently been nearly zero, not significantly positive, as the life-cycle theory might suggest. Of course, one might argue that were it not for the Baby Boom, the effect of the high stock market would have been to make savings, as measured, strongly negative, since the capital gains on stocks would be considered income not included in the national income, income that people could normally be expected to spend from.[13]

Another theory as to why Boomers may be less risk averse is that the Boomers, who have no memory of the Great Depression of the 1930s or of World War II, have less anxiety about the market and the world. There is indeed some evidence that shared experiences in formative years leave a mark forever on a generation's attitudes.[14] Over the course of the bull market since 1982, Boomers have gradually replaced as prime investors those who were teens or young adults during the depression and the war.

Although there is no doubt at least some truth to these theories of the Baby Boom's effects on the stock market, it may be public *perceptions* of the Baby Boom and its presumed effects that are most responsible for the surge in the market. The impact of the Baby Boom is one of the most talked-about issues relating to the stock market, and all this talk in and of itself has the potential to affect stock market value. People believe that the Baby Boom represents an important source of strength for the market today, and they do not see this strength faltering any time soon. These public perceptions contribute to a feeling that there is a good reason for the market to be high and a confidence that it will stay that way for some time to come. Congratulating themselves on their cleverness in understanding and betting on these population trends in their stock market investments, many investors fail to appreciate just how common their thinking really is. Their perceptions fuel the continuing upward spiral in market valuations.

The most prominent exponent of the Baby Boom theory of the stock market has been Harry S. Dent. He began with a 1992 book entitled *The Great Boom Ahead: Your Comprehensive Guide to Personal and Business Profit in the New Era of Prosperity,* which was so successful that he has written several sequels. His 1998 book, *The Roaring 2000s: Building the Wealth & Lifestyle You Desire in the Greatest Boom in History,* was on the *New York Times* best-seller list for four weeks in 1998. His 1999 book, *The Roaring 2000s Investor: Strategies for the Life You Want,* is as of this writing ranked within the top 100 in sales among all books according to Amazon.com. This book predicts that the stock market will continue to boom until 2009, when the number of people who are 46 starts to decline, and then the market will drop.

Dent's success with the Baby Boom theme has predictably spawned a number of imitators—all extolling the wonderful opportunities now to get rich in the stock market—with titles like *Boomernomics: The Future of Your Money in the Upcoming Generational Warfare* by William Sterling and Stephen Waite (1998) and *Boom, Bust & Echo: How to Profit from the Coming Demographic Shift* by David K. Foot and Daniel Stoffman (1996). Discussions of the Baby Boom and its effects on the stock market are everywhere, and their general tone is that the Boom is good for the stock market now and will be for years to come.

### *An Expansion in Media Reporting of Business News*

The first all-news television station, the Cable News Network (CNN), appeared in 1980 and gradually grew, with viewership boosted by such events as the Gulf War in 1991 and the O. J. Simpson trial in 1995, both stories that fueled great demand for uninterrupted coverage. The public acquired the habit of watching the news on television throughout the day (and night), not simply at the dinner hour. CNN was followed by the business networks. The Financial News Network, founded in 1983, was later absorbed into CNBC. Then came CNNfn and Bloomberg Television. Together, these networks produced an uninterrupted stream of financial news, much of it devoted to the stock market. So pervasive was their influence that traditional brokerage firms found it necessary to keep CNBC running in the lower corners of their brokers' computer screens. So many clients would call to ask about something they had just heard on the networks that brokers (who were supposed to be too busy working to watch television!) began to seem behind the curve.

Not merely the scope but also the nature of business reporting has changed in recent years. According to a study by Richard Parker, a senior fellow at Harvard University's Shorenstein Center, newspapers in the past twenty years have transformed their formerly staid business sections into enhanced "Money" sections, which dispense useful tips about personal investing. Articles about individual corporations that used to be written as if they would be of interest only to those involved in the industry or the corporations themselves now are written with a slant toward profit opportunities for individual investors. Articles about corporations regularly include analysts' opinions of the implications of the news for investors.[15]

Such enhanced business reporting leads to increased demand for stocks, just as advertisements for a consumer product make people more familiar with the product, remind them of the option to buy, and ultimately motivate them to buy. Most advertising is really not the presentation of important facts about the product but merely a reminder of the product and its image. Given the heightened media coverage of investments, a stock market boom should come as no greater surprise than increased sales of the latest sports utility vehicle after a major ad campaign.

### *Analysts' Increasingly Optimistic Forecasts*

According to data from Zacks Investment Research about analysts' recommendations on some 6,000 companies, only 1.0% of recommendations were "sells" in late 1999 (while 69.5% were "buys" and 29.9% were "holds"). This situation stands in striking contrast to that indicated by previous data. Ten years earlier, the fraction of sells, at 9.1%, was nine times higher.[16]

Analysts are now reluctant to recommend that investors sell anything. One reason often given for this reluctance is that a sell recommendation might incur the wrath of the company involved. Companies can retaliate by refusing to talk with analysts whom they view as submitting negative reports, excluding them from information sessions, and not offering them access to key executives as they prepare earnings forecasts. This situation represents a change in the fundamental culture of the investment industry, and in the tacit understanding that recommendations are as objective as the analyst can make them.

Another reason that many analysts are reluctant to issue sell recommendations is that an increasing number of them are employed by firms that underwrite securities, and these firms do not want their analysts to do anything that might jeopardize this lucrative side of the business. Analysts affiliated with investment banks give significantly more favorable recommendations on firms for which their employer is the co- or lead underwriter than do unaffiliated analysts, even though their earnings forecasts are not usually stronger.[17]

Those who know the ropes realize that today's hold recommendation is more like the sell recommendation of yesteryear. According to James Grant, a well-known market commentator, "Honesty was never a profit center on Wall Street, but the brokers used to keep up appearances. Now they have stopped pretending. More than ever, securities research, as it is called, is a branch of sales. Investor, beware."[18]

Analysts' recommendations have been transformed by something analogous to grade inflation in our schools: C used to be an average grade, yet now it is considered as bordering on failure. Many of us know that such inflation happens, and we try to correct for it in interpreting our children's grades. Similarly, in the market we factor inflation into analysts' recommendations. But not everyone is going to make adequate corrections for analysts' newly hyperbolic language, and so the general effect of their changed standards will be to encourage the higher valuation of stocks.

Moreover, it is not just a change in the units of measurement that infects analysts' reports. Even their quantitative forecasts of earnings growth show an upward bias. According to a study by Steven Sharpe of the Federal Reserve Board, analysts' expectations of growth in the S&P 500 earnings per share exceeded actual growth in sixteen of the eighteen years between 1979 and 1996. The average difference between the projected and actual growth rate of earnings was 9 percentage points. The analysts breezed through both the steep recession of 1980–81 and the recession of 1990–91 making forecasts of earnings growth in the 10% range.[19]

This bias in analysts' forecasts is a characteristic of their one-year forecasts; they are usually more sober in predicting the next earnings announcement just before it is released. Analysts tend to comply with firms' wishes to see positive earnings surprises each quarter, by issuing estimates that fall slightly short of the actual number. Firms may, just before making earnings announcements, talk with analysts whose forecasts are on the high side, urging them down, while neglecting to talk with analysts whose forecasts are on the low side, thereby creating a downward bias in the average earnings forecast without being blatantly untruthful.[20] Casual evaluation of analysts' forecasts by clients would most naturally take the form of comparing the latest earnings announcement with the latest forecast, and therefore analysts do not sharply overestimate earnings just before they are announced, which would be an obvious embarrassment to them.

Analysts' upward bias comes to the fore in predicting the vague, undifferentiated future, not immediate quarterly or yearly outcomes. And it is expectations for the vague, undifferentiated future, even far beyond one-year forecasts, that lie behind the high market valuations we see. Analysts have few worries about being uniformly optimistic regarding the distant future; they have concluded that such generalized optimism is simply good for business. Certainly they perceive that their fellow analysts are demonstrating such long-run optimism, and there is, after all, safety in numbers. Glibly and routinely offering "great-outlook-for-the-U.S." patter to the investing public, they perhaps give little thought to its accuracy.

### *The Expansion of Defined Contribution Pension Plans*

Changes over time in the nature of employee pension plans have encouraged people to learn about, and eventually accept, stocks as investments. Although these changes do not technically favor stocks over other investments for retirement, they have—by forcing people to make explicit choices among their retirement investments, choices that previously were made for them—worked in the direction of encouraging investment in stocks. Making such choices teaches people about stocks and increases their level of familiarity with them.

The most revolutionary change in these institutions in the United States has been the expansion of defined contribution pension plans at the expense of defined benefit plans. An important milestone came in 1981, when the first 401(k) plan was created; it was soon ratified by a landmark ruling by the Internal Revenue Service.[21] Prior to that date, employer pension plans had usually been of the defined benefit type, in which the employer merely promised a fixed pension to its employees when they retired. Reserves to pay the defined benefit were managed by the employer. With 401(k) plans (as well as such analogues as 403(b) plans), employees are offered the opportunity to have contributions to a tax-deferred retirement account deducted from their paychecks. They then own the investments in their 401(k) accounts and must allocate them among stocks, bonds, and money market accounts. The tax law encourages employers to make matching contributions to their employees' 401(k) accounts, so there is a powerful incentive for employees to participate.

Various factors have also encouraged the growth of defined contribution pension plans since the bottom of the market in 1982. Labor unions have traditionally sought defined benefit plans for their members as a way of ensuring their welfare in retirement, and the decline of unions has meant diminishing support for these plans. The importance of the manufacturing sector, long a stronghold of labor unions and defined benefit pensions, has shrunk. Defined benefit plans have also become less popular with management, because so-called overfunded plans sometimes make companies vulnerable to takeovers. Defined contribution plans are seen as less costly to administer than defined benefit plans. Moreover, defined contribution plans have become more popular with those employees who like to monitor their investments, and therefore companies have tended to offer the plans to all employees.

Through these tax incentives for participation in plans offering choices between stocks and bonds, the government has forced working people to learn about the advantages of stocks versus bonds or money market investments. Any incentive to learn about an investment vehicle is likely to boost demand for it. In 1954, when the New York Stock Exchange carried out a marketing study to understand how to promote public interest in the stock market, it concluded that most people did not know very much about stocks: only 23% of the public even knew enough to define what a share is. Moreover, the survey revealed a vague public distrust of the stock market.[22] So the exchange held a series of public information seminars to try to remedy this lack of knowledge and this prejudice against stocks as an investment. But no set of seminars that the exchange could ever afford could compare with the learning-by-doing effects of the defined contribution plan in encouraging public knowledge about and interest in stocks.

If one's attention to the stock market is filtered through the lens of a pension plan, it may encourage longer-term thinking. The stated purpose of a 401(k) plan is to prepare for retirement, which is, for most workers, many years away. A 401(k) plan sponsor does not call participants with tips about short-run investment opportunities, and statements about portfolio value are mailed out only infrequently. The participant cannot check his or her portfolio value every day in the newspaper. This longer-term thinking may boost stock market valuations by diverting investors from preoccupation with short-term fluctuations.

Encouraging longer-term thinking among investors is probably, all in all, a good thing. But an additional effect of 401(k) plans as they are structured today may be to boost demand for stocks further through another psychological mechanism. By offering multiple stock market investment *categories* for employees to choose among, employers can create demand for stocks. An effect of categories on ultimate investment choices was demonstrated by economists Shlomo Benartzi and Richard Thaler. They found, using both experimental data and data on actual pension fund allocations, that people tend to spread their allocations evenly over the available options, without regard to the *contents* of the options. For example, if a 401(k) plan offers a choice of a stock fund and a bond fund, many people will put 50% of their contributions into each. If the plan instead offers a choice between a stock fund and a balanced fund (with, say, 50% stocks and 50% bonds in it) then people will still tend to put 50% into each, even though they are now really putting 75% of their portfolio into stocks.[23]

The options offered as part of 401(k) plans tend to be heavily weighted in favor of stocks. In contrast, most 401(k) plans do not have any real estate options; only one plan, that offered by TIAA-CREF, has an option for genuine, direct investment in real estate. In this way the growth of 401(k) plans has encouraged the growth of public interest in the stock market relative to the real estate market. Indeed the typical 401(k) plan today offers choices among a stock fund, a balanced fund (typically 60% stocks and 40% bonds), company stock (investments in the employer itself), possibly a specialized stock fund such as a growth fund, a bond fund, and a money market fund, as well as fixed-income guaranteed investment contracts. It is not surprising, from the findings of the Benartzi and Thaler study, that people put proportionately more into the stock funds, given that so many stock-related choices are laid out before them. Moreover, since there are more interesting "flavors" of stocks—just as, in the corner liquor store, there are more varieties of wine than of vodka—more attention is likely to be drawn to them.

It is in such subtle ways that the *interest value* or *curiosity value* of stocks, not any kind of rational decision-making process, encourages investors to want to buy more of them than they otherwise would. And this seemingly unconscious interest has helped bid up the price of the stock market.

### *The Growth of Mutual Funds*

The stock market boom has coincided with a peculiar growth spurt in the mutual fund industry and a proliferation of advertising for mutual funds. In 1982, at the beginning of the recent long-term bull market, there were only 340 equity mutual funds in the United States. By 1998, there were 3,513—more equity mutual funds than stocks listed on the New York Stock Exchange. In 1982, there were 6.2 million equity mutual fund shareholder accounts in the United States, about one for every ten U.S. families. By 1998, there were 119.8 million such shareholder accounts, or nearly two accounts per family.[24]

Mutual funds are a new name for an old idea. Investment companies arose in the United States as early as the 1820s, though these were not called mutual funds.[25] The Massachusetts Investors Trust, generally regarded as the first mutual fund, was created in 1924. It was different from the other investment trusts in that it published its portfolio, promised prudent investment policies, and was self-liquidating when investors demanded cash for their investments. But this first mutual fund got off to a slow start: investors were not quick to appreciate its advantages. The 1920s bull market instead saw the proliferation of many other investment trusts: investment companies without the safeguards we associate with mutual funds today, many of them dishonest operations and some of them even, effectively, Ponzi schemes (see Chapter 3).

After the stock market crash of 1929, many of these became even more worthless than the market as a whole, and the public soured on investment trusts. In particular, they felt betrayed by the managers of the trusts, who were often pursuing their own interests in flagrant conflict with those of their investors. The Investment Company Act of 1940, which established regulations for investment companies, helped restore a measure of public confidence. But people needed more than just government regulations; they needed a new name, one that did not carry the unsavory associations of investment trusts. The term *mutual fund,* with its similarity to the mutual savings bank and the mutual insurance company—venerable institutions that had survived the stock market crash largely untouched by scandal—was much more reassuring and attractive to investors.[26]

The mutual fund industry was given new impetus by the Employee Retirement Income Security Act of 1974, which created Individual Retirement Accounts. But the industry really took off after the recent bull market began in 1982.

Part of the reason that equity mutual funds proliferated so rapidly after that date is that they are used as part of 401(k) pension plans. As people invest their plan balances directly in mutual funds, they develop greater familiarity with the concept; they are thus more inclined to invest their non-401(k) savings in mutual funds as well.

Another reason for the funds' explosive growth is that they have paid for a great deal of advertising. Television shows, magazines, and newspapers frequently carry advertisements for them, and active investors receive unsolicited ads in the mail. Mutual funds encourage more naïve investors to participate in the market, by leading them to think that the experts managing the funds will steer them away from pitfalls.

The proliferation of equity mutual funds has therefore focused public attention on the market, with the effect of encouraging speculative price movements in stock market aggregates, rather than in individual stocks.[27] The emerging popular concept that mutual fund investing is sound, convenient, and safe has encouraged many investors who were once afraid of the market to want to enter it, thereby contributing to an upward thrust in the market. (See Chapter 10 for a further discussion of public attitudes toward mutual funds.)

### *The Decline of Inflation and the Effects of Money Illusion*

The outlook for U.S. inflation, as measured by the percentage change in the Consumer Price Index, has gradually improved since the bull market began. In 1982, even though U.S. inflation was then around 4% a year, there was still considerable uncertainty as to whether it would return to the high level (nearly 15% for the year) experienced in 1980. The most dramatic stock price increases of this bull market occurred once the inflation rate had settled down into the 2–3% range in the mid-1990s, and it then dropped below 2%.

The general public pays a lot of attention to inflation, as I discovered in my interview studies of public attitudes toward it.[28] People widely believe that the inflation rate is a barometer of the economic and social health of a nation. High inflation is perceived as a sign of economic disarray, of a loss of basic values, and a disgrace to the nation, an embarrassment before foreigners. Low inflation is viewed as a sign of economic prosperity, social justice, and good government. It is not surprising, therefore, that a lower inflation rate boosts public confidence, hence stock market valuation.

But from a purely rational standpoint, this stock market reaction to inflation is inappropriate. In 1979 Nobel laureate Franco Modigliani, with Richard Cohn, published an article arguing that the stock market reacts inappropriately to inflation because people do not fully understand the effect of inflation on interest rates.[29] When inflation is high—as it was when they wrote, near the bottom of the stock market in 1982—nominal interest rates (the usual interest rates we see quoted every day) are high because they must compensate investors for the inflation that is eroding the value of their dollars. Yet real interest rates (interest rates as corrected for the effects of inflation) were not high then, and therefore there should not have been any stock market reaction to the high nominal rates. Modigliani and Cohn suggested that the market tends to be depressed when nominal rates are high even when real rates are not high because of a sort of "money illusion," or public confusion about the effects of a changing monetary standard. When there is inflation, we are changing the value of the dollar, and therefore changing the yardstick by which we measure values. Faced with a changing yardstick, it is not surprising that many people become confused.

Modigliani and Cohn also argued (and this is a more subtle point) that people fail to take account of a bias in measured corporate profits due to the fact that corporations deduct from their profits the total interest paid on their debt, and not just the real (inflation-corrected) interest. In inflationary times, part of this interest paid may be viewed merely as a prepayment of part of the real debt, rather than a cost to the company. Few investors realize this and make corrections for this effect of inflation. Their failure to do so may be described as another example of money illusion.[30]

Public misunderstanding about inflation at the present time encourages high expectations for real (inflation-corrected) returns. Most data on past long-run stock market returns is reported in the media in nominal terms, without correction for inflation, and people might naturally be encouraged to expect that such nominal returns would continue in the future. Inflation today is under 2%, compared with a historical average Consumer Price Index level of inflation that has averaged 4.4% a year since John Kennedy was elected president in 1960. Therefore expecting the same nominal returns we have seen in the stock market since 1960 is expecting a lot more in real terms.

Plots of historical stock price indexes in the media are almost invariably shown in nominal terms, not the real inflation-corrected terms shown in the figures in this book. Consumer prices have increased six-fold since 1960 and seventeen-fold since 1913. This inflation imparts an strong upward trend to long-run historical plots of stock price indexes, if they are not corrected for inflation. Thus the extraordinary behavior of the real stock market at the turn of the millennium, the spike up in stock prices that was visible in Figure 1.1, does not stand out in the long historical plots we see in the media. In fact, viewing these plots encourages us to think that nothing at all unusual is going on now in the stock market.

The reason news writers generally do not make corrections for inflation is probably that they think such adjustments are esoteric and would not be widely appreciated by their readers. And they are probably right. The general public has not by and large taken Economics 101, and those who did sit through it have probably forgotten much of what they learned. Thus they have not assimilated the basic lesson that there is nothing natural about measuring prices in dollars when the quantity, and value, of those dollars has been highly unstable. The public at large does not fully appreciate that the more meaningful measure of the stock market level is in terms of some broad basket of goods, as the level is measured if it is corrected for consumer price inflation.[31]

### *Expansion of the Volume of Trade: Discount Brokers, Day Traders, and Twenty-Four-Hour Trading*

The turnover rate (the total shares sold in a year divided by the total number of shares) for New York Stock Exchange stocks nearly doubled between 1982 and 1999, from 42% to 78%.[32] The NASDAQ market, which emphasizes high-technolgoy stocks, shows an even greater turnover rate increase, from 88% in 1990 to 221% in 1999.[33] The higher turnover rate may be symptomatic of increased interest in the market as a result of other factors mentioned here. But another reason for the rising turnover rate in the stock market is the declining cost of making a trade. After competitive brokerage commissions were mandated by the Securities and Exchange Commission (SEC) in 1975, there was an immediate drop in commission rates, and discount brokers came into being. Technological and organizational changes were also set in motion. Such innovations as the Small Order Execution System, introduced by NASDAQ in 1985, and new order handling rules issued by the SEC in 1997 have resulted in ever lower trading costs. SEC regulations encouraging equal access to the markets have now spawned a growing number of amateur investors who can "day trade," that is, try to make profits by rapidly trading stocks using the same order execution systems used by professionals.

The significant growth of online trading services coincides roughly with the most spectacular increases in the stock market since 1997. According to a study by the SEC, there were 3.7 million online accounts in the United States in 1997; by 1999 there were 9.7 million such accounts.[34] The growth of online trading, as well as the associated Internet-based information and communication services, may well encourage minute-by-minute attention to the market. After-hours trading on the exchanges also has the potential to increase the level of attention paid to the market, as investors can track changing prices in their living rooms during their leisure time.

Speculative prices seem to get a volatility nudge whenever markets are open. The magnitude of price changes tends to be lower over two-day intervals that include a day when markets are closed (as, for example, during a time when the New York Stock Exchange closed on Wednesdays).[35] It is therefore plausible to expect that the expansion of online trading and the opening of markets for longer hours will raise their volatility. Whether it will raise or lower the level of prices is less certain.

There is, however, some evidence suggesting that more frequent exposure to price quotes might in fact diminish demand for stocks. Economists Shlomo Benartzi and Richard Thaler have shown that the time pattern of attention to market prices can have important effects on the demand for stocks. In experimental situations, if people are shown daily data on stock prices they express much less interest in investing in stocks than if they are shown only longer-run returns.[36] Witnessing the day-to-day noise in stock prices apparently encourages more fear about the inherent risk of investing in stocks. Thus institutional innovations that encourage viewing the market price more frequently might tend to depress the price level of the market.

On the other hand, the increased frequency of reporting of stock prices caused by recent institutional and technological changes may have just the opposite effect to that observed in the experimental situation crafted by Benartzi and Thaler. In a nonexperimental setting, where people's focus of attention is not controlled by an experimenter, the increased frequency of price observations may tend to increase the demand for stocks by attracting attention to them. And changing public attention is a critical factor in the valuation of investments, a point that will be elaborated in Chapter 8.

### *The Rise of Gambling Opportunities*

There has been a dramatic increase in gambling opportunities in the United States in recent years. Most forms of gambling and lotteries were outlawed by states in the 1870s after a scandal in the

Louisiana lottery, and the Louisiana national lottery itself was effectively shut down by an 1890 act of Congress prohibiting the sale of lottery tickets by mail. From then until 1970, opportunities to gamble legally were confined largely to racetracks, a form of gambling that has limited public appeal and which at the time required travel to a racetrack. But by 1975, there were thirteen state lotteries, and by 1999 there were thirty-seven, offering very convenient and easy means of wagering. Until 1990, legalized casinos operated only in Nevada and Atlantic City. By 1999 there were nearly 100 riverboat and dockside casinos and 260 casinos on Indian reservations. Over the same interval, betting at racetracks has also expanded dramatically, with the development of off-track betting, relying on satellite broadcasts of the races. Cable and Internet wagering on races is now possible from home. There has also been a proliferation of electronic gambling devices, including slot machines, video poker, video keno, and other stand-alone devices. In some states these may even be found at truck stops, convenience stores, and lottery outlets. The ubiquity and convenience of gambling opportunities, and the strength of the marketing campaign undertaken to promote gambling, are unprecedented in U.S. history. According to the 1999 report of the National Gambling Impact Study Commission, 125 million Americans gambled in 1998—a figure that represents most of the adult population.[37] Moreover, 7.5 million Americans were estimated to be either problem or pathological gamblers.

The rise of gambling institutions, and the increased frequency of actual gambling, have potentially important effects on our culture and on changed attitudes toward risk taking in other areas, such as investing in the stock market. The legalization of gambling in the form of state lotteries has sometimes been observed to help the illegal numbers business, rather than replace it,[38] and thus it might also promote other capricious risk-taking activities. Gambling suppresses natural inhibitions against taking risks, and some of the gambling contracts, in particular the lotteries, superficially resemble financial markets: one deals with a computer, one receives a certificate (the lottery ticket), and, in the case of the so-called mega-lottos, one participates in a much-talked-about national phenomenon. Having established a habit of participating in such gambling, it would be natural to graduate to its more upscale form, speculation in securities.

The period of highest U.S. stock market volatility was 1929 to 1933, when volatility was more than twice as high as had ever been recorded before. This period of volatility occurred during a "gambling craze" that was brought on not by legalization but by the organized crime that was inadvertently created by the prohibition of alcoholic beverages during the period 1920–33.[39] The criminal gangs that grew after 1920 to satisfy the nation's thirst for alcohol found it natural to branch out into numbers games or speakeasy versions of craps and roulette. Organized crime developed a modern and efficient distribution, marketing, and retail system to supply the nation at large with liquor, going far beyond its traditional neighborhood strongholds, and this same infrastructure served to facilitate illegal gambling activities on a much larger scale. Certainly the widespread disrespect for the law fostered by Prohibition helped legitimize gambling.

A spillover from gambling to financial volatility may come about because gambling, and the institutions that promote it, yield an inflated estimate of one's own ultimate potential for good luck, a heightened interest in how one performs compared with others, and a new way to stimulate oneself out of a feeling of boredom or monotony. Today we are constantly subjected to highly professional advertisements that try to foster such attitudes, even radio and television advertisements that depict typical gamblers' self-justifications as expressed by professional actors. These marketing efforts, and the experience of gambling or seeing others gamble, may well have the effect of encouraging frivolous risk-taking behavior in the stock market as well. Such ads may be startlingly explicit. A Connecticut billboard advertising off-track betting touts it, in big letters, as being "Like the Stock Market, Only Faster."

### *Summing Up*

Looking back at the list of potential precipitating factors for the stock market boom, it is worth remembering that there is no air-tight science of stock market pricing. Economists have certainly made progress in understanding financial markets, but the complexity of real life continues to prevail.

Many of the foregoing factors have a self-fulfilling aspect to them, and they are thus difficult, if not impossible, to capture in predictive scientific explanations. Yet many of them also have indisputable markers. The Internet boom, the rise of online trading, the Republican Congress, and the proposed capital gains tax cut occurred just as the market started its most breathtaking ascent. Other factors—including the rise of defined contribution pension plans, the growth of mutual funds, the decline of inflation, and the expansion of the volume of trade—were clearly associated with events that unfolded since the bottom of the market in 1982. Beyond these, our culture clearly reflects further developments that have accompanied the surge in stocks. For example, studies reveal that the degree of materialism has risen steadily in the past generation, that patriotic zeal following the demise of Communism has contributed to our confidence in the capitalist system, and perhaps most interestingly, that gambling has been on the rise during the 1990s. Many of these factors are present in Europe and in other countries as well as the United States, and so a theory that they are responsible for the stock market boom in the United States is not inconsistent with the fact that the boom is shared substantially by these other countries.[40]

Correlation is certainly not causation, nor should it be construed as such. But when exuberance, irrational or otherwise, is the order of the day, it is essential to take account of the self-fulfilling psychology of stocks in making the policy decisions that will affect our society for decades to come.

# Three

# *Amplification Mechanisms: Naturally Occurring Ponzi Processes*

In the previous chapter we examined a number of disparate factors that have precipitated the present speculative bubble. In this chapter we consider how the effect of these factors is amplified by mechanisms involving investor confidence, investor expectations for future market performance, and related influences on investor demand for stocks. To provide context and concreteness, we shall first examine evidence about investor confidence and expectations.

The amplification mechanisms work through a sort of feedback loop; later in this chapter they will also be described as a type of naturally occurring Ponzi process. Investors, their confidence and expectations buoyed by past price increases, bid up stock prices further, thereby enticing more investors to do the same, so that the cycle repeats again and again, resulting in an amplified response to the original precipitating factors. The feedback mechanism is widely mentioned in popular discourse as merely a hypothesis, often regarded as unproven. In fact, there is some evidence in support of such a feedback mechanism, as we shall see.

### *High Investor Confidence*

A striking feature of the recent bull market has been the high levels of investor confidence in the stock market. My 1999 mail questionnaire survey of random samples of wealthy individuals in the United States showed that most people believe that stocks are the best investment for the long run.[1] One of the questions on the survey, and the 1999 results from 147 respondents, were as follows:

> Do you agree with the following statement? "The stock market is the best investment for long-term holders, who can just buy and hold through the ups and downs of the market."
>
> | | |
> |---|---|
> | 1. Strongly agree | 76% |
> | 2. Agree somewhat | 20% |
> | 3. Neutral | 2% |
> | 4. Disagree somewhat | 1% |
> | 5. Strongly disagree | 1% |

Agreement with this question is obviously very strong. Fully 96% of the respondents agreed at least somewhat in 1999. The percentage who agreed strongly in 1999 is also remarkably high, at 76%. I also asked this question of wealthy individuals in 1996, and the results were only slightly less dramatic then: of the 134 respondents, 94% agreed at least somewhat, and 69% agreed strongly.

A 96% level of agreement on just about any survey question is remarkable, and it is all the more so on a question about something as personal as investing strategy.[2] Many people used to think (for example, in the 1970s and 1980s) that real estate was the best investment or (for example, in making decisions about investments for retirement before the recent bull market) that government bonds were the best investment.[3] One might have thought that more than a few of the respondents would believe that investing in gold or diamonds or other commodities, investing in antiques or art, or even investing in education or self-improvement would be the best strategy. But no: almost all agree on the stock market.

Associated with this view is a feeling that the stock market is a very safe place. Another question on the survey, and the 1999 results from 147 respondents, were as follows:

How much do you agree with this statement? "If there is another crash like October 19, 1987, the market will surely be back up to its former levels in a couple years or so."

| | |
|---|---|
| 1. Strongly agree | 47% |
| 2. Agree somewhat | 44% |
| 3. Neutral | 3% |
| 4. Disagree somewhat | 5% |
| 5. Strongly disagree | 1% |

There is an overwhelming tendency to show concord with this statement: 91% of the wealthy individual investors agreed at least somewhat in 1999. Almost no one really disagrees, as they should if they believe that markets are unpredictable. When I asked this same question of wealthy individuals in 1996, there were 135 answers, and of these 82% agreed at least somewhat.

It is curious that people do not seem to believe in the converse of the premise of the above question: they do not believe that the market will surely go back down in a couple of years if it goes up dramatically, as it has done recently.[4] Their belief in the resilience of the market seems to stem from a generalized feeling of optimism and assurance, rather than a belief in the long-run stability of prices.

Here, then, captured in the responses to these two questions, we see the extraordinary public confidence in the stock market that underlies recent market valuations. People seem to think that they have discovered a safe and lucrative investment, one that cannot lose. They perceive no real downside risk, and this explains their willingness to buy stocks even when, by conventional measures such as price-earnings ratios, they are so greatly overvalued.

Although I have been surveying investors since the mid-1980s, it did not occur to me to ask these questions until 1996. I suppose I did not think to ask before then whether investors thought a stock market crash would surely be reversed because such highly optimistic investor thinking was not so flagrantly in evidence then. So I have no way to prove that the public did not believe even back then that any stock market crash would surely soon be reversed. I did, however, ask a somewhat similar question starting in 1989. The question and the 1999 results from 145 wealthy individual respondents, plus the 1996 results from 132 respondents and the 1989 results from 116, were as follows:

> If the Dow dropped 3% tomorrow, I would guess that the day after tomorrow the Dow would:

| | *1999* | *1996* | *1989* |
|---|---|---|---|
| 1. Increase | 56% | 46% | 35% |
| 2. Decrease | 19% | 24% | 34% |
| 3. Stay the same | 12% | 18% | 13% |
| 4. No opinion | 13% | 11% | 18% |

The percentage who thought in 1999 that the Dow would increase is nearly three times the percentage who thought it would decrease. It was not always so. In 1996, there was about a 2:1 ratio between the percentage predicting an increase and that predicting a decrease. In 1989, the percentage predicting an increase was about the same as the percentage predicting a decrease. Thus, over this ten-year interval, it is clear that there has been a sharp increase in the confidence among individual investors that any one-day drop in the market will be quickly reversed.[5]

There is some evidence suggesting that many people in 1929 felt equally certain about reversals of stock market drops. Although we do not have questionnaire survey data of the time, we do have contemporary accounts of investor confidence. Frederick Lewis Allen, in his 1931 history of the 1920s, *Only Yesterday,* wrote:

> As people in the summer of 1929 looked back for precedents, they were comforted by the recollection that every crash of the past few years had ultimately brought prices to a new high point. Two steps up, one step down, two steps up again—that was how the market went. If you sold, you had only to wait for the next crash (they came every few months) and buy in again. And there was really no reason to sell at all: you were bound to win in the end if your stock was sound. The really wise man, it appeared, was he who "bought and held on."[6]

### *Some Reflections on Investor Confidence*

It is important to consider the nature, and likely sources, of this current investor confidence, not only to understand the present situation but also to lead us into a discussion, later in this chapter, of feedback loops. We will see that the feedback that reinforces investor confidence occurs in the context of a complex social and psychological environment.

Where did people get the idea that, if there is ever a crash, the market is sure to rise to past levels within a couple of years or so? History certainly does not suggest this. There are many examples of markets that have done poorly over long intervals of time. To pick just one from recent memory, the Nikkei index in Japan is still selling at less than half its peak value in 1989. Other examples are the periods after the 1929 and 1966 stock market peaks discussed in Chapter 1. But these examples of persistent bad performance in the stock market are not prominent in the public mind.

One reason that the recent domestic market performance is more prominent in investors' minds is simply that they have *experienced* these domestic stock prices every day; they have watched and reacted to a rising U.S. market since 1982. U.S. investors today have not had the same experience with Japanese stocks, or with the U.S. market in decades past. Many people fix their attention on plots of rising stock prices in newspapers every day, and they seem to come away with an intuitive feeling that every decline is reversed, to be followed swiftly by new highs. The same human pattern-recognition faculty that we used when we learned to ride a bike or to drive a car, giving us an intuitive sense of what to expect next, has been applied to our expectations for the market. For investors in their twenties, thirties, or forties, this upward trend has been present during most of the years they have been observing or investing in the market.

The subjective experience over the years of seeing stock market declines consistently reverse themselves has a psychological impact on our thinking that is hard to appreciate, or reconstruct, after the fact. Those who thought the market would go down and stay down became sensitized to their bad feelings from being repeatedly wrong, year after year. Those who consistently predicted a decline became painfully aware of a loss of reputation from being so wrong so often. Since our satisfaction with our views of the world is part of our self-esteem and personal identity, it is natural for the formerly pessimistic to want to settle on a different view, or at least to present themselves to the public with a different theme. Thus the changed emotional environment will have an impact on their views—or certainly the expression of them—that is independent of any objective evidence supporting or refuting those views.

Even if they have not personally paid attention to the stock market since 1982, today's investors are living in a time and place where recitations of the feelings of others who have experienced the market are heard regularly. It is helpful, to appreciate this sense, to quote one person's argument against market timing, from the 1999 book *Dow 40,000* by David Elias:

> An example of what can happen when an individual waits for the Dow to indicate "the perfect time" to invest is the saga of Joe, a friend of mine. Joe started calling me in 1982 when the Dow was just over 1000, looking for the right time to get into equities. Over the years, he continued to seek a pullback that would be his perfect moment. Today, at age 62, Joe still has his money parked in bank CDs. He has missed the entire bull market and all its thousand-point milestones. Even now, Joe does not realize that there never is a perfect time. When the market recovers from a pullback, it generally goes to new highs.[7]

There is something superficially convincing about this passage, especially when it is combined, as in the next paragraph in Elias's book, with illustrations of the power of compound interest when returns are high (as they have recently been in the stock market), suggesting that the stock market is your chance to become really and truly rich. The tale has emotional immediacy, as would a story about a driving mistake that led to a serious accident or a story about the advantages of asking the boss for a raise.

A related reason why an argument built around such a story has such appeal is that—by presenting successful investing as a process of mastering one's own internal impulses rather than taking account of our present situation in history—it invites the reader to forget what is special about the present time in terms of the level of the market. Normal people think a lot about controlling their own impulses—for example, about disciplining themselves to good work rather than dissipation, about staying slim rather than getting fat—and so arguments that appeal to such self-control have more resonance than articles about the history of price-earnings ratios. The appeal of Elias's argument is also that it calls to mind the pain of regret, the emotional reasons we have for investing *now,* a point to which I will return later in this chapter. When arguments become so detached from an analysis of historical data, the only impact on people's thinking made by actual data is a vague sense, from casual inspection of very recent data, that the market has always reversed declines.

Many media accounts routinely tell stories about the satisfaction felt by those who have invested in stocks in years past, with the clear suggestion to the reader that "you can do it too." To cite only one among numerous examples, a 1999 article in *USA Weekend,* a national Sunday magazine insert for newspapers, carried an article entitled "How to (Really) Get Rich in America." The article gives examples of investor successes and offers the hypothetical story of a twenty-two-year-old college graduate earning $30,000 a year with annual real income raises of 1%. "If she saved only 10% of her income and invested the savings in an S&P index fund she'd have a net worth of $1.4 million on retirement at age 67, in today's dollars."[8] These calculations assume that the S&P index fund earns a riskless 8% real (inflation-corrected) return. There is no mention of the possibility that the return might not be so high over time, and that she might *not* end up a millionaire. An article with a very similar title, "Everybody Ought to Be Rich," appeared in the *Ladies' Home Journal* in 1929.[9] It performed some very similar calculations, yet similarly omitted to describe the possibility that anything could go wrong in the long term. The article became notorious after the 1929 crash.

These seemingly convincing discussions of potential increases in the stock market are rarely offered in the abstract, but instead in the context of stories about successful or unsuccessful investors, and often with an undertone suggesting the moral superiority of those who invested well. A strong public admiration for those who make money patiently and slowly, unfazed by market fluctuations, has evolved. It is a theme developed in many popular books. Notable among these is *The Millionaire Next Door: The Surprising Secrets of America's Wealthy* by Thomas Stanley and William Danko, which was on the *New York Times* hardcover best-seller list for eighty-eight weeks after its publication in 1996 and continues on the *Times* paperback best-seller list as of this writing. The book, which extols the virtues of patience and frugality, has sold over a million copies.

Indeed such stories of patient investing transcend U.S. borders. In Germany, the 1999 best-seller *The Road to Financial Freedom: A Millionaire in Seven Years* by Bodo Schäfer sets a seven-year horizon for investors and gives as the first of ten "golden rules" the dictum that any stock market decline must soon be reversed. Another German book from 1999, *No Fear of the Next Crash: Why Stocks Are Unbeatable as Long-Term Investments* by Bernd Niquet, devotes itself entirely to the theme that patient investing in stocks always wins.[10]

In viewing the popular expressions of confidence in the market, whether from the 1990s or the 1920s, and in trying to understand how people felt about them at the time, it is important to bear in mind that in most cases the statements of confidence in the stock market that we see are not the focal point of attention in the contexts in which they appear. Thus, for example, Suze Orman, a highly successful investment adviser in the 1990s and a best-selling author, with books like *The 9 Steps to Financial Freedom* (1997) and *The Courage to Be Rich: Creating a Life of Material and Spiritual Abundance* (1999), has built a remarkable reputation for herself on television, appearing often on shows like Oprah Winfrey's, by stressing the emotional and spiritual steps one should take to acquire a fortune. Her concrete advice is to get out of debt and into stocks, and her example of the power of compound interest with a rate of return of 10% is never the focus of attention. Most of her audience is apparently interested in her spiritual message, and her confronting their difficulty in saving is on target and attention-grabbing for them. Her assumption that the market will surely produce a return of 10% a year is mere background information that her viewers and readers do not have the time or the inclination to examine. Yet the repetition that she and others like her give to this assumption nonetheless promotes it to the status of conventional wisdom.

Other factors lie behind today's strong investor confidence—factors that only muddy their thinking. An important one has been the inexorable rise in the Consumer Price Index (CPI), noted in the preceding chapter, which has put upward pressure on all prices, thereby tending to wipe out nominal declines in any speculative market. The inflation consequently disguises the fact that in real inflation-corrected terms the speculative asset may not have regained its real value. People no doubt think back to the experience they have had with their homes. In the northeast United States, for example, where home prices declined at the beginning of the 1990s, home prices in many regions are back up to their 1988–90 peaks. People tend to forget that we have had 25–30% inflation in the CPI since then, so that real (inflation-corrected) home values are still way down. Of course, with today's lower inflation this feeling should be diminished, but people still have memories of higher-inflation environments, and they will have them for some time to come. The present situation, with sharply lower but still positive inflation, may be especially conducive to high market valuation: people are optimistic for the future economy because of low inflation, but they are still expecting the same tendency for stock prices to rebound from falls that they showed during inflationary periods.

Another important factor is the current economic expansion, the longest such peacetime expansion in U.S. history. Those who predicted a recession have been almost as soundly discredited as those who predicted a stock market drop, and this only serves as further intuitive confirmation of an optimistic view for the market. Indeed the evidence we see of public confidence in the stock market mirrors evidence of confidence in the overall economy. The consumer confidence measures of both the Conference Board and the Survey Research Center at the University of Michigan have been close to record levels in recent years.

### *Evidence for Undiminished Expectations Despite a High Market*

In my surveys of investors, I have found that the current high market has not diminished average expectations. I ask investors, in open-ended questions, for their expectations for the Dow for various horizons. I do not ask them to select from categories or ranges of price increase; they must come up with a number on their own, without my suggesting anything. In my surveys of high-income individual investors, in 1989, the average expected one-year-ahead change in the Dow was 0.6%. In 1996, it was 5.0%, and in 1999, it was 4.6%, about the same as in 1996. Thus, despite a sharply rising stock market over the past decade, average expectations among high-income individual investors have on the whole also been rising since 1989. Among institutional investors, I find no particular trend to expectations for one-year-ahead stock market returns, and so they too are not becoming discouraged by the higher market.

Some might be surprised at how modest the average reported expectations are today. Looking at the individual answers, it is obvious why the averages are so low. Most investors are answering that the market will increase something like 10–15% over the next year, which is roughly the average historical nominal return over the last fifty years. Very few of them answer that it will do better than this. Something like a third of the individuals answer that the market will go down, typically by 10%, some saying by 20%. Thus, given these answers, the *average* of the expectations has been an approximately 5% market price increase. In 1989, many more respondents thought that the market would go down 10% or 20%, so that the average expectation for the market was about zero.

It is not surprising that few people answer that they expect the market to go up 20% or 30% in the next year. That is just not a respectable answer, not something one would expect to see validated in media accounts. The respectable thing to say is that it will continue to post the same impressive returns it has on average over the past thirty years or more. It is equally respectable to venture that there could be a correction—one hears that in the media, too—hence the predictions of a decline by some respondents. Do people in fact believe the answers they write on the questionnaire? Probably most of them do not know what to believe, and possibly they consider their own answers as good as anything else to believe.

The PaineWebber/Gallup polls have reported much more optimistic average expectations among individual investors. Their July 1999 surveys showed that these investors expected on average a 15.0% return on the stock market over the next twelve months. This sounds like quite an optimistic expectation, much higher than that in my surveys. The difference in results may have to do with subtle differences in wording. Their question was: "Thinking about the stock market more generally, what overall rate of return do you think the stock market will provide investors during the coming twelve months?" Mine was: "How much of a change in percentage terms do you expect in the following (use a + before your number to indicate an expected increase, a – to indicate an expected decrease, leave blanks where you do not know)" and the questionnaire then provided spaces to give answers for the Dow Jones Industrial Average for one month, three months, six months, one year, and ten years. Note the different *sounds* of the two questions. PaineWebber/Gallup asks respondents for a percentage return. Perhaps this suggests to their respondents that a return should be a positive number. I ask for a percentage change in price. My question mentions the possibility that the answer could be negative. Answers to survey questions can be sensitive to the wording of those questions (although if the wording is kept unchanged over time on the questionnaires, the changes in the answers over time may be indicative of the direction of changes in expectations).

Montgomery Asset Management carried out quarterly surveys of mutual fund investors in 1998 that were widely reported in the press as having found yet more extravagant expectations for the stock market. One survey concluded that expectations were for 34% annual returns on average for the next ten years. However, their methodology was apparently flawed, as was revealed in a *Wall Street Journal* article.[11] The question they posed to interviewees did not make it clear whether they should give an annual return for the next ten years or the ten-year total return. A total return of 34% for the next ten years would be on the order of 3% a year, not a high expectation. Moreover, their reported median expectation was only 15% a year, and so their reported 34% a year average expectation must have been caused by a few wild answers that brought the average up.

Overall expectations for the market among most investors are therefore not so extravagantly high as suggested by some polls. But expectations do appear to be somewhat higher and at least remain as strong as they were in 1989, despite a very high market.

### *Some Reflections on Investor Expectations and Emotions*

Economists usually like to model people as calculating optimally their investment decisions based on expectations of future price changes and estimates of the risk in alternative investments. However, in fact, the typical investor's actual decision about how much to allocate to the stock market overall, and into other asset classes such as bonds, real estate, or other investments, tends not to be based on careful calculations. Investors are not often assembling forecasts for these different asset class returns and weighing these against measured risks.

Part of the reason they are not is that investors more often feel that experts have little or no idea what to expect of future price changes for these asset classes, or how much risk there is in each. After all, experts disagree all the time, and one might easily conclude that there is no great loss in ignoring what they are currently saying about the outlook for any given asset class. Investors must therefore base their judgments on basic principles on which most experts seem always to agree.

The evidence used by experts to predict the relative returns on broad asset classes has little immediacy for most people. Experts talk about the potential actions of the Federal Reserve Board in Washington, about shifts in the Phillips curve, or about distortions on aggregate earnings caused by inflation and conventional accounting procedures. Most individuals have little interest in such esoterica.

And yet investors must make some decisions. What factors might then enter into one's mind when making a decision about how much to put into the stock market? The feeling that the stock market is "the only game in town," in some emotional sense, might play a pivotal role at this point in the decision making.

One knows that the stock market *could* repeat the performance of recent years. That possibility seems quite real, just as real as the possibility of a major correction in the market. But how does one feel about the decision at this point? How does one feel, for example, when one knows, late at night, that it is time to fill out the 401(k) allocation form, and one is tired and annoyed by the necessity to make such an important decision based on so little solid information?

How one feels certainly depends on one's recent experience in investing. If one has been out of the market and has not participated in the profits that others have recently enjoyed, one may be feeling a sharp pain of regret. And regret is an emotion that, psychologists have found, provides considerable motivation.[12] Envy of others who may have made more in the stock market than one earned at work in the past year is a related painful feeling, especially so in that it diminishes one's ego. If these people who made so much in the market were really smarter and knew better, then one really feels like a laggard. Even if they were not smarter, just lucky—smiled on by God—it may not feel much better. One may feel that if one can participate in just one more year of an advancing stock market—assuming it advances for another year—that will help assuage the pain. Of course, one also thinks that the market may well go down. But how does one weigh the potential emotional expense of such a possible loss at the time that one is making the asset allocation decision?

Perhaps one feels that the potential loss will not be much more diminishing to one's ego than the failure to participate has already been. Of course, one likely realizes that one takes the risk of entering the market just as it begins a downward turn. But the psychological cost of such a potential future loss may not be so much greater relative to the very real regret at having been out of the market in the past. Therefore—although there are many other ways to deal with the thought that one is a "loser," such as rediscovering the importance of being a good friend, spouse, or parent, or pursuing the simple things in life—it may well end up that the only really emotionally satisfying decision to make now is to get into the stock market.

Of course if one has been in the stock market, and is deciding today whether to stay in the market, one has a very different emotional frame of mind. One feels satisfaction and probably some pride in one's past successes, and one certainly feels wealthier. One may feel as gamblers do after they have raked in winnings: that one is "playing with the house money" and therefore has nothing to lose emotionally by wagering again.[13]

The emotional state of investors when they decide on their investments is no doubt one of the most important factors causing the bull market. Although their emotional state may be in part a consequence of the factors described in the previous chapter, such as the rise of materialistic sentiment and individualism, it is also amplified by the psychological impact of the increasingly strong uptrend observed in the market.

### *Public Attention to the Market*

The level of public interest in and attention to the market changes significantly over time, just as the public's interest jumps from one newsworthy topic to another. Attention shifts from news stories about Jacqueline Kennedy to stories about O. J. Simpson to stories about Princess Diana. Interest in the stock market goes through fads in just the same way, depending on the story quality of the precipitating events.

Some writers have indicated that 1929 was a time of dramatically heightened investor attention to the stock market. John Kenneth Galbraith, in his book *The Great Crash: 1929,* wrote:

> By the summer of 1929 the market not only dominated the news. It also dominated the culture. That *recherché* minority which at other times has acknowledged its interest in Saint Thomas Aquinas, Proust, psychoanalysis and psychosomatic medicine then spoke of United Corporation, United Founders and Steel. Only the most aggressive of the eccentrics maintained their detachment from the market and their interest in autosuggestion or communism. Main Street had always had one citizen who could speak knowingly about buying or selling stocks. Now he became an oracle.[14]

That public attention was focused on the stock market in the late 1920s is supported by many other such commentaries. One should bear in mind that Galbraith's argument contains some journalistic overstatement that he no doubt could not have gotten away with had he been writing in the 1920s. But Galbraith is on the right track in terms of the direction of change over the 1920s.

If one looks at the *Reader's Guide to Periodical Literature* year by year throughout the 1920s, one sees that only a tiny percentage of the articles in periodicals, always less than 0.1%, were about the stock market in any given year. People were thinking about plenty of other things besides the market. However, the percentage of articles concerning the stock market grew markedly over the course of the decade. There were 29 articles about the stock market in 1922–24, or 0.025% of all articles listed; 67 articles in 1925–28, or 0.035% of all articles listed; and 182 articles in 1929–32, or 0.093% of all articles listed. Thus over the 1920s the percentage of articles about the stock market almost quadrupled.

We see a similar pattern of changed interest in the stock market from an identical study of the *Reader's Guide* in the recent bull market, although the percentage of articles that are about the stock market is higher throughout this period than in the 1920s. In 1982, at the bottom of the stock market, there were 242 articles about the stock market, or 0.194% of all articles. In 1987, the year of the crash, there were 592 articles, or 0.364% of all articles, almost twice as many. After the crash, interest waned again, and there were only 255 articles, or 0.171% of all articles, in 1990. In 1996, 1997, and 1998 the number of articles rose again, to 580 articles in 1998, or 0.293% of all articles.

Another source of evidence on investor attention to the market is the number of investment clubs, as reported by the National Association of Investors Corporation (NAIC). Investment clubs are small social groups, typically meeting at members' homes in the evening, that together invest small sums of money for fun and for the purpose of learning about investments. The NAIC was founded in 1951 by four investor clubs at the beginning of the 1950s bull market; the number of clubs grew to 953 by 1954, reached a peak of 14,102 in 1970 (near the top of the market), and fell with the market to 3,642 in 1980 (near the bottom of the market). Now the number of clubs is up well beyond its prior peak, to 37,129.[15] The crude conformity of the number of investment clubs to the performance of the market is noteworthy, suggesting that investors' attention is indeed attracted by bull markets.

Further evidence that past successes in the market encourage attention to the market can be seen in the behavior of the volume of sales in the stock market. Volume of sales, measured by dollar trading volume over total market value on the New York Stock Exchange, rose sharply in the early years of the bull market after 1982, but declined for a couple of years after the 1987 crash, thereafter to resume its upward path. Economists Meir Statman and Steven Thorley have shown with a statistical analysis that high returns in the stock market continue to promote high volume for many months afterward, and that while high volatility in market prices also promotes volume of trade, the effect of volatility on volume of trade is more transient. Statman and Thorley conclude that this persistent effect of returns on volume is due to the impact of higher returns on investor confidence.[16] Even though a rising market "lifts all boats," there is still a tendency for investors to interpret their investing success as confirmation of their own abilities, and this reinforces their interest in trading stocks.

When people experience success in any area, there is of course a natural tendency for them to take new initiatives and develop their skills in hopes of achieving more such success. In a study of investors who switched from phone to online trading, comparing them with investors who continued to use telephones to make their trades, economists Brad Barber and Terrance Odean found that the switchers on average had beat the market by over 2% a year. After they went on line, these switchers traded more speculatively and actively, and then proceeded to lag the market by more than 3% annually.[17] This finding may be interpreted as showing that overconfidence from past success encouraged people to expend the fixed cost of learning about online trading. Having acquired these capabilities and interests, they are likely to pay greater attention to the market for a sustained period, measured in years, in order to see their skills investment "pay off."

If one watches casually for discussions of the stock market, they typically come at some point during a dinner party, cookout, or other social event. Bringing up the stock market is seen as an accepted, even mildly exciting, conversational gambit. It is an agreeable topic. Twenty years ago, bringing up the stock market at such an occasion would have seemed like an intrusion, a *faux pas*, a poorly judged attempt to mix business with pleasure. The difference between now and then is subtle, but nevertheless revelatory of the fundamental change in investor enthusiasm for the market.

### *Feedback Theories of Bubbles*

In feedback loop theory, initial price increases (caused, for example, by the kinds of precipitating factors described in the previous chapter) lead to more price increases as the effects of the initial price increases feed back into yet higher prices through increased investor demand. This second round of price increases feeds back again into a third round, and then into a fourth, and so on. Thus the initial impact of the precipitating factors is amplified into much larger price increases than the factors themselves would have suggested. Such feedback loops may be a factor not only in the historic bull and bear markets for the aggregate stock market but also, with some differences in details, in the ups and downs of individual investments.

The feedback theory is, as I have noted, widely known, but most people do not use the term *feedback loop* to describe it. The phrase is a scientist's term for what might popularly be called a vicious circle, a self-fulfilling prophecy, a bandwagon effect. Although the phrase *speculative bubble* has more than one meaning in common discourse, it usually appears to refer to such feedback.

In the most popular version of the feedback theory, one that relies on *adaptive expectations,* feedback takes place because past price increases generate expectations of further price increases.[18] In another version of the feedback theory, feedback takes place because of increased *investor confidence* in response to past price increases. Usually, such feedback is thought to occur in response not so much to a sudden price increase as to a pattern of consistency in price increases.

The evidence discussed earlier in this chapter is consistent with both the adaptive expectation and investor confidence feedback theories playing a role in the current stock market situation. The feedback can also occur for emotional reasons, reasons unconnected with either expectations or confidence. The effect of "playing with the house's money," as discussed previously, can result in a sort of feedback: this frame of mind may reduce investors' inclination to sell after a price increase, thus amplifying the effects of the precipitating factors on price.

Economists John Campbell and John Cochrane have proposed a theory of habit formation that may also serve to amplify stock market responses. In their model, people become slowly habituated to the higher level of consumption that they can expect from a more highly valued stock market. After a stock market increase, people may be newly experimenting with higher consumption levels, but not yet habituated to them. Investors who have made profits in the market may be willing to take more risks, because they still feel they could give up the higher consumption level if investment losses forced them to do so. Again, their willingness to hold stocks at higher prices may amplify the effects of the precipitating factors.[19]

Regardless of which feedback theory applies, the speculative bubble cannot grow forever. Investors' demand for a stock cannot grow forever, and when it stops growing price increases will stop. According to the popular version of the expectation feedback theory, at that point we would expect a drop in the market for the stock, a bursting of the bubble, since investors no longer think prices will continue to rise and therefore no longer see a good reason to hold the stock. However, other versions of the feedback theory do not suggest a sudden bursting of the bubble, since they are not predicated on continually increasing prices.

Indeed, even according to the most popular versions of the feedback theory, there is actually no reason to think that there should be sudden bursts of bubbles. There must be some noise in investor demand, some unpredictability of response to past price changes, some lack of synchrony across investors. Moreover, the enticement to enter or exit the market that past price changes create is not likely to be determined only by the most recent change in price. It is plausible that investors will look back over many days, weeks, or months of price changes in deciding whether they find recent market performance enticing. Thus the simple feedback theory is consistent with a price pattern that shows many interruptions and jiggles.[20]

With any of these feedback theories, it would also seem that *negative* bubbles should occur, in which feedback occurs in a downward direction, as initial price declines discourage some investors, causing further price declines, and so on.[21] (The term *negative bubble* always reminds me of watching a sealed plastic soda bottle filled with warm air gradually implode as it cools, and seeing it pop back into shape when the cap is loosened—though this metaphor is really no more apt than the soap bubble metaphor for the positive speculative events.) Price continues to decline until further price decreases begin to seem unlikely, at which point there is no reason for people to want to stay away from the stock and the negative bubble bursts back up—even though, as with positive bubbles, the burst will probably not be sudden.

Feedback loop dynamics can generate complex and even apparently random behavior. The so-called random number generators in some types of computer software are really just simple nonlinear feedback loops, and even some quite simple feedback loops have been demonstrated to yield behavior that looks so complicated as to suggest randomness. If we suppose that there are other kinds of feedback loops operating in the economy, besides simple price-increase-to-further-price-increase feedback, then we may conclude that the apparent randomness of the stock market, the tendency it has to create sudden moves for no apparent reason, might not be so inexplicable after all. The branch of mathematics that studies nonlinear feedback loops, called *chaos theory,* may be applicable to understanding the complexity of stock market behavior.[22]

### *Perceptions of Feedback and Bubbles among Investors*

The feedback theory of speculative bubbles is so widely known as to be considered part of our popular culture. It is natural to wonder, therefore, whether public perceptions of such a bubble might be influenced by the recent high pricing of the market. Conceivably, the current bubble might exist only because people *think* that there is a temporary bubble and want to ride with it for a while.

By looking at a series of indicators from my semiannual surveys of institutional investors, I have constructed a *bubble expectations index.* The indicators I look at are the percentages of the respondents who say that the market is too high but will go up in the short term, that the market will rise and then decline, that it is advisable to stay in the market only for the short run, that one must be careful not to be influenced by others' optimism, and that the market will increase in the short run, although the probability of a stock market crash in the next six months is greater than 10%. Substantial percentages of the respondents, averaging from 10% to 50%, say these things in answer to my questions. The bubble expectations index shows substantial oscillations, indicating that the percentage of institutional investors exhibiting bubble sentiment has fluctuated over time. The level of the index seems to be related to the change in the stock market over the prior six months, meaning that expectations of a temporary bubble are higher whenever the market has been going up more in the preceding six months. However, the index shows no strong trend over the decade since 1989.

A *Barrons* Big Money Poll of professional money managers in April 1999 asked, "Is the stock market in a speculative bubble?" Seventy-two percent of the respondents said yes, only 28% no.[23] This result may seem surprising, given that I found no substantial upward trend in the bubble expectations index, but their question is rather ambiguous, since it does not define a bubble, and no comparison is made with earlier years. Their other survey questions do not ask the respondents if they have bubble expectations as I define them, and their survey finds relatively optimistic expectations overall.

In fact I find little evidence that people have been thinking, during the recent market highs at the dawn of the new millennium, that we are in a temporary speculative bubble. The conspicuous feature of the current high pricing is high confidence that the market will always do well.

### *Ponzi Schemes as Models of Feedback and Speculative Bubbles*

It is very hard to prove that a simple mechanical price feedback model, producing heightened investor attention and enthusiasm, is actually a factor in financial markets. We may have a casual impression that investors are showing enthusiasm for investments in response to past price increases, but we do not see any concrete evidence that such feedback actually affects their decisions.

In order to provide evidence that such feedback mechanisms do play a role in financial markets, it is helpful to look at the example of Ponzi schemes, or pyramid schemes, by means of which hoaxers create positive feedback from putative current investment returns to future investment returns. These schemes have been perpetrated so many times that governments have had to outlaw them, yet they still keep popping up. They are particularly interesting since they are, in a way, controlled experiments (controlled by the hoaxer!) that demonstrate characteristics of the feedback that cannot be seen so plainly either in normal markets or in the experimental psychologist's laboratory.

In a Ponzi scheme, the manager of the scheme promises to make large profits for investors by investing their money. But little or no investment of contributors' funds in any real assets is actually made. Instead, the manager pays off the initial investors with the proceeds of a sale to a second round of investors, and the second round with the proceeds from a sale to a third, and so on. The name of the scheme derives from a particularly famous (though certainly not the first) example, perpetrated by one Charles Ponzi in the United States in 1920. A Ponzi scheme entices initial investors, after they have made a lot of money, to tell their success stories to another round of investors, who then invest even more in the scheme, allowing the hoaxer to pay off the second round of investors, whose success story entices an even larger round of investors, and so on. This scheme must end eventually, since the supply of investors cannot increase forever, and the perpetrator of the scheme no doubt knows this. The perpetrator may hope to exit, not having paid off the last and largest round of investors, and then hide from the law. (Or, possibly, he or she may imagine that with luck, fantastic investment opportunities will be found later, thereby saving the scheme.)

We know that Ponzi schemes have been successful in making their perpetrators rich, at least until they were apprehended. Charles Ponzi attracted 30,000 investors in 1920 and issued notes totaling $15,000,000, all within seven months.[24] In a recent celebrated story, a former housewife, Raejean Bonham, set up an enormous Ponzi scheme on her own in the tiny town of Fox in rural Alaska. She promised to pay 50% returns in two months and enticed 1,200 investors in forty-two states to pay her a total of between $10 and $15 million between 1989 and 1995.[25]

A particularly dramatic story emerged in Albania in 1996 and 1997 when a number of Ponzi schemes promising fantastic rates of return enticed a good share of the people of that country. Seven Ponzi schemes accumulated some $2 billion, or 30% of Albania's annual gross domestic product.[26] Enthusiasm for the schemes was so intense that in the 1996 local elections members of the ruling government party included symbols of the Ponzi scheme funds on their campaign posters, apparently wanting to gain some credit for the new wealth sources. When the schemes failed in 1997, enraged protesters looted banks and burned buildings, and the government was forced to call out the army to restore peace; a number of rioters were killed. The collapse of the schemes forced the resignation of Prime Minister Aleksander Meksi and his cabinet.[27]

As part of their strategy, successful Ponzi schemes present to investors a plausible story about how great profits can be made. Charles Ponzi told investors that he was able to make money for them by exploiting an arbitrage profit opportunity involving international postage reply coupons. These coupons were sold by postal services so that the purchaser could enclose the coupon in a letter to another country and thereby prepay a reply. There were apparently some genuine potential profit opportunities in buying postage reply coupons in Europe and selling them in the United States, because the currency exchange rate did not correspond exactly to the rate implicit in the coupons. Ponzi's story of profit opportunities from trading the coupons, eventually published in newspapers during the scheme, sounded plausible to some influential people. But the actual profit opportunities were not realizable since there was no easy way to sell the coupons, and the hoax began to unravel when the New York postmaster declared that the world's supply of international postage reply coupons was not enough to make the fortune Ponzi claimed to have made.

Raejean Bonham in Alaska claimed she was buying unused frequent-flier miles from large companies, repackaging them as discount tickets, and then selling them at a large profit. The Albanian investment company VEFA was supposedly making a number of conventional investments in a reviving economy. (There was also a rumor in Albania at the time that VEFA was a front for money-laundering, an activity that also sounded like a plausible source of big money to many investors.)[28]

A critical observation to be made about these examples of Ponzi schemes is that initial investors were reportedly very skeptical about the schemes and would invest only small amounts. A story about an arbitrage profit opportunity in postage reply coupons, if merely told directly, without the evidence that it had made others a lot of money, would not sound credible enough to entice many investors. Investors do not become truly confident in the scheme until they see others achieving large returns.

The possibility that the so-called investment payoffs are in fact coming only from new money is typically raised repeatedly and publicly well before the collapse of these schemes, and the hoaxers must of course deny the claim publicly. This was the case both for the original Ponzi scheme and for the Albanian example. The fact that many people continue to believe in the scheme afterward seems puzzling, and to outside observers the believers in the scheme may seem quite foolish.[29] But this only shows the powerful effect on people's thinking of seeing others having made substantial sums of money. That others have made a lot of money appears to many people as the most persuasive evidence in support of the investment story associated with the Ponzi scheme—evidence that outweighs even the most carefully reasoned argument against the story.

### *Speculative Bubbles as Naturally Occurring Ponzi Processes*

It would appear, by extrapolation from examples like those given in the previous section, that speculative feedback loops that are in effect naturally occurring Ponzi schemes do arise from time to time without the contrivance of a fraudulent manager. Even if there is no manipulator fabricating false stories and deliberately deceiving investors in the aggregate stock market, tales about the market are everywhere. When prices go up a number of times, investors are rewarded sequentially by price movements in these markets, just as they are in Ponzi schemes. There are still many people (indeed, the stock brokerage and mutual fund industries as a whole) who benefit from telling stories that suggest that the market will go up further. There is no reason for these stories to be fraudulent; they need only emphasize the positive news and give less emphasis to the negative. The path of a naturally occurring Ponzi scheme—if we may call speculative bubbles that—will be more irregular and less dramatic, since there is no direct manipulation, but the path may sometimes resemble that of a Ponzi scheme when it is supported by naturally occurring stories. The extension from Ponzi schemes to naturally occurring speculative bubbles appears so natural that one must conclude, if there is to be debate about speculative bubbles, that the burden of proof is on skeptics to provide evidence as to why Ponzi-like speculative bubbles *cannot* occur.

Many of the major finance textbooks today, which promote a view of financial markets as working rationally and efficiently, do not provide arguments as to why feedback loops supporting speculative bubbles cannot occur. In fact, they do not even *mention* bubbles or Ponzi schemes.[30] These books convey a sense of orderly progression in financial markets, of markets that work with mathematical precision. If the phenomena are not mentioned at all today, then students are not given any way to judge for themselves whether or not they are in fact influencing the market.

### *Irrational Exuberance and Feedback Loops Today*

Perceived long-term risk is down. Expected returns are not down, despite a high-flying market. Emotions and heightened attention to the market create a desire to get into the game. Such is irrational exuberance today in the United States.

There are many ultimate causes for this exuberance, as detailed in the previous chapter, and the effects of these causes can be amplified by a feedback loop, a speculative bubble, as we have seen in this chapter. As prices continue to rise, the level of exuberance is enhanced by the price rise itself.

In this chapter we have only begun to describe the process of feedback. We have seen that feedback does not merely come about as individuals look at past price increases and make arithmetical calculations to adjust for individual levels of confidence and expectations. The changes in thought patterns infect the entire culture, and they operate not only directly from past price increases but also from auxiliary cultural changes that the past price increases helped generate. For a better understanding of how precipitating factors exert their effects and how they are amplified, we turn, in the next part, to a broader discussion of the cultural changes that accompanied the recent stock market boom and other speculative booms.

*Part Two*

# Cultural Factors

# Four

# The News Media

The history of speculative bubbles begins roughly with the advent of newspapers.[1] One can assume that, although the record of these early newspapers is mostly lost, they regularly reported on the first bubble of any consequence, the Dutch tulip mania of the 1630s.[2]

Although the news media—newspapers, magazines, and broadcast media, along with their new outlets on the Internet—present themselves as detached observers of market events, they are themselves an integral part of these events. Significant market events generally occur only if there is similar thinking among large groups of people, and the news media are essential vehicles for the spread of ideas.

In this chapter, I consider the complexity of the media's impact on market events. As we shall see, news stories rarely have a simple, predictable effect on the market. Indeed, in some respects, they have less impact than is commonly believed. However, a careful analysis reveals that the news media do play an important role both in setting the stage for market moves and in instigating the moves themselves.

## *The Role of the Media in Setting the Stage for Market Moves*

The news media are in constant competition to capture the public attention they need to survive. Survival for them requires finding and defining interesting news, focusing attention on news that has word-of-mouth potential (so as to broaden their audience), and, whenever possible, defining an ongoing story that encourages their audience to remain steady customers.

The competition is by no means haphazard. Those charged with disseminating the news cultivate a creative process, learning from each others' successes and failures, that aims to provide emotional color to news, to invest news stories with human interest appeal, and to create familiar figures in the news. Years of experience in a competitive environment has made the media professions quite skillful at claiming public attention.

The news media are naturally attracted to financial markets because, at the very least, the markets provide constant news in the form of daily price changes. Certainly other markets, such as real estate, are sources of news. But real estate does not typically generate daily price movements. Nothing beats the stock market for sheer frequency of potentially interesting news items.

The stock market also has star quality. The public considers it the Big Casino, the market for major players, and believes that on any given day it serves as a barometer of the status of the nation—all impressions that the media can foster and benefit from. Financial news may have great human interest potential to the extent that it deals with the making or breaking of fortunes. And the financial media can present their perennial lead, the market's performance, as an ongoing story—one that brings in the most loyal repeat customers. The only other regular generator of news on a comparable scale is sporting events. It is no accident that financial news and sports news together account for roughly half of the editorial content of many newspapers today.

## *Media Cultivation of Debate*

In an attempt to attract audiences, the news media try to present debate about issues on the public mind. This may mean creating a debate on topics that experts would not otherwise consider deserving of such discussion. The resulting media event may convey the impression that there are experts on all sides of the issue, thereby suggesting a lack of expert agreement on the very issues that people are most confused about.

I have over the years been called by newspeople asking me if I would be willing to make a statement in support of some extreme view. When I declined, the next request would inevitably be to recommend another expert who *would* go on record in support of the position.

Five days before the 1987 stock market crash, the MacNeil/Lehrer NewsHour featured Ravi Batra, author of *The Great Depression of 1990: Why It's Got to Happen, How to Protect Yourself.* This book took as its basic premise a theory that history tends to repeat itself in exact detail, so that the 1929 crash and subsequent depression had to repeat themselves. Despite Batra's significant scholarly reputation, this particular book of his is not one that would be viewed with any seriousness by most reputable scholars of the market. But it had been on the *New York Times* best-seller list for fifteen weeks by the time of the crash. On the NewsHour, Batra confidently predicted a stock market crash in 1989 that would "spread to the whole world"; after it, he declared, "there will be a depression."[3] Batra's statements, made as they were on a highly respected show, may—even though they predicted a crash two years hence—have contributed in some small measure to an atmosphere of vulnerability that brought us the crash of 1987. Although Batra's appearance on the NewsHour just before the crash might be considered a coincidence, one must keep in mind that predictions of stock market crashes are actually quite rare on national news shows. The proximity of his appearance to the actual crash is at the very least highly suggestive.

Should the media be faulted for presenting debates on topics of little merit? One can argue that they ought to focus on a variety of topics of interest to general audiences, so that the public can refine their views. Yet in doing so the media seem often to disseminate and reinforce ideas that are not supported by real evidence. If news directors followed only their highest intellectual interests in judging which views to present, the public might indeed find its consciousness constructively broadened. But that is apparently not how the media see their mission—nor do competitive pressures encourage them to rethink the matter.

### *Reporting on the Market Outlook*

There is no shortage of media accounts that try to answer our questions about the market today, but there *is* a shortage within these accounts of relevant facts or considered interpretations of them. Many news stories in fact seem to have been written under a deadline to produce something—*anything*—to go along with the numbers from the market. The typical such story, after noting the remarkable bull market, focuses on very short-run statistics. It generally states which groups of stocks have risen more than others in recent months. Although these stocks are described as leaders, there is no good reason to think that their performance has caused the bull market. The news story may talk about the "usual" factors behind economic growth, such as the Internet boom, in glowing terms and with at least a hint of patriotic congratulation to our powerful economic engine. The article then finishes with quotes from a few well-chosen "celebrity" sources, offering their outlook for the future. Sometimes the article is so completely devoid of genuine thought about the reasons for the bull market and the context for considering its outlook that it is hard to believe that the writer was other than cynical in his or her approach.

What are the celebrity sources quoted as saying in these articles? They typically give numerical forecasts for the Dow Jones Industrial Average in the near future, tell stories or jokes, and dispense their personal opinions. For example, when Abby Joseph Cohen of Goldman Sachs & Co. coins a quotable phrase—as with her warnings against "FUDD" (fear, uncertainty, doubt, and despair) or her phrase "Silly Putty Economy"—it is disseminated widely. Beyond that, the media quote her opinions but pay no critical attention to her analysis. In fact, although she no doubt has access to a formidable research department and performs extensive data analysis before forming her opinions, they are ultimately reported as just that—her opinions. Of course she should not be faulted for this, for it is the nature of the sound-bite-driven media that superficial opinions are preferred to in-depth analyses.

### *Record Overload*

The media often seem to thrive on superlatives, and we, their audience, are confused as to whether the price increases we have recently seen in the stock market are all that unusual. Data that suggest that we are setting some new record (or are at least close to doing so) are regularly stressed in the media , and if reporters look at the data in enough different ways, they will often find *something* that is close to setting a record on any given day. In covering the stock market, many writers mention "record one-day price changes"—measured in points on the Dow rather than percentage terms, so that records are much more likely. Although the media have become increasingly enlightened about reporting in terms of points on the Dow in recent years, the practice still persists among some writers.

This *record overload*—the impression that new and significant records are constantly being set—only adds to the confusion people have about the economy. It makes it hard for people to recognize when something truly and importantly new really *is* happening. It also, with its deluge of different indicators, encourages an avoidance of individual assessment of quantitative data—a preference for seeing the data interpreted for us by celebrity sources.

### *Do Big Stock Price Changes Really Follow Big News Days?*

Many people seem to think that it is the reporting of specific news events, the serious content of news, that affects financial markets. But research offers far less support for this view than one would imagine.

Victor Niederhoffer, while he was still an assistant professor at Berkeley in 1971 (before he became a legendary hedge fund manager), published an article that sought to establish whether days with news of significant world events corresponded to days that saw big stock price movements. He tabulated all very large headlines in the *New York Times* (large type size being taken as a crude indicator of relative importance) from 1950 to 1966; there were 432 such headlines. Did these significant-world-event days correspond to big movements in stock prices? As the standard of comparison, Niederhoffer noted that the S&P Composite Index over this period showed substantial one-day increases (of more than 0.78%) on only 10% of the trading days, and substantial one-day decreases (of more than 0.71%) on only another 10% of the trading days. Of the 432 significant-world-event days, 78 (or 18%) showed big price increases, and 56 (or 13%) showed big decreases. Thus such days were only slightly more likely to show large price movements than other days.[4]

Niederhoffer claimed that, on reading the stories under these headlines, many of the world events reported did not seem likely to have much impact on the fundamental value represented by the stock market. Perhaps what the media *thought* was big national news was not what was really important to the stock market. He speculated that news events that represented crises were more likely to influence the stock market.

Defining a crisis as a time when five or more large headlines occurred within a seven-day period, Niederhoffer found eleven crises in the sample interval. These were the beginning of the Korean war in 1950, the capture of Seoul by the Communists in 1951, the Democratic National Convention of 1952, Russian troops' threatening Hungary and Poland in 1956, the Suez crisis of 1956, Charles de Gaulle's taking office as French premier in 1958, the entry of U.S. marines into Lebanon in 1958, Russian premier Nikita Khrushchev's appearance at the United Nations in 1959, Cuban tensions in 1960, the Cuban arms blockade in 1962, and President John Kennedy's assassination in 1963. During these crises, so defined, 42% of the daily price changes were "big" changes, as compared with 20% for other, "normal" time periods. Thus the crisis periods were somewhat, but not dramatically, more likely to be accompanied by big stock price changes.

Note that there were only eleven such weeks of "crisis" in the whole sixteen years of Niederhoffer's sample. Very few of the aggregate price movements in the stock market show any meaningful association with headlines.

### *Tag-Along News*

News stories occurring on days of big price swings that are cited as the causes of the changes often cannot, one suspects, plausibly account for the changes—or at least not for their full magnitude. On Friday, October 13, 1989, there was a stock market crash that was clearly identified by the media as a reaction to a news story. A leveraged buyout deal for UAL Corporation, the parent company of United Airlines, had fallen through. The crash, which resulted in a 6.91% drop in the Dow for the day, had begun just minutes after this announcement, and so it at first seemed highly likely that it was the cause of the crash.

The first problem with this interpretation is that UAL is just one firm, accounting for but a fraction of 1% of the stock market's total value. Why should the collapse of the UAL buyout have such an impact on the entire market? One interpretation at the time was that the deal's failure was viewed by the market as a watershed event, portending that many other similar pending buyouts would also fail. But no concrete arguments were given in support of this view; rather, dubbing it a watershed seemed to have been nothing more than an effort to make sense after the fact of the market's move in response to the news.

To try to discover the reasons for the October 13, 1989, crash, survey researcher William Feltus and I carried out a telephone survey of 101 market professionals on the Monday and Tuesday following the crash. We asked: "Did you hear about the UAL news before you heard about the market drop on Friday afternoon, or did you hear about the UAL news later as an explanation for the drop in the stock market?" Only 36% said they had heard about the news before the crash; 53% said they had heard about it afterward as an explanation for the drop; the rest were unsure when they had heard about it. Thus it appears that the news story may have *tagged along* after the crash, rather than directly caused it, and therefore that it was not as prominent as the media accounts suggested.

We also asked the market professionals to interpret the news story. We queried:

> Which of the following two statements better represents the view you held last Friday:
>
> 1. The UAL news of Friday afternoon will reduce future takeovers, and so the UAL news is a sensible reason for the sudden drop in stock prices.
> 2. The UAL news of Friday afternoon should be viewed as a focal point or attention grabber, which prompted investors to express their doubts about the market.

Of the respondents, 30% chose 1 and 50% chose 2; the rest were unsure. Thus they were mostly reacting to the news as an *interpretation of the behavior of investors.*[5] It may be correct to say that the news event was *fundamental* to this stock market crash, in that it represented a "story" that enhanced the feedback from stock price drops to further stock price drops, thereby preserving the feedback effect for a longer period than would otherwise have been the case. Yet it was unlikely to have been its *cause.*

### *The Absence of News on Days of Big Price Changes*

We can also look at days of unusually large price movements and ask if there were exceptionally important items of news on those days. Following up on Niederhoffer's work, in 1989 David Cutler, James Poterba, and Lawrence Summers compiled a list of the fifty largest U.S. stock market movements, as measured by the S&P Index, since World War II, and for each tabulated the explanations offered in the news media. Most of the so-called explanations do not correspond to any unusual news, and some of them could not possibly be considered serious news. For example, the reasons given for large price movements included such relatively innocuous statements as "Eisenhower urges confidence in the economy," "further reaction to Truman victory over Dewey," and "replacement buying after earlier fall."[6]

Some would argue that perhaps we should not expect to see prominent news on days of big price changes, even if markets are working perfectly. Price changes in a so-called efficient market occur, so the argument goes, as soon as the information becomes public; they do not wait until the information is reported in the media. (This is a topic to which I return in Chapter 9.) Thus it is not surprising, according to this line of reasoning, that we often do not find new information in the newspaper on the day of a price change: earlier information, appearing to the casual observer as tangential or irrelevant, has already been interpreted by perceptive investors as significant to the fundamentals that should determine share prices.

Another argument advanced to explain why days of unusually large stock price movements have often not been found to coincide with important news is that a confluence of factors may cause a significant market change, even if the individual factors themselves are not particularly newsworthy. For example, suppose certain investors are informally using a particular statistical model that forecasts fundamental value using a number of economic indicators. If all or most of these particular indicators point the same way on a given day, even if no single one of them is of any substantive importance by itself, their combined effect will be noteworthy.

Both of these interpretations of the tenuous relationship between news and market movements assume that the public is paying continuous attention to the news—reacting sensitively to the slightest clues about market fundamentals, constantly and carefully adding up all the disparate pieces of evidence. But that is just not the way public attention works. Our attention is much more quixotic and capricious. Instead, news functions more often as an *initiator* of a chain of events that fundamentally change the public's thinking about the market.

## *News as the Precipitator of Attention Cascades*

The role of news events in affecting the market seems often to be delayed, and to have the effect of setting in motion a *sequence of public attentions*. These attentions may be to images or stories, or to facts that may already have been well known. The facts may previously have been ignored or judged inconsequential, but they can attain newfound prominence in the wake of breaking news. These sequences of attention may be called *cascades,* as one focus of attention leads to attention to another, and then another.

At 5:46 A.M. on Tuesday, January 17, 1995, an earthquake measuring 7.2 on the Richter scale struck Kobe, Japan; it was the worst earthquake to hit urban Japan since 1923. The reaction of the stock markets of the world to this event provides an interesting case study since in this case we know without doubt that the precipitating event, the earthquake, was truly exogenous and not itself generated by human activity or business conditions—not a response to a subtle hint of economic change nor the result of a confluence of unusual values of conventional economic indicators. In the Cutler-Poterba-Summers list of media explanations for the fifty largest postwar movements in the S&P Index in the United States, discussed earlier, not a single one of the explanations referred to any substantial cause that was definitely exogenous to the economy.[7]

The earthquake took 6,425 lives. According to estimates by the Center for Industrial Renovation of Kansai, the total damage caused by the earthquake was about $100 billion. The reaction in financial markets was strong, but delayed. The Tokyo stock market fell only slightly that day, and prices of construction-related companies generally rose, reflecting the expected increased demand for their products and services. Analysts reported at that time that the probable effects of the earthquake on corporate value were as yet ambiguous, since the wave of rebuilding after the quake might stimulate the Japanese economy.

The biggest reaction to the earthquake did not come until a week later. On January 23, the Japanese Nikkei index fell 5.6% on no apparent news except the gradual unfolding of numerous news accounts of earthquake damage. Over the ten days following the earthquake, the Nikkei lost over 8% of its value. If viewed as the direct result of the earthquake damage alone, the loss of value would be an overreaction.

What was going on in investors' minds over the ten days following the earthquake? Of course, there is no rigorous way to find out. We know only that over this period the Kobe earthquake dominated the news, created new and different images of Japan, and may have led to very different impressions about the Japanese economy. Moreover, the quake sparked discussions about the risk of an earthquake centered in Tokyo. Despite the fact that geological evidence suggesting that Tokyo is at risk for a major earthquake was already known, greater attention was now focused on this potential problem. The damage that an earthquake of the severity of the 1923 quake could cause to modern-day Tokyo was put at $1.25 trillion by Tokai Research and Consulting Inc.[8]

Even more puzzling than the direct effect of the Kobe earthquake on the domestic Japanese markets was its effect on foreign stock markets. On the day that the Nikkei fell 5.6%, the FT-SE 100 index in London fell 1.4%, the CAC-40 in Paris fell 2.2%, and the DAX in Germany fell 1.4%. The Brazilian and Argentine stock markets both fell about 3%. These diverse countries around the world suffered no earthquake damage on this occasion.

The best interpretation of the effects of the Kobe earthquake on the stock markets of the world is that news coverage of the earthquake, and of the accompanying stock market declines, engaged the attention of investors, prompting a cascade of attentions that brought to the fore some more pessimistic factors.

Another market reaction to news illustrates how media attention may, through a cascade of attentions, lead many investors to eventually take seriously news that would normally be considered nonsense and irrelevant. A sequence of news stories about Joseph Granville, a flamboyant market forecaster, appear to have caused a couple of major market moves. The only substantive content of these media stories was that Granville was telling his clients to buy or sell, and that Granville himself was influential.

Granville's behavior easily attracted public attention. His investment seminars were bizarre extravaganzas, sometimes featuring a trained chimpanzee who could play Granville's theme song, "The Bagholder's Blues," on a piano. He once showed up at an investment seminar dressed as Moses, wearing a crown and carrying tablets. Granville made extravagant claims for his forecasting ability. He said he could forecast earthquakes and once claimed to have predicted six of the past seven major world quakes. He was quoted by *Time* magazine as saying, "I don't think that I will ever make a serious mistake in the stock market for the rest of my life," and he predicted that he would win the Nobel Prize in economics.[9]

The first Granville episode took place on Tuesday, April 22, 1980. With the news that he had changed his recommendation from short to long, the Dow rose 30.72 points, or 4.05%. This was the biggest increase in the Dow since November 1, 1978, a year and a half earlier. The second episode occurred on January 6, 1981, after Granville's investor service changed from a long recommendation to a short recommendation. The Dow took its biggest dive since October 9, 1979, over a year earlier. There was no other news on either of these occasions that might appear responsible for the market change, and on the second occasion both the *Wall Street Journal* and *Barrons* squarely attributed the drop to Granville's recommendation.

Can we be sure that media reporting of Granville and his supposed powers of prognostication caused these changes? Many people wondered if the Granville effect was not just a coincidence that the news media exaggerated. We *can* be sure that a sequence of news stories about Granville's pronouncements, with their substantial word-of-mouth potential, had a cumulative effect on national attention, and that public reactions to his pronouncements and to market declines at the time of his announcements were fundamentally altered by this cascade.[10]

### News during the Crash of 1929

The role of the news media in causing the stock market crash of 1929 has been debated almost since the crash itself. In fact the puzzle facing historians and economists has been, by some interpretations, that just before the crash there was no significant news at all. But, people have wondered ever since, how could this record stock market crash get under way with no news? What common concerns were on the minds of sellers that caused so many of them to try to sell at the same time?

The Monday, October 28, 1929, stock market crash was the biggest single-day drop (measured between the closing price the previous trading day and the closing price on the day) in the Dow until the October 19, 1987, crash. On October 28, 1929, the Dow fell 12.8% in one day (13.01% measured from the high to the low on that day). The second-biggest drop in history (until 1987) occurred the following day, when the Dow dropped 11.7% (15.9% measured from the high to the low on that day). The combined close-to-close drop in those two days in 1929 was 23.1%. What news had arisen that might rationally account for such a sizable stock market decline?

On reading the major newspapers over that weekend and on into the morning of Tuesday, October 29, one is easily led to conclude that nothing of any consequence for the fundamentals of the market was happening. Indeed that was the conclusion reported in the newspapers themselves. On the morning of October 29, newspapers around the country carried an Associated Press story that said in part, "In the absence of any adverse news developments over the week-end, and in the face of the optimistic comments on business forthcoming from President Hoover and leading industrial and banking executives, Wall Street's only explanation of today's decline was that a careful checking up of accounts over the week-end disclosed numerous weak spots, which had been overlooked in the hectic sessions of last week." The *New York Times* attributed the drop only to a "general loss of confidence." The *Wall Street Journal* reported that "business in general shows no signs of disintegration" and that the decline was due to "necessitous liquidation of impaired accounts."[11]

What else was in the news on those days? As of Monday morning there was news that the Interstate Commerce Commission would proceed with its plan to recapture some excess railroad income. There was a favorable report on the earnings of U.S. Steel. New information was reported on charges that the Connecticut Manufacturer's Association had succeeded in introducing into a tariff bill provisions favoring Connecticut. Mussolini had made a speech saying that the "men and institutions of fascism can face any crisis, even if it is sudden." A new aspirant to the French premiership, Edouard Daladier, announced the foreign minister of his prospective cabinet. A British airliner was lost at sea with seven aboard. The *Graf Zeppelin* planned a trip to explore the Arctic. Richard Byrd's party was making progress toward the South Pole.

After Black Monday, early on Tuesday morning, the second day of the crash, it was reported that prominent financiers had asserted that heavy banking support would come into the market that day, in search of bargains. If this was significant news at all, one would think it was good news. Other news on Tuesday morning was that two senators had called on President Hoover to declare his position on duties on agricultural and industrial products, that Senator Hiram Bingham had complained that the Lobby Inquiry had treated him unfairly, a Hungarian count and countess had been given the right to enter the country, and another airliner had been lost with five aboard.

All of these stories sound very typical. If there really was a good reason for the drop in the market, then certainly there must have been *something* happening at the time that people knew about. And one would think that such concerns would have made it into the news in some form. Perhaps one must read the papers more carefully. One author, Jude Wanniski, indeed claimed that there was a story in the *New York Times* on the morning of Monday, October 28, 1929, that might conceivably account for such a decline. This front-page story was an optimistic report on the likelihood of passage of the Smoot-Hawley tariff, then still in committee. The story was picked up by the Associated Press and United News the following day and given front-page treatment around the country on Tuesday, October 29.[12]

It is conceivable that the Smoot-Hawley tariff might have been expected to hurt the outlook for U.S. corporate profits. One could have thought that it would generally benefit corporations, many of whom actively sought the tariff. But it has been argued by historians of the 1929 crash that the tariff might have been expected to have the opposite effect, given the retaliation from other countries that it would engender. Allan Meltzer in fact argued that the tariff could be the reason "why the 1929 recession did not follow the path of previous monetary contractions but became the Great Depression."[13] However, other economists, including Rudiger Dornbusch and Stanley Fischer, pointed out that exports were only 7%

of the gross national product (GNP) in 1929 and that between 1929 and 1931 they fell by only 1.5% of 1929 GNP. This hardly seems like the cause of the Great Depression. Moreover, they pointed out that it is not clear that the Smoot-Hawley tariff was responsible for the decline in exports. The depression itself might be held responsible for part of the decline. Dornbusch and Fischer showed that the 1922 Fordney-McCumber tariff increased tariff rates as much as the Smoot-Hawley tariff, and the Fordney-McCumber tariff was of course followed by no such recession.[14]

Even if we were to allow that the possibility of passage of the Smoot-Hawley tariff was important enough to account for a decline in share values of this magnitude, one must still ask whether there was any news over the weekend that would substantially alter one's estimation of the likelihood that the tariff would be passed. Just what was the content of the story in the *New York Times?* On Saturday, October 26, Senator David Reed declared that the Smoot-Hawley tariff bill was "dead" in committee. This provoked denials by Senators Reed Smoot and William Borah. The *Times* quoted Senator Smoot as saying, "If that is Senator Reed's opinion, I suppose he has a right to express it. But it isn't the view of the Finance Committee." Senator Borah said, "My opinion is that the tariff bill is not going to die." The next morning, October 29, the *Times* reported that Senator Reed had reiterated his conviction that the bill was dead and went on to cite other opinions on both sides of the issue. Although the original *Times* story had sounded optimistic for the bill, the United News version of the story published on October 29 was pessimistic. The *Atlanta Constitution,* when it ran the story on October 29, carried the headline, "Senate Gives Up Hope of Enacting New Tariff Bill."

Nonetheless, it is hard to see that this interchange among senators, so typical of political wrangling, amounts to important news. The same sort of news accounts had been coming out all along with regard to the tariff bill. A week earlier, on October 21, the *Times* had quoted Senator James Watson, Republican leader of the Senate, offering his view that the Senate would pass the bill within another month. On October 13, Senator Smoot was reported as telling President Hoover that there was a chance the bill would pass by

November 20. Alternately optimistic and pessimistic news on the tariff bill had been coming in since Hoover's election.

Far more significant than news about fundamentals among the newspaper stories on Monday, October 28, 1929, are clues to the importance attached in people's minds to the events of just a few days earlier, when the stock exchange had seen a record decline in share prices. That was the so-called Black Thursday, October 24, 1929, when the Dow had fallen 12.9% within the day but recovered substantially before the end of trading, so that the closing average was down only 2.1% from the preceding close. This event was no longer news, but the memory of the emotions it had generated was very much part of the ambience on Monday. The *New York Times* noted in its Monday morning edition that Wall Street, "normally deserted and quiet on Sunday as a country graveyard, hummed with activity as bankers and brokers strove to put their houses in order after the most strenuous week in history. . . . When the bell clangs at 10 o'clock this morning for the resumption of trading, most houses will be abreast of their work and ready for what may come." The atmosphere of that Sunday on Wall Street was described: "Sightseers strolled from street to street, gazing curiously at the Stock Exchange Building and the Morgan banking offices across the way, centers of last week's dramatic financial happenings. Here and there a sightseer picked up from the street a vagrant slip of ticker tape, as visitors seize upon spent bullets on a battlefield as souvenirs. Sightseeing buses made special trips through the district."[15]

Indeed, on that same Monday morning of the crash the *Wall Street Journal* saw fit to run a front-page editorial stating that "everybody in responsible positions says that business conditions are sound."[16] The editorial staff of the *Journal* must have had reasons to suspect that reassurance was needed if the market was to remain stable. Presumably they had heard snippets of popular conversation, or could at least guess how people might react following the weekend, given the huge debacle on Thursday.

So perhaps what happened on Monday, October 28, 1929, was just an echo, albeit a very exaggerated one, of what had happened the previous week. What had the media said about this? Again, the newspapers seemed to think that there was no important news. The *Chicago Tribune* wrote, on Sunday, October 27, 1929, "It has been the collapse of a vastly inflated bubble of speculation, with little or no cause in the country's general situation. A top-heavy structure has collapsed of its own weight—there has been no earthquake." The *New York Times* said, "The market smash has been caused by technical rather than fundamental considerations." The *Guaranty Survey*, published by the Guaranty Trust Company, remarked that "to suppose that the selling wave of the last few weeks was due to adverse developments of corresponding importance in the general business situation would be a fundamental error."[17]

Let us go back in time and look at the news on the morning of Black Thursday, October 24, 1929. Once again, the news does not seem to be very significant. President Hoover had announced a plan to develop inland waterways. Atlantic Refinings' earnings for the year were reported to be its highest ever. The president of a sugar company had told a Senate committee investigating lobbying that $75,000 had been spent by the sugar lobby since December in a campaign to reduce duties on sugar. Negotiators had reported a setback in efforts to establish the Bank for International Settlements. A Carnegie Fund report decried the subsidization of college athletes. The America's Cup committee had announced the rules for the next running of the yacht race. An amateur pilot attempting a solo flight across the Atlantic was reported lost. President Hoover had taken a trip on a picturesque river boat down the Ohio River.

Nothing here seems remotely to suggest anything fundamental about the outlook for the stock market. But let us look back yet another day. There was news on the Wednesday before Black Thursday that there had been a major drop in the market (the Dow closed on Wednesday down 6.3% from Tuesday's close) and that total transactions had had their second highest day in history. Should we then look for the cause in the news of October 23, 1929? Again there was no national news of any apparent significance, but again there were references to past market moves. The most significant concrete news stories in the newspapers seem consistently to have been about previous moves of the market itself. The most prominent content in the news appears to have been interpretations of the reasons for these previous moves, often in terms of investor psychology.

There is no way that the events of the stock market crash of 1929 can be considered a response to any real news stories. We see instead a *negative bubble,* operating through feedback effects of price changes, and an *attention cascade,* with a series of heightened public fixations on the market. This sequence of events appears to be fundamentally no different from those of other market debacles—including the notorious crash of 1987, to which we now turn.

### *News during the Crash of 1987*

When the stock market crashed on October 19, 1987—setting a new record one-day decline that nearly doubled that of either October 28 or October 29, 1929 (to this day it is the all-time record one-day price drop)—I considered it a unique opportunity to inquire directly of investors what they considered to be the significant news on that day. It was no longer necessary, as it had been for those who studied the 1929 crash, to rely on media interpretations suggesting what was the important news on investors' minds. As far as I have been able to determine, no one else took advantage of this opportunity. The results of my questionnaire survey, sent out to a sample of institutional investors and a sample of individual investors the week of the crash, were the only published findings of a survey asking investors what they were thinking on the day of the crash.[18]

In my 1987 survey, I listed all the news stories published in the few days preceding the crash that seemed at all relevant to the changing opinions of the market, ending with news that had appeared in the papers on the morning of the crash. I asked the investors:

> Please tell us how important each of the following news items was to you personally on October 19, 1987, in your evaluation of stock market prospects. Please rate them on a one-to-seven scale, 1 indicating that the term was completely unimportant, 4 indicating that it was of moderate importance, 7 indicating that it was very important. Please tell how important *you* then felt these were, and not how others thought about them.

I included ten news stories, and in the eleventh position a space marked "Other" where respondents could write in their own choices.

The results were broadly similar between institutional and individual investors, and between those who had actually bought or sold on October 19. Respondents rated everything as relevant. They thought that most of the news stories rated at least a 4, that is, they were of moderate importance. The only news story that merited an average score less than 3 was the sell signal that investment guru Robert Prechter was reported to have given on October 14, and even that received a score around 2. Even the news that the United States had attacked an Iranian oil station, a minor skirmish reported on October 19, received a rating over 3. Respondents were not very forthcoming with other news stories in the "Other" category. They tended to mention concerns, rather than news stories that broke at the time of the crash. The most common write-in answer was a concern about too much indebtedness, referring variously to the federal deficit, the national debt, or taxes. Such a response was offered by a third of the individual investors who wrote in answers and a fifth of the institutional investors.

But the striking result was that the most highly rated news stories among those I listed were those about *past price declines themselves*. The most important news story, according to the respondents, was the 200-point drop in the Dow on the morning of October 19, a news story that yielded an average score of 6.54 among individual sellers on October 19 and 6.05 among institutional sellers on October 19. The preceding week's news of the record (in terms of points lost) stock market declines was considered the second most important story.

One of the questions asked respondents to give their recollections of the interpretations they had attached to the price declines on the day of the crash: "Can you remember any specific theory you had about the causes for the price declines October 14–19, 1987?" Respondents were given space to write answers in their own words, which I read and categorized. Odd as it may seem from the perspective of today's much higher market, the most common theme in the answers to this open-ended question was that the market had been overpriced before the crash. Overpricing was mentioned by 33.9% of the individual investors and 32.6% of the institutional investors. Although this response accounts for fewer than half the answers, it is noteworthy that so many thought to mention this in answer to an open-ended question. (I also asked them directly elsewhere on the questionnaire whether they thought, just before the crash, that the market was overpriced, and 71.7% of the individual investors [91.0% of those who had sold on October 19] and 84.3% of the institutional investors [88.5% of those who had sold on October 19] said yes.)[19] Another important theme in answer to the open-ended question was one of institutional stop-loss, identified by the presence of the words *institutional selling, program trading, stop-loss,* or *computer trading;* 22.8% of the individuals and 33.1% of the institutional investors mentioned such a theme. There was also an investor irrationality theme, identified by statements to the effect that investors were crazy or that the fall was due to investor panic or capricious changes in opinion; 25.4% of the individuals and 24.4% of the institutional investors touched on this theme. None of these major themes had anything to do with breaking news events other than the crash itself.

Immediately after this question, I asked on the questionnaire, "Which of the following better describes your theory about the declines: a theory about investor psychology [or] a theory about fundamentals such as profits or interest rates?" Most—67.5% of the institutional investors and 64.0% of the individual investors—picked a theory about investor psychology.

Thus it appears that the stock market crash had substantially to do with a *psychological feedback loop* among the general investing public from price declines to selling and thus further price declines, along the lines of a negative bubble, as discussed in Chapter 3. The crash apparently had nothing particularly to do with any news story other than that of the crash itself, but rather with theories about other investors' reasons for selling and about their psychology.

President Ronald Reagan, reacting to the crash, set up a study commission headed by former Treasury Secretary Nicholas Brady. He asked the Brady Commission to tell him what had caused the crash and what should be done about it. Investment professionals are generally uncomfortable going on record to explain the causes of such events, and many reports about the crash tended to focus the inquiry away from its ultimate causes. But the members of the Brady Commission were under orders from the president of the United States to face the matter head on. As a result, we have in their report the only major effort to collect all the relevant facts and explain the crash of 1987. They wrote in their summary the following explanation for the crash:

> The precipitous market decline of mid-October was "triggered" by specific events: an unexpectedly high merchandise trade deficit which pushed interest rates to new high levels, and proposed tax legislation which led to the collapse of the stocks of a number of takeover candidates. This initial decline ignited mechanical, price-insensitive selling by a number of institutions employing portfolio insurance strategies and a small number of mutual fund groups reacting to redemptions. The selling by these investors, and the prospect of further selling by them, encouraged a number of aggressive trading-oriented institutions to sell in anticipation of further market declines. These institutions included, in addition to hedge funds, a small number of pension and endowment funds, money management firms and investment banking houses. This selling, in turn, stimulated further reactive selling by portfolio insurers and mutual funds.[20]

This conclusion by the Brady Commission sounds in some ways very much like the one I drew from my own survey-based study of the crash. By "price-insensitive selling" they mean selling that comes in response to a price drop but is insensitive to how low the price goes before the sale is concluded—selling at any price. The commission was saying here, most prominently, that the crash was caused by what I have called a feedback loop, with initial price declines influencing more investors to exit the market, thereby creating further price declines. The Brady Commission was saying, in effect, that the crash of 1987 was a negative bubble.

A strength of the Brady Commission's study of the crash relative to my own was their unparalleled access to major investing institutions. Their study complements my own in reaching the conclusion that a feedback loop was at work in the crash. However, their conclusion sounds a bit different from mine in that it gives prominence to the substantive content of news stories. In addition, theirs suggests that much of the selling was "mechanical" or "reactive," rather than psychological or herdlike.

Based on the results of my study, the news stories that the Brady Commission mentions about the merchandise trade deficit and about new highs in interest rates cannot be considered central to investors' thinking. In my survey, I included these in my list of news stories and got a lukewarm response from respondents (mostly 4s). Moreover, if one looks at long-term plots of both the trade deficit and interest rates, it is very clear that there was no sudden break in either of these series that could possibly be seen as standing out in a historical perspective. Virtually nothing happened to either the trade deficit or interest rates.

The proposed tax legislation that the Brady Commission mentions had completely escaped my notice as an important news story to include on my list. The news had broken on October 14, five days before the crash, and it had not seemed to me to be the subject of significant public comment in the days leading up to the crash. Representative Dan Rostenkowski's House Ways and Means Committee was considering tax changes that would have had the effect of discouraging corporate takeovers. Changing capital gains tax provisions struck many would-be interpreters of the crash after the fact as having fundamental importance for stock prices in an efficient market.

When I learned of the potential importance of this news story, I went back over the questionnaires I had received to see how many respondents had mentioned it in their answers under "Other." I found no mention at all among the 605 individual responses, and only three mentions among the 284 institutional responses. Clearly, this news story does not deserve to be singled out as a major cause of the crash.[21]

The Brady Commission puts quite a bit of stress on a tool of institutional investors called "portfolio insurance." Portfolio insurance is a strategy for limiting losses that was invented by Professors Hayne Leland and Mark Rubinstein at the University of California at Berkeley and successfully marketed by them to many institutional investors in the 1980s. Portfolio insurance is really a misnomer; the strategy is merely a plan for selling stocks. It involves impressive mathematical models, but in fact it is nothing more than a formalized procedure for getting out of the market by selling stocks when they start to go down. Leland himself, in his classic 1980 article on portfolio insurance, admits as much: "Some 'rules of thumb' such as 'run with your winners, cut your losses' and 'sell at a new high, buy at a new low,' will be shown to approximate the optimal dynamic trading strategies for certain types of investors."[22] So, by using portfolio insurance, investors are merely doing what has always come naturally, only with a little more mathematical precision and careful planning. But with the fancy new name "portfolio insurance," which suggests that the strategy is prudent and sensible, and with its high-tech image, the advent of this strategy quite likely made many investors more reactive to past price changes.

The adoption of portfolio insurance by many institutional investors was a sort of fad—a sophisticated fad, but a fad nonetheless. Since it has a distinctive name (the term *portfolio insurance* had essentially not been used before 1980), it is possible to trace the course of this investor fad by means of word counts in the press. I performed such a count on ABI/INFORM, a database of business periodicals, and found no more than 1 reference to portfolio insurance in each of the years 1980–83, 4 in 1984, 6 in 1985, 41 in 1986, and 75 in 1987. References to portfolio insurance were growing along the type of steady growth path that characterizes simple word-of-mouth epidemic models, which will be discussed in Chapter 8.[23]

So the development of portfolio insurance changed the way some investors reacted to past price changes just before the crash of 1987. There were probably other changes in the nature of the feedback loop that, because they were not so concretely programmed as portfolio insurance, we could not observe directly. But the important point is that *it was the changed nature of the feedback loop, not the news stories that broke around the time of the crash,* that was the essential cause of the crash.

Feedback can be modified by many factors, and the news media themselves can certainly have an impact on it. The *Wall Street Journal,* on the morning of the 1987 crash, ran a plot showing the Dow in the 1980s and, just below it, a plot showing the Dow in the

1920s up to and for a month after the crash of 1929.[24] The two plots were aligned so that the current date lined up with the date of the 1929 crash, and so the plot suggested that the crash of 1929 might be about to repeat itself. Investors had the opportunity to see this plot at breakfast a matter of minutes before the crash of 1987 actually started. The *Journal* was openly suggesting the possibility of a crash starting that day. True, this was not a front-page story, and no one story by itself is decisive in causing a crash. But this little story and the accompanying plot, appearing as they did on the morning of the crash, probably did help prime investors to be more alert to suggestions of a crash.

When the big price declines on the morning of October 19, 1987, began, the archetype that was the 1929 crash encouraged many people to question whether "it" was happening again—the "it" being the Great Crash as illustrated in the *Journal*, not the crash of 1907, nor the upcrash of 1932, nor any of the numerous other historical stock market events that by then had been almost completely forgotten. The mental image of the biggest crash in history possibly happening on that very day had the potential to enhance the feedback from initial price declines to later price declines. The image also provided a suggestion of how far the market would decline before it rebounded, a crucial factor in determining how far the market actually did fall. In fact, in the crash of October 19, 1987, the Dow actually fell in one day almost the same amount as it did on October 28–29, 1929—22.6% in 1987 versus 23.1% in 1929. That it fell roughly the same amount on both occasions might be regarded as just a coincidence, especially since the 1987 crash took two days rather than one, and few investors in 1987 even knew exactly how far the market fell in 1929. On the other hand, many did have a rough impression of the extent of the 1929 plunge, and there was little other concrete information available to investors on October 19, 1987, to suggest when the market should stop falling.

The changed feedback that occurred at the time of the 1987 crash should be thought of as just one example of continually changing price-to-price feedback, as investors' theories and methods change over time. It would be a mistake to describe the changed feedback as the result only of the technological innovation represented by portfolio insurance. Despite the use of computers in executing portfolio insurance strategies, it is still people who decide to deploy the tool and who decide how quickly it will take effect in a declining market. And there are of course many other people who, aware that portfolio insurance is being used, adjust their own informal responses to past price changes depending on their perceptions of other investors' use of the strategy. Portfolio insurance is of interest to us in this context only because it shows us concretely how people's thinking can change in ways that alter the manner in which feedback from stock price changes affects further stock price changes, thereby creating possible price instabilities.

### *The Role of News Media in Propagating Speculative Bubbles*

The role of the news media in the stock market is not, as commonly believed, simply as a convenient tool for investors who are reacting directly to the economically significant news itself. The media actively shape public attention and categories of thought, and they create the environment within which the stock market events we see are played out.

The examples given in this chapter illustrate that the news media are fundamental propagators of speculative price movements through their efforts to make news interesting to their audience. They sometimes strive to enhance such interest by attaching news stories to stock price movements that the public has already observed, thereby enhancing the salience of these movements and focusing greater attention on them. Or they may remind the public of past market episodes, or of the likely trading strategies of others. Thus the media can sometimes foster stronger feedback from past price changes to further price changes, and they can also foster another sequence of events, referred to here as an attention cascade.

This is not to say that the news media are a monolithic force pushing ideas onto a purely passive audience. The media represent a channel for mass communication and the interpretation of popular culture, but popular culture has an inherent logic and process of its own. We turn next to a study of some of the basic ideas in our culture, whose transformation over time bears a relation to the changing speculative situation in stock markets.

## *Five*

# *New Era Economic Thinking*

Stock market expansions have often been associated with popular perceptions that the future is brighter or less uncertain than it was in the past. The term *new era* has periodically been used to describe these times.

Of course, there is some obvious validity to the new era notion. The general trend over the twentieth century has been a rise in the standard of living and a decline in the impact of economic risks on individuals. By many measures the world has indeed been gradually growing into a new and better era. But the most salient characteristic of popular new era thinking is that it is not continuously in evidence; rather, it occurs in pulses.

In contrast to the irregular references to a new era in popular culture, economists or other influential commentators who have proclaimed a new era at various times in history have usually been quite cautious in their choice of words. Often, they merely seem to be betting on the continuation of long-term trends.

Impressions that the public is affected in different ways at different times by new era thinking—or for that matter by any other popular economic theory—are hard to pin down. For example, it is difficult to trace the evolution of ideas through questionnaire survey work, because one only knows to question the public about specific ideas *after* those ideas have attracted a good deal of attention.

We can do word counts of publications using computerized databases, and thereby get some idea of the changing frequency with which certain economic terms are used, but such searches are crude and miss the often subtle ways in which the use of the terms changes over time. When I tried to establish how often the phrase *new era* has been used in the past few years, I found that the term has been used in so many different contexts that a search on this phrase alone is not meaningful for our purposes. On the other hand, I have established from the Nexis database that the term *new era economy* did not have any currency until a *Business Week* cover story in July 1997 attributed this term to Alan Greenspan, marking an alleged turning point in his thinking since the "irrational exuberance" speech some months earlier.[1] The term *new era economy* has been in regular use ever since. (The association of this term with one powerful figure provides yet another striking example of how individual actors or media events can change public thinking.)

The recent use of the term *new era* in this context actually preceded the *Business Week* article, for a pair of articles in the *Boston Globe* in June 1997 used the terms *new era thesis, new era theorists,* and *new era school* and identified Ralph Acampora, technical research director at Prudential Securities, as a member of the so-called school. In August 1997, a much-talked-about article by Paul Krugman in the *Harvard Business Review* attacked the newly prominent new era theory, and this of course gave the term even greater currency.[2] In the decade before 1997, the Nexis search reveals that the term *new era* was used only rarely to denote optimistic economic outlooks; in those years the term apparently had little currency.

All of these uses of the term *new era* to describe the economy occurred after the 1990s stock market had advanced far enough that it was beginning to amaze people, and all the new era stories feature the stock market.[3] It was not as if some economists proclaimed a new era after looking at national income data or other data relevant to the real economic outlook. The new era theory emerged principally as an after-the-fact interpretation of a stock market boom. This is surely no surprise. A stock market boom is a dramatic event that calls for an equally dramatic interpretation. In contrast, an increase in the growth rate of the gross domestic product—from, say, 2% to 3%—although perhaps exciting to economists, does not make the same impression on the general public. It is insubstantial, esoteric, and simply cannot hold its own against the flashier news offerings bombarding the public.

Whenever the market reaches a new high, public speakers, writers, and other prominent people suddenly appear, armed with explanations for the apparent optimism seen in the market. Reporters may not always get the timing right, and they may suggest that it was the words spoken by these great men and women that caused the market shifts. Although prominent people can certainly move markets, often their wisdom merely tags along with market moves. Nevertheless, the new era thinking they promote is part of the process by which a boom may be sustained and amplified—part of the feedback mechanism that, as we have seen, can create speculative bubbles.

A defender of markets' rationality might point out that even if discussions of a new era really are the cause of the boom, it does not follow that news accounts of these discussions must precede the boom. Technically, of course, it is possible—in spite of the fact that most media discussions of new era theories seem to coincide with or come after stock market booms—that the *word-of-mouth* discussions did in fact precede and cause the booms. The news media might have been late to recognize the discussions.

But that defense of markets' rationality is not very plausible if we consider the nature of the thought patterns observed among the general investing public. There is such lack of interest among the public in reasoned arguments about the future course of the corporate sector that it is highly unlikely that the public could have been harboring secret thoughts of a new era in corporate profits unrelated to past stock price increases.

It appears that most people are not interested in long-run economic growth forecasts for the aggregate economy. Economic theory would suggest that they should be interested, if they are behaving rationally. But in fact the topic is too abstract, boring, or technical. The public is interested in expansive descriptions of future technology—for example, in what amazing new capabilities computers will soon have—not in gauging the level of U.S. corporate earnings in coming years. In fact, it is doubtful that more than a small percentage of the populace today could give an estimate of aggregate U.S. corporate earnings accurate within an order of magnitude. They are hardly likely to be interested in predicting changes in those same earnings.

History does show that there are at times strong unseen forces within public opinion that are not revealed in the media or in public discussions until some key event brings them out of the woodwork. But such currents in public opinion typically relate to naïve theories based on personal observations or ill-founded prejudices against minority groups or foreign countries. The public simply does not harbor secret opinions about the economic growth rate.[4]

Conventional wisdom interprets the stock market as reacting to new era theories. In fact, it appears that the stock market often *creates* new era theories, as reporters scramble to justify stock market price moves. The situation reminds one of the Ouija board, in which players are encouraged to interpret the meaning of movements in their trembling hands and to distill forecasts from them. Or the stock market is seen as an oracle, issuing mysterious and meaningless pronouncements, which we then ask our leaders to interpret, mistakenly investing their interpretations with authority.

In this chapter I analyze the "new era" thinking that accompanied previous market peaks in the United States. I also offer some indications of the public's thinking in the times when the "new eras" had run their course. I make liberal use of contemporary quotations, since these provide the most direct evidence of people's thoughts and concerns.

### *The 1901 Optimism: The Twentieth-Century Peak*

As noted in Chapter 1, the first of the three major peaks in the price-earnings ratio since 1881 occurred in June 1901, right at the dawn of the twentieth century. Prices had achieved spectacular increases over the preceding twelve months, and in mid-1901 observers reported real speculative fervor: "The outburst of speculation during April, 1901, was something rarely paralleled in the history of speculative manias. . . . The newspapers were full of stories of hotel waiters, clerks in business offices, even doorkeepers and dressmakers, who had won considerable fortunes in their speculations. The effect on the public mind may be imagined."[5]

With the beginning of the century in January 1901, there was much talk of the future and of technological progress to come: "trains [will be] running at 150 miles per hour, . . . newspaper publishers will press the buttons and automotive machinery will do the rest, . . . phonographs as salesmen will sell goods in the big stores while automatic hands will make change."[6] Guglielmo Marconi made the first transatlantic radio transmission in 1901, and there were predictions that we would soon be in radio communication with the planet Mars.

The Pan-American Exposition in Buffalo, New York, from May 1 to November 1, 1901, emphasized high technology. It had as its centerpiece the 375-foot Electric Tower, illuminated by 44,000 light bulbs powered by faraway generators at Niagara Falls. The tower was "indescribably brilliant" and held visitors "spellbound."[7] The exposition's Electricity Building featured exhibits about the wonders of electricity. There was an electrograph, a machine that transmitted pictures by wire (forerunner of the fax machine), and a tel-autograph, a machine that enabled one to transmit one's signature over long distances (forerunner of credit card signature-verification devices). The exposition even offered a simulated trip to the moon on the airship *Luna:* the visitor could take a stroll through the streets and shops of the moon before returning to earth.

In a sense, the high-tech age, the computer age, and the space age seemed just around the corner in 1901, though the concepts were expressed in different words than we would use today. People were upbeat, and in later years the first decade of the twentieth century came to be called the Age of Optimism, the Age of Confidence, or the Cocksure Era. The mood was perhaps similar to that of today, a century later and near the dawn of the twenty-first century. Given the modern media's exploitation of anniversary or threshold events, and the human tendency to consider such events as symbolic new beginnings, investing them with exaggerated hopes and expectations, the transitions to new centuries may tend to be optimistic times. The 1901 example suggests that new-century optimism might in fact extend for years beyond 2001.

But there was another reason why people in 1901 thought that the stock market ought to be highly valued. The most prominent business news in the papers in recent years had been about the formation of numerous combinations, trusts, and mergers in a wide variety of businesses, stories such as the formation of U.S. Steel out of a number of smaller steel companies. Many stock market forecasters in 1901 saw these developments as momentous, and the term *community of interest* was commonly used to describe the new economy dominated by them. An April 1901 editorial in the *New York Daily Tribune* explained:

> But a new era has come, the era of "community of interest," whereby it is hoped to avoid ruinous price cutting and to avert the destruction which has in the past, when business depression occurred, overtaken so many of the competing concerns in every branch of industry. In the great iron and steel industry, for example, which, as Andrew Carnegie has said, has been the prince and the pauper of the industrial world, now highly prosperous again and again deeply depressed, consolidations of scores of scattered concerns into a dozen larger ones within the last two years have now been followed by the combination of the latter into the most gigantic combination the world has ever known, a combination which, if the expectations of its projectors are fulfilled, will result in the avoiding of much economic waste through eliminating the possibility of the erection of unnecessary plants for competitive reasons, in the effecting of many economies through the abolishing of duplicate official positions and establishment of a uniform price list, and in the enlargement of export trade by reason of the lower prices which can be fixed in consequence of the various economies coincident to consolidation.
>
> In the railroad field, too, combination is the ruling idea, and for the same reasons. Competing roads are being consolidated or leased, with resulting economy of operation and permanent cessation of rate cutting, and representatives of powerful roads are going into the boards of heretofore incorrigible rate cutting lines, in which bodies they have an influence potent, if not controlling.[8]

These reasons for optimism for the stock market are certainly plausible. It is easily believable that elimination of competition might create monopoly profits for corporations, thus boosting their share prices.

But the editorial does not mention the potential for antitrust law to end the "community of interest" era. In September 1901, the pro-business president William McKinley was assassinated while visiting the Pan-American Exposition; he was succeeded by his "cowboy" vice president, Teddy Roosevelt. It was only six months later, in March 1902, that Roosevelt dusted off the almost-forgotten Sherman Antitrust Act of 1890 and used it against the Northern Securities Company. Over the next seven years he embarked on a vigorous antitrust policy. When the defects of the Sherman Act became apparent, the Clayton Antitrust Act of 1914 furthered the government's assault on corporate combinations.

The premise of the "community of interest" theory of stock prices turned out to be wrong; those who expressed high optimism for stocks on this basis were not thinking of all that could go wrong. People were not considering the possibility that society would not tolerate this shift of wealth toward stockholders. Presumably they did not consider this because there had not yet been any concrete antitrust activity. Yet in thinking about the level of the stock market, one must of course consider the long-run earnings, spread over future decades, that the market represents, and of the potential for society to make adjustments, positive or negative, to control this earnings stream.

Rarely do discussions of the level of the stock market consider the possibility of government reaction to the level of profits, even though government policy toward corporations has changed substantially and dramatically over time. The corporate profits tax alone has been adjusted many times, from 0% in 1901, to 1% in 1911, to 10% in 1921, to 14% in 1931, to 31% in 1941, to 50.75% with a 30% excess-profits tax in 1951, to 35% today. Despite the fact that the U.S. government's past actions raised the corporate profits tax from 0% to 50.75%, effectively nationalizing more than half the stock market, potential future adjustments in this tax are rarely mentioned in discussing the outlook for the market.

The 1901 example illustrates one way in which new era thinking can go wrong: such thinking concentrates attention on the effects of events currently prominent in the news. Little attention is paid to "what-ifs," even if they have substantial probability.

There was another important theme in 1901: that stocks were now being held in "strong hands." "The ownership of stocks has changed hands. The public speculators do not now own them. They are owned by people who are capable of protecting them under any circumstances, such as the Standard Oil, Morgan, Kuhn Loeb, Gould and Harriman Interests. These people who are the foremost financiers of the country evidently know when they go into a proposition what ultimate results may be expected."[9] This theory, like theories expressed at other market peaks, finds it inconceivable that there could be a selling panic. In the shortest run, perhaps this theory was right. But those strong hands did not stop the stock market crash of 1907, nor the dramatic slide of stock values between 1907 and 1920.

### *The 1920s Optimism*

The bull market of the 1920s was apparently a time of relatively great public enthusiasm for and interest in the stock market, and the enthusiasm seemed to peak in 1929 with the market. In his 1931 book *Only Yesterday,* Frederick Lewis Allen wrote of 1929:

> The rich man's chauffeur drove with his ears laid back to catch the news of an impending move in Bethlehem Steel; he held 50 shares himself on a twenty-point margin. The window cleaner at the broker's office paused to watch the ticker, for he was thinking of converting his laboriously accumulated savings into a few shares of Simmons. Edwin Lefevre (an articulate reporter on the market at this time who could claim a considerable personal experience) told of a broker's valet who made nearly a quarter of a million in the market; of a trained nurse who cleaned up thirty thousand following the tips given her by grateful patients; of a Wyoming cattleman, thirty miles from the nearest railroad, who bought or sold a thousand shares a day.[10]

Although this account may create an exaggerated impression of the level of public attention to the stock market, there is no question that attention was much keener in the 1920s than at other times, and that enthusiastic investors were not hard to find.

The 1920s were a time of rapid economic growth and, in particular, of the widespread dissemination of some technological innovations that had formerly been available only to the wealthy. The automobile came into common use at roughly this time. In 1914 there had been only 1.7 million automobiles registered in the United States, but by 1920 there were 8.1 million and by 1929 there were 23.1 million. The automobile brought with it a new sense of freedom and possibility, and a widespread awareness that these personal values could be attained by new technology.

The 1920s were also the time when the electrification of the country was extended beyond the major cities, which had already been electrified. By 1929, 20 million U.S. homes were wired. Kerosene lamps were out; electric light bulbs were in. By 1929, nearly half of all wired homes had vacuum cleaners, and a third had washing machines. Moreover, the 1920s saw the expansion of radio broadcasting and the development of radio as a mature national entertainment medium. In 1920 there were only three radio stations in the entire United States; by 1923 there were over five hundred. Nationally known radio stars like Rudy Vallee and nationally popular shows like *Amos 'n' Andy* appeared in the 1920s. The National Broadcasting Company formed the first national network in 1926, and regular shows created a sense of national culture previously unknown. Sound also invaded our movies. Lee De Forest invented the sound-on-film system in 1923, and talkies had completely displaced silent movies by the end of the decade. Because these innovations had such an impact on everyday lives, affecting people in their homes and in their hours of leisure, the 1920s were a time when massive technological progress was unusually apparent to even the most casual observer.

There were, at the time of the 1920s stock market boom, many clear statements proclaiming a new era for the economy. For example, as early as 1925 we hear, "There is nothing now to be foreseen which can prevent the United States from enjoying an era of business prosperity which is entirely without equal in the pages of trade history."[11]

John Moody, head of Moody's Investors Service, a rating agency, said in an article about the stock market in 1928, "In fact, a new age is taking form throughout the entire civilized world; civilization is taking on new aspects. We are only now beginning to realize, perhaps, that this modern, mechanistic civilization in which we live is now in the process of perfecting itself."[12]

Given the public enthusiasm for stocks and the enormous run-up in the market, there was a corresponding demand for books that interpreted and justified the market boom. In 1929, Charles Amos Dice, in *New Levels in the Stock Market,* gave a number of reasons to expect the increase to continue. He preferred the term *new world* to *new era,* but the idea was the same. He wrote of a "new world of industry," referring to techniques of mass production, large research departments, the beginning of the electrical age, the industrialization of the South, the emergence of large-scale production, and the mechanization of agriculture. Furthermore Dice wrote of a "new world of distribution," predicting the proliferation of installment credit, the chain-store movement, new techniques of advertising that would stimulate demand, and new market research techniques. He also spoke of a "new world of finance," referring to the expansion of investment banking to provide new sources of funds for corporations, the rise of the holding company as a tool to make financing more flexible, and advances in the Federal Reserve System's understanding of how to stabilize business. Dice described the Federal Reserve as analogous to the governor on a steam engine, regulating the speed of the economy.[13]

The Dice book, curiously, was printed in August 1929, a month before the peak of the market prior to the onset of the depression. The timing of the book's appearance seems even more remarkable when one finds attached at page 69 a small slip of paper entitled "Errata." The slip, apparently added after the text was printed but before the book was bound, notes that the Dow Jones Industrial Average rose on September 3, 1929, to over 20 points above the level indicated in the book. The slip of paper instructs the reader to adjust upward the projections for the Dow given in the printed book by 15 to 20 points. Thus Dice managed to time his book for the exact peak of the market, and thus to make the most catastrophic error possible in forecasting the market.

Prof. Irving Fisher at Yale, who has been described as one of America's most eminent economists, argued that the U.S. stock market was not at all overvalued. He was quoted as saying just before the peak in 1929 that "stock prices have reached what looks like a permanently high plateau." He wrote a book entitled *The Stock Market Crash—And After,* with a preface dated less than two months after Black Thursday. Fisher must have been working on this book at the same time as Dice was writing his, but his timing was not so bad. The 1929 crash came while he was still at work on the book. Yet Fisher was still able to be optimistic after the crash, especially since the market had gone down only a fraction of the distance it ultimately would by 1932, and the crash did not yet seem to signal anything like the end of an era.

Fisher argued in his book that the outlook was for rapidly increasing earnings for a number of reasons, some of them parallel to those cited by Dice. First, he pointed out that the merger movement of the 1920s allowed economies of large-scale production. He noted that "the economies from mergers take time to develop, while the effect on the stock market of their formation is instant." Scientific research and invention were proceeding at a faster pace than before. The advantages of the automobile were only just beginning to be exploited, with the development of a rapidly widening network of surfaced highways. Much was being learned about the efficient use of waste products. In agriculture, recent inventions included subsoil plowing, better fertilizers, enhanced breeds of farm animals, and new and improved crops. As all of these inventions came gradually to be applied, further earnings increases could be anticipated from them. Fisher also maintained that the management of American corporations was improving, thanks to the application of "scientific" methods, improved layouts of manufacturing facilities, and more sophisticated management techniques. Businesses were able to plan better for the future, he claimed, partly because of his own invention of "master-charting," a pencil-and-paper method of priority planning for executives. Fisher also was encouraged by his perception that labor unions were now accepting joint responsibility for the solution of industrial problems.[14]

Others argued that the market valuations of the 1920s were sound because we were in a more sober time—and not just figuratively. The prohibition of alcoholic beverages was thought to be a sign of greater steadiness and intelligence: "Many different things contributed to this happy result. . . . [including] the elimination from our national life of the saloon and its destructive elements, and consequent comparative sobriety among the population as a whole. Most of the money formerly spent in the saloon has since gone into continually higher standards of living, investments and savings banks."[15]

Of course, optimistic sentiments for the market were not the only sentiments expressed at the time. The high price of the market relative to rough measures of fundamental value did not go unnoticed in 1929. The *New York Times* and the *Commercial and Financial Chronicle* consistently pointed out what they interpreted as speculative excess. Paul M. Warburg of the International Acceptance Bank decried the "unrestrained speculation."[16] Yet we know, from the level of the stock market itself, that the weight of public sentiment was overwhelmingly positive in the 1920s.

## *New Era Thinking of the 1950s and 1960s*

New era thinking also seemed, judging from media accounts, to undergo a sudden surge in the mid-1950s, when the market increased 94.3% in real (inflation-corrected) terms between September 1953 and December 1955. The market had been stalled during most of the early 1950s, amid lingering fears that the economy might sink back into a depression now that the stimulus of increased World War II production was absent. But the sudden near-doubling in the stock market, supported by a solid growth in earnings, apparently caused the investing public to forget such fears and to indulge in genuine new era thinking. In May 1955 *U.S. News and World Report* wrote:

> Once again the feel of a "new era" is in the air. Confidence is high, optimism almost universal, worry largely absent.
>
> War is receding as a threat. Peace is a growing prospect. Jobs are quite plentiful. Pay never was so good. The promise is that taxes will be cut. Everywhere things are in a rising trend.

> Three times in 10 years a depression scare has come and gone without amounting to much. The first scare came in 1946, right after World War II. Military spending was cut drastically with scarcely a ripple. The second scare came in 1949. The public went right on buying, oblivious to the worries of businessmen, and this scare faded. The third scare began in mid-1953. It now is little more than a memory.[17]

The sense that investors were terribly optimistic and confident of the market was in and of itself part of the new era thinking. *Newsweek* wrote in December 1955 that "basic to the upsurge [in the stock market] was an investor faith in the overwhelming strength of the economy—and the fact that corporations were cashing in on this prosperity."[18]

In a development strongly paralleling the evolution of radio in the 1920s as the vehicle for a mass national culture, the early 1950s had seen the widespread introduction of television. In 1948 only 3% of U.S. families owned television sets; by 1955 76% did. Like the Internet, television was a vivid technological innovation that captured the imagination of almost everyone. It was evidence for technological progress that could not be overlooked; within a few short years the majority of Americans began regularly spending hours watching an electronic device.

Inflation was very low at the time, and people credited this to newly enlightened Fed policy. Treasury Secretary George Humphrey boasted in 1955 that

> In the past 2-3/4 years, the value of the dollar has changed only one-half of one cent. We have kept inflation's hand out of your savings almost entirely.
>
> We regard inflation as a public enemy of the worst type. But we have not hesitated, either, to ease or restrict the basis of credit when need was indicated. The full force of monetary policy has been made effective more promptly than ever before to respond to natural demands. This has been done by the timely use of monetary policy and credit; by the return to the public of purchasing power through the biggest tax cut in the history of the nation; by cutting unjustified Government spending; by timely encouragement to construction, home building and needed improvements.[19]

Something analogous to the "strong hands" theme seen in the 1920s—the idea that the demand for stocks was stable enough to prevent any downturn—was present in the 1950s as well. *Newsweek* wrote in 1955:

> Many financial men like to think that the nation has developed a "new capitalism" with an ever-broadening base. Some 7.5 million people hold stock in publicly owned corporations, compared with 6.5 million three years ago. Assets of mutual funds, which give the small investor a chance to spread his risk, have soared from $1.3 billion in 1946 to $7.2 billion. Thousands of workers have become owners of the firms they work for via employee stock-purchase plans.
>
> All this may not add up to an absolute guarantee against another '29, but most experts are confident that it goes a long way.[20]

The idea that Irving Fisher had presented in the 1920s as a reason for optimism, that businesses were able to plan better for the future, was floated again as a new idea in the 1950s: "there is a new attitude of business itself that promises to avoid deep depressions in the future. Business firms today make long-term plans and appear to be less influenced than in the past by short-term fluctuations in activity."[21]

The Baby Boom was seen as another important factor driving prosperity and the market, because people needed to spend money on their babies (just as the grown-up babies themselves, despite having fewer children, are now perceived as bidding up stock prices as they save for their retirement): "It is this boom in babies that is being counted on now to make the latest 'new era' different from the last one. Families are growing bigger. Good roads and fine automobiles are opening the countryside. The urge is toward suburban living and for houses with three or four bedrooms instead of one or two."[22]

The increase in the use of consumer credit was also cited, as it had been in the 1920s, as a reason to expect prosperity: "This willingness to lay out cash amounted, in the opinion of one influential Washington individual, to a 'consumer spending revolution.' . . . In spending his money, the average individual's wants have gradually been upgraded."[23]

With the election of John Kennedy as president in 1960, and given his advocacy of economic stimulus measures, it was generally thought that the economy ought to do especially well. Kennedy inspired confidence beginning with his initial State of the Union message in 1961. He was perceived as showing vision and optimism, and he hit upon a dramatic symbol for that vision by promising, in a special message to Congress in May 1961, that the United States would land men on the moon before 1970. Americans expected that such an achievement would be remembered for centuries, marking as it would humankind's first escape from its planet of origin. Kennedy was viewed as the incarnation of our national optimism and of the strength of the stock market: "Wall Street has a simple description for the phenomenal strength of stock prices, 'The Kennedy Market.'" The confidence inspired by the Kennedy economic program led some to conclude that the country was entering a "new economy" in which "businessmen can enjoy reasonably continuous prosperity indefinitely" and that there was "more justification for confidence" in monetary policy than in times past.[24] The Kennedy initiatives were expanded on by the "Great Society" program of his successor, Lyndon Johnson, beginning in 1964; Johnson's program set as its primary goals nothing less than an end to poverty and urban decay.

In the 1960s, the theory that the stock market is the "best investment" was prominent: "Investors feel that stocks are the best investment medium—as a hedge against possible inflation, as a means of participating in the future growth of business." "Investors seem to be betting that inflation will accompany recovery—and that common stocks, even at present prices, represent the only real hedge."[25] At that time, investors believed that if inflation broke out, the stock market would go up, rather than down, as is now commonly thought, and that therefore the prospect of inflation was a reason to own stocks. There was concern in the early 1960s that, even though there was virtually no inflation, the Kennedy-Johnson economic programs could become inflationary.

A possibly significant factor behind the 1960s market peak was the Dow's approach to 1,000. That the approach of a new milestone such as a four-digit Dow would have an impact on the public imagination may seem silly, but, given the lack of any other solid basis for the market's valuation, talk of such an arbitrary level provided a solid anchor for people's expectations.

Even before the Dow got close to 1,000, the press was counting the milestones. A 1965 *Business Week* article noted that "Like the four-minute mile, psychological barriers are made to be cracked. It's no less so in Wall Street, where the 900 'magic' mark on the Dow-Jones industrial average (as the 600, 700, and 800 marks before it) will probably crumble sooner or later." *Newsweek* wrote that the 900 barrier had reached "almost mystical significance in the minds of many observers." In 1966, when the 1,000 level loomed, *Time* wrote that "At week's end the average had reached 986.13, less than 14 points from the 1000 mark that the Street considers a mystical number. Even though that number may be more mystical than meaningful, the date of the breakthrough will appear in history books of decades, or perhaps even centuries, to come—and the date is not far off."[26] The market appears to have raced to just under 1,000, but it would not pass the magic number for a long time. Although the Dow was not then computed on a minute-by-minute basis, it finally rose above 1,000 (if computed using the highs for the day) in January 1966. It was not until 1972, the eve of the stock market crash, that it closed above 1,000, and even then it stayed above 1,000 only briefly.

The Dow did not rise solidly above 1,000 until 1982, and, if one computes a real stock price, it did not rise above the 1966 high in real terms—and stay above it—until January 1992, twenty-six years later.[27] The period from January 1966 to January 1992 was one of low returns, confined as it was (with no capital gain) to income from dividends; the average annual real stock market return was only 4.1% per year.[28] These are signs consistent with a notion that the market was in some sense "reaching" toward 1,000 in 1966, and that it became relatively overpriced.

### *New Era Thinking during the Bull Market of the 1990s*

I have already described some of the new era thinking that characterized the 1990s in Chapter 2. Here I make just a few additional observations and then contrast the modern new era thinking with that during the new eras described in this chapter.

As with all major stock market booms, there have been writers during the 1990s who offer new era theories to justify the market. Michael Mandel, writing in *Business Week* in 1996 in an article entitled "The Triumph of the New Economy," listed five reasons for his belief that the market is not crazy: increased globalization, the boom in high-tech industries, moderating inflation, falling interest rates, and surging profits.[29]

A prominent theory during this boom has been that low inflation makes for a strong market outlook. In the 1990s, theories about inflation dominated discussion of the market outlook just as they did in the 1960s, but now the prevalent theory has been reversed. In the 1990s, it was thought that if inflation were to break out the market would go down rather than up. The idea that the stock market is a good investment because it is a hedge against inflation (i.e., that it will go up if there is an outbreak of inflation) was dead.

Why did people in the 1990s think that inflation would push the market down, whereas in the 1960s they thought it would push it up? In the 1990s, investors may have been reacting to a literature published by economists showing that economies do more poorly during sudden outbursts of very high inflation. In fact, these studies do not show much of a relation between moderate or long-run inflation and real economic performance; over the relevant range, they would suggest that the 1960s-era theory was right—that the real value of the stock market should be relatively immune to news of inflation, and that the stock market should move with consumer prices, not against them.[30] More likely, people in the 1990s were reacting to the fact that the stock market had in recent years moved against inflation, rather than with it.

Many of the same themes that appeared in the 1920s, 1950s, and 1960s after stock market booms were repeated in the 1990s.

Roger Bootle, in his 1998 book *The Death of Inflation,* argued that the "inflationary era," during which "managed capitalism" and strong labor unions have induced an inflationary spiral, is drawing to a close. In "managed capitalism," "prices were decided, not determined by the interplay of interpersonal supply and demand." Now, Bootle declared, we are entering the "zero era," brought on by global capitalism, privatization, and the decline of labor unions, all of which make it impossible for prices to be decided by committee.[31]

Steven Weber, with his 1997 article "The End of the Business Cycle" in the public policy journal *Foreign Affairs,* argued that macroeconomic risks are lower now: "Changes in technology, ideology, employment and finance, along with the globalization of production and consumption, have reduced the volatility of economic activity in the industrialized world. For both empirical and theoretical reasons in advanced industrial economies the waves of the business cycle may be becoming more like ripples." Weber presented a number of reasonable-sounding arguments. For instance, he noted that the economy has come to be dominated by the service sector in a way that it was not thirty years ago, and he pointed out that service employment has always been more stable than industrial production.[32]

Downsizing and restructuring—terms describing so-called managerial revolutions in the 1980s—were thought then to be important reasons for the growth of profits since 1982. The thought that they are still sources of profit growth still lingers in some people's minds. Yet there has also been substantial skepticism about these managerial revolutions, as exemplified by the comic strip *Dilbert,* which dwells on petty labor-management conflicts in the new era economy.

It should be noted that not all stories in the media in the 1990s were slanted toward new era emphases when compared with stories during earlier episodes of high pricing. I could not find 1990s accounts that were as expansively and breathlessly optimistic as some in 1901 or 1929, and although there is much optimism in the media in the 1990s, it is usually a matter of background presumption rather than bold assertion. There appears to have been a media attitude change, and optimistic hyperbole was out in the 1990s. Many writers seemed, if anything, rather more influenced by concerns about market overpricing and speculative mania. In fact, many media accounts in the mid- to late 1990s have focused on what they consider the craziness of investors. For example, a *Fortune* story in April 1996 told of reporters stopping random people on the street and asking them for stock tips. They stopped a policeman, a Starbucks barista, a carpenter on a billboard crew, and an ID checker at a fitness club, and all them offered expansive stock recommendations. They could not find a shoeshine boy, but otherwise their experience mirrored that of Bernard Baruch before the crash of 1929, who remarked that he had received stock tips from the shoeshine boy and interpreted that as a sign of market excess.[33] Articles with titles like "Gamblers High: Is This a Market Where Yesterday's Yardsticks Don't Apply?" or "It's Tulip Time on Wall Street" or "Say Goodbye to the Last Bear" abounded. The possibility that the stock market boom is a speculative bubble was certainly thrust before the minds of readers in the 1990s.

### *The Ends of New Eras*

Despite the suggestion inherent in the phrase *speculative bubble* that there may be a dramatic burst—a stock market crash—speculative bubbles and their associated new era thinking do not end definitively with a sudden, final crash. Upon reflection this is not surprising, given that stock prices are essentially formed in the minds of the millions of investors who buy and sell stocks, and it is unlikely that so many people would simultaneously arrive at sudden and enduring changes in their long-run perceptions.

People today remember the stock market crash of 1929 as occurring in one or two days. In fact, after that crash, the market recovered almost all of its lost ground by early 1930. The significance of 1929 is not the one-day drops in October, but the fact that that year marked the beginning of the end: the beginning of the three-year period that reversed much of the stock market gains of the 1920s. The same is true of other stock market drops. One-day events do not figure prominently, except as symbols of the malaise in the markets.

I noted in Chapter 1 that the high pricing of the market in 1901 was not followed by any immediate or dramatic price decline, but rather that prices ceased to increase and that eventually, after some twenty years had elapsed, the market had lost most of the real value it had had in 1901. The change took so long to work itself out that it is rather more generational in character, and therefore it is hard to find comment about in the media.

If we look at 1920–21, when the real stock market was at its lowest since 1901, discussions of the stock market centered on what had gone wrong; the glowing descriptions of future prosperity seen in 1901 were no longer to be found. The biggest factor in most commentary of the period centers on the 1920–21 recession, which was unusually severe. Coverage centered on recent losses by businessmen and on paper fortunes that had disappeared. In place of the "community of interest" keeping prices up, there was instead discussion of hostility from farmers and shippers toward railroads, of customers demanding reductions in rates. The cancellation of government contracts following the world war was thought to have revealed weakness in existing businesses. Strained political conditions abroad following the war were also viewed as a negative factor for the U.S. economy. The actions of "conscienceless" short sellers or bear raiders were considered negative influences on the market, as were the effects of tax-loss selling for income tax purposes.

There is some evidence that investors in 1921 had learned not to be influenced by exaggerated claims and inflated schemes. A 1921 article in the *Saturday Evening Post* by Albert Atwood describes highly speculative prices as a thing of the past and quotes a stockbroker as saying that "the promotions of the last few years have been neither as wild nor as fantastic as those of the boom period of 1900 and 1901."

Another theme running through accounts of the period is that market psychology somehow mysteriously changes, and that it had, at that time, become inexplicably negative. Atwood quotes a banker in 1921: "All the world got together to drive down prices, and when the whole world makes up its mind, when everyone thinks alike and is determined that prices shall go lower, nothing can resist the movement."[34]

The end of the 1929 new era thinking was more dramatic and directly tied to the Great Depression that followed; by 1932 it was already plain that the United States was into the deepest depression it had ever experienced, and there seemed to be *prima facie* evidence that the new era was over. The optimists who had been extolling a bright future for the economy were silenced by events that deviated so markedly from their forecasts that it seemed they could not be explained by any convenient adjustments in theories. Economic forecasters demonstrated extreme uncertainty about the future, and observers of consumer behavior claimed that consumer uncertainty had stalled demand.[35]

The depression of the 1930s was a time of widespread concern that our economic system was failing. Oscar Lange, a University of Chicago professor of economics, wrote in the *American Economic Review* in 1939 that "the view is widely held that the American economy has lost its momentum of expansion and reached a stage of more or less permanent stagnation."[36]

The perceived failure of capitalism ushered in the heyday of Communism in the United States. Communism seemed to many to be the wave of the future, even inevitable. Many of the best writers of the era became openly sympathetic to Communism in the 1930s, including Kenneth Burke, Erskine Caldwell, Robert Cantwell, Jack Conroy, Edward Dahlberg, John Dos Passos, James Farrell, Langston Hughes, and William Saroyan.[37]

Further evidence of the loss of hope for the uncontrolled capitalist economy can be seen in the ascendance of radical political movements abroad. The rise of Nazism in Germany is itself a telling symptom of the widespread despair that took hold of many people's thinking after 1929. The change in mindset of the German public within the space of a few years seems astonishing, and it is a useful reminder of how changeable any public mood may be.

The end of 1965 new era thinking was associated with the appearance of high inflation. The Kennedy administration's claim that it could lower unemployment through high-pressure economics was found to be false; in fact we entered a period of "stagflation," with both high unemployment and high inflation. In 1974, Arthur Okun, who had been a staff member of the Council of Economic Advisors under President Kennedy and later its chairman, called the attempt at high-pressure economics "one of the greatest failures of economic analysis in modern times." Inflation was seen as a significant brake on the economic outlook. Arthur Burns, the chairman of the Federal Reserve Board, said, "No country that I know of has been able to maintain widespread economic prosperity once inflation got out of hand."[38] Even though this fact is unsupported by economic analysis, there was a general perception that it was true.[39]

By the early 1980s, there was a widespread feeling that the United States was losing its preeminence to Japan. In a *USA Today* article entitled "How Japan Is Taking Over Our Markets," an expert is quoted as saying, "The only problem is that no targeted industry in history—not autos, not steel, ball bearings, televisions, motorcycles—has been able to cope with the onslaught from the Japanese." Japan was seen then as especially strong in the high-tech fields, in which our past successes had always been integral to our national self-esteem and identity.

Ends of new eras seem to be periods when the national focus of debate can no longer be upbeat. At such times, a public speaker may still think that it would be good business to extol a vision of a brilliant future for our nation's economy, but it is simply not credible to do so. One could, at such times, present a case that the economy must recover, as it always has, and that the stock market is underpriced and should go up, but public speakers who make such a case cannot achieve the command of public attention they do after a major stock market run-up and economic boom. There are times when an audience is receptive to optimistic statements and times when it is not.

# Six

## New Eras and Bubbles around the World

Large stock market moves like the U.S. examples I discussed in the last chapter have also occurred in many other countries over the years, affording us numerous other observations. These suggest that speculative bubbles—periods of exaggerated but temporary investor enthusiasm, often associated with "new era" theories—are in fact commonplace.

In this chapter, I examine the largest recent stock market moves around the world. For some of these, I rely on accounts by the news media. Of course, media accounts are not always reliable, and I cannot claim to have done exhaustive research on any of these examples. However, they illustrate the significance in these countries of factors I have identified in previous chapters as important in U.S. stock market moves. I show that the record price movements in these countries have tended to be reversed afterward—as one would expect if bubbles were common among them.

### The Largest Recent Stock Market Events

Table 6.1 shows the twenty-five largest recent (until 1999) one-year real stock price index increases for thirty-six countries, and Table 6.2

*Table 6.1*
***Largest Recent One-Year Real Stock Price Index Increases***

| Country | Percentage increase | One-year period | Price change over subsequent one-year period (percent) |
|---|---|---|---|
| 1. Philippines | 683.4 | Dec. 1985–Dec. 1986 | 28.4 |
| 2. Taiwan | 400.1 | Oct. 1986–Oct. 1987 | 65.7 |
| 3. Venezuela | 384.6 | Jan. 1990–Jan. 1991 | 33.1 |
| 4. Peru | 360.9 | Aug. 1992–Aug. 1993 | 15.8 |
| 5. Colombia | 271.3 | Jan. 1991–Jan. 1992 | –19.9 |
| 6. Jamaica | 224.5 | Apr. 1992–Apr. 1993 | –59.2 |
| 7. Chile | 199.8 | Jan. 1979–Jan. 1980 | 38.9 |
| 8. Italy | 166.4 | May 1985–May 1986 | –15.7 |
| 9. Jamaica | 163.4 | Aug. 1985–Aug. 1986 | 8.7 |
| 10. Thailand | 161.9 | Oct. 1986–Oct. 1987 | –2.6 |
| 11. India | 155.5 | Apr. 1991–Apr. 1992 | –50.3 |
| 12. Italy | 147.3 | Apr. 1980–Apr. 1981 | –32.1 |
| 13. Austria | 145.4 | Feb. 1989–Feb. 1990 | –19.8 |
| 14. Finland | 128.3 | Sept. 1992–Sept. 1993 | 46.3 |
| 15. Denmark | 122.9 | Apr. 1971–Apr. 1972 | –12.4 |
| 16. Spain | 119.8 | Dec. 1985–Dec. 1986 | 4.2 |
| 17. Luxembourg | 113.4 | Dec. 1992–Dec. 1993 | –10.8 |
| 18. Sweden | 111.5 | Aug. 1982–Aug. 1983 | –9.6 |
| 19. Portugal | 103.8 | Apr. 1997–Apr. 1998 | –34.1 |
| 20. Luxembourg | 103.6 | Jan. 1985–Jan. 1986 | 2.6 |
| 21. Hong Kong | 101.0 | Jan. 1993–Jan. 1994 | –38.5 |
| 22. Hong Kong | 99.1 | Feb. 1975–Feb. 1976 | –3.4 |
| 23. Korea | 98.8 | Feb. 1975–Feb. 1976 | 31.9 |
| 24. Hong Kong | 98.6 | Nov. 1979–Nov. 1980 | –22.4 |
| 25. Sweden | 96.6 | Aug. 1977–Aug. 1978 | –50.8 |

shows the twenty-five largest decreases for the same countries. Table 6.3 shows the twenty-five largest recent five-year real stock price increases, and Table 6.4 shows the twenty-five largest decreases. The tables are based on monthly data starting at varying dates for the different countries, but for over half the thirty-six countries, the data begin in or before 1960.[1]

*Table 6.2*
***Largest Recent One-Year Real Stock Price Index Decreases***

| Country | *Percentage decrease* | *One-year period* | *Price change over subsequent one-year period (percent)* |
|---|---|---|---|
| 1. Taiwan | –74.9 | Oct. 1989–Oct. 1990 | 85.1 |
| 2. Jamaica | –73.8 | Jan. 1993–Jan. 1994 | 69.6 |
| 3. Sweden | –63.6 | Aug. 1976–Aug. 1977 | 96.6 |
| 4. United Kingdom | –63.3 | Nov. 1973–Nov. 1974 | 72.7 |
| 5. Thailand | –62.8 | Aug. 1997–Aug. 1998 | 71.9 |
| 6. South Africa | –62.1 | July 1985–July 1986 | 48.9 |
| 7. Philippines | –61.9 | Oct. 1973–Oct. 1974 | –14.1 |
| 8. Korea | –61.9 | June 1997–June 1998 | 167.0 |
| 9. Pakistan | –59.5 | Oct. 1990–Oct. 1991 | 9.0 |
| 10. India | –58.4 | Nov. 1963–Nov. 1964 | –18.8 |
| 11. Denmark | –56.0 | July 1969–July 1970 | –15.3 |
| 12. Hong Kong | –55.5 | Aug. 1997–Aug. 1998 | 90.0 |
| 13. Hong Kong | –55.1 | Dec. 1981–Dec. 1982 | 7.7 |
| 14. Norway | –54.2 | May 1967–May 1968 | 39.9 |
| 15. Spain | –54.1 | Oct. 1976–Oct. 1977 | –15.6 |
| 16. Norway | –53.6 | Jan. 1974–Jan. 1975 | –2.1 |
| 17. Australia | –53.0 | Oct. 1973–Oct. 1974 | 33.6 |
| 18. France | –49.0 | Sept. 1973–Sept. 1974 | 25.3 |
| 19. Indonesia | –48.1 | Mar. 1997–Mar. 1998 | –45.1 |
| 20. Canada | –47.9 | June 1981–June 1982 | 69.4 |
| 21. Finland | –47.5 | Feb. 1990–Feb. 1991 | 6.3 |
| 22. Colombia | –47.1 | Jan. 1980–Jan. 1981 | 74.2 |
| 23. Italy | –46.1 | Apr. 1974–Apr. 1975 | –31.3 |
| 24. Norway | –46.1 | Dec. 1989–Dec. 1990 | 68.6 |
| 25. Denmark | –45.8 | Sept. 1973–Sept. 1974 | 14.7 |

It is clear that very large stock price movements are commonplace by world standards. Many are much larger, in the percentage terms shown, than those we have recently experienced in the United States. Indeed, no example from the United States even appears in any of the tables. (We should bear in mind that the U.S. market is the largest in the world, and there are a few near misses

*Table 6.3*
***Largest Recent Five-Year Real Stock Price Index Increases***

| Country | Percentage increase | Five-year period | Price change over subsequent five-year period (percent) |
|---|---|---|---|
| 1. Philippines | 1,253.2 | Nov. 1984–Nov. 1989 | 43.5 |
| 2. Peru | 743.1 | Sept. 1991–Sept. 1996 | Not available |
| 3. Chile | 689.7 | Mar. 1985–Mar. 1990 | 104.2 |
| 4. Jamaica | 573.9 | Dec. 1980–Dec. 1985 | 38.7 |
| 5. Korea | 518.3 | Mar. 1984–Mar. 1989 | –36.6 |
| 6. Mexico | 501.7 | Jan. 1989–Jan. 1994 | –50.9 |
| 7. Taiwan | 468.1 | May 1986–May 1991 | –12.7 |
| 8. Thailand | 430.7 | May 1986–May 1991 | 17.0 |
| 9. Colombia | 390.7 | Apr. 1989–Apr. 1994 | –52.0 |
| 10. Spain | 381.9 | Oct. 1982–Oct. 1987 | –33.7 |
| 11. India | 346.1 | Apr. 1987–Apr. 1992 | 58.4 |
| 12. Finland | 336.3 | Sept. 1992–Sept. 1997 | Not available |
| 13. Austria | 331.3 | Jan. 1985–Jan. 1990 | –39.7 |
| 14. Portugal | 329.1 | Apr. 1993–Apr. 1998 | Not available |
| 15. Finland | 291.0 | Sept. 1982–Sept. 1987 | –55.5 |
| 16. Jamaica | 280.2 | July 1984–July 1989 | 10.9 |
| 17. Japan | 275.6 | Aug. 1982–Aug. 1987 | –48.5 |
| 18. France | 262.6 | Mar. 1982–Mar. 1987 | 10.2 |
| 19. Finland | 262.5 | Feb. 1968–Feb. 1973 | –68.2 |
| 20. Hong Kong | 261.6 | Jan. 1975–Jan. 1980 | –17.2 |
| 21. Netherlands | 256.6 | July 1993–July 1998 | Not available |
| 22. Norway | 253.1 | Sept. 1982–Sept. 1987 | –18.9 |
| 23. Norway | 248.4 | Oct. 1992–Oct. 1997 | Not available |
| 24. Sweden | 247.1 | Aug. 1982–Aug. 1987 | –36.9 |
| 25. Hong Kong | 230.9 | Oct. 1982–Oct. 1987 | –14.6 |

even in percentage terms. For example, the 184.8% real U.S. stock market increase from April 1994 to April 1999 almost makes the list of the biggest five-year price increases. In addition, the U.S. stock market fell 44.1% in real terms from October 1973 to October 1974, which almost puts it on the list of biggest one-year drops. And the real 113.9% rise from June 1932 to June 1933 would qualify for the list of biggest one-year increases, except that this period, from

*Table 6.4*

***Largest Recent Five-Year Real Stock Price Index Decreases***

| Country | Percentage decrease | Five-year period | Price change over subsequent five-year period (percent) |
|---|---|---|---|
| 1. Spain | –86.6 | Dec. 1974–Dec. 1979 | 0.1 |
| 2. Jamaica | –85.5 | July 1973–July 1978 | 185.2 |
| 3. Venezuela | –84.9 | May 1977–May 1982 | 138.9 |
| 4. Thailand | –84.0 | Jan. 1994–Jan. 1999 | Not available |
| 5. Philippines | –83.1 | Feb. 1980–Feb. 1985 | 1,000.0 |
| 6. Italy | –80.7 | June 1973–June 1978 | 72.6 |
| 7. Pakistan | –78.3 | Feb. 1994–Feb. 1999 | Not available |
| 8. Norway | –77.1 | July 1973–July 1978 | 74.1 |
| 9. Jamaica | –76.9 | Jan. 1993–Jan. 1998 | Not available |
| 10. Philippines | –76.6 | Sept. 1969–Sept. 1974 | –40.7 |
| 11. India | –74.6 | Aug. 1962–Aug. 1967 | 0.7 |
| 12. United Kingdom | –73.5 | Dec. 1969–Dec. 1974 | 81.5 |
| 13. South Africa | –73.4 | Apr. 1981–Apr. 1986 | 16.6 |
| 14. Colombia | –73.3 | July 1971–July 1976 | –24.8 |
| 15. Colombia | –72.7 | July 1979–July 1984 | 36.9 |
| 16. Chile | –72.6 | June 1980–June 1985 | 587.9 |
| 17. Philippines | –72.2 | Apr. 1976–Apr. 1981 | 24.4 |
| 18. Finland | –71.3 | Oct. 1973–Oct. 1978 | 99.0 |
| 19. Korea | –68.3 | June 1993–June 1998 | Not available |
| 20. Portugal | –67.9 | Jan. 1988–Jan. 1993 | 222.6 |
| 21. Jamaica | –64.2 | Nov. 1969–Nov. 1974 | –68.9 |
| 22. Korea | –63.6 | Aug. 1978–Aug. 1983 | 375.0 |
| 23. Italy | –62.6 | Jan. 1970–Jan. 1975 | –46.1 |
| 24. France | –62.5 | Jan. 1973–Jan. 1978 | 5.7 |
| 25. Italy | –62.3 | Sept. 1960–Sept. 1965 | –0.5 |

the depths of the Great Depression to the beginnings of recovery, occurred much earlier than the sample period used to construct the tables.)

The rightmost column in each of the tables also shows, whenever possible, what happened during the twelve months or five years after each of these periods of dramatic price change.[2] As can be seen, there is considerable variability across these countries as to whether the market continued in the same direction over the subsequent interval or reversed itself. At the end of this chapter, I describe what we know about the sequelae of the large price changes tabulated here.

### *Stories Associated with the Largest Price Changes*

It is easier to find stories associated with one-year price changes than with five-year price changes. Five years is such a long time that factors underlying the rise or decline in stock markets are often lost from public consciousness, being seen as underlying trends rather than salient events. Fortunately for our purposes, fourteen of the twenty-five five-year intervals of real price increase shown in Table 6.3 contain twelve-month intervals shown in Table 6.1, and eleven of the twenty-five five-year intervals of real price decline shown in Table 6.4 contain twelve-month intervals shown in Table 6.2.

Some of the twelve-month price increases seem to be associated with good reasons for a rational price change. This is especially so for the very largest one-year changes: typically something very unusual was going on. But even in these cases, there often seems to be a suggestion of some market overreaction to events.

The biggest one-year real stock market increase of all, in the Philippines from December 1985 to December 1986, was an amazing 683.4%. The biggest five-year real price change, of 1,253%, also occurred in the Philippines. The five-year period, from November 1984 to November 1989, included the record one-year period.

During the twelve-month period from December 1985 to December 1986 the regime of Ferdinand Marcos collapsed, Marcos fled the country, and a new government led by Corazon Aquino took charge of the country. In the period just before the price increase, a Communist insurgency had threatened to turn the country into another Vietnam. The Marcos government had assassinated Corazon Aquino's husband. There were demonstrations in the streets. It was in general a time of enormous uncertainty about the future. With the new government in place, the country developed renewed hope: a "new era" certainly seemed at hand. Moreover, the price changes were not reversed during the subsequent one- or five-year intervals, as can be seen from the tables.

One might suspect that the very low values for the Philippine stock market in December 1985, at the beginning of the record twelve-month period, were the result of a sort of negative bubble. Indeed, three of the top twenty five-year price decreases shown in Table 6.4 occurred in the Philippines by 1985. The Philippine stock market had a truly dismal record prior to its spectacular increase. Newspaper accounts in 1985 and earlier puzzled over the unusually low price-earnings ratios, often around 4. When viewed from this perspective, the largest stock increase in our tables was but a reversal of a series of decreases.

The second biggest one-year increase (October 1986 to October 1987) and the biggest one-year decrease (October 1989 to October 1990) both occurred in Taiwan. Taiwan is also the home of the seventh-largest five-year increase, from May 1986 to May 1991, and to the twenty-seventh-largest five-year decrease, from October 1988 to October 1993.

During the year of the highest speculative increase in Taiwan, October 1986 to October 1987, there were some impressive "new era" reasons for optimism. Booming exports had pushed economic growth rates into the double-digit range, and it was widely predicted that with this steep growth trajectory the economy would soon be producing such high-tech items as computer chips. The new affluence was visible everywhere: expensive foreign cars cruised the streets of Taipei and businessmen freely downed $100 bottles of wine at glamorous new restaurants. Even so, the savings rate was very high, and the country was investing heavily in its future.

In the fall of 1987, after a series of antigovernment street demonstrations, the government finally lifted the martial law that had been in force since 1949 and also allowed the formation of opposition parties for the first time. Later in that twelve-month period, in September 1987, the government made two historic and highly visible announcements: permitting foreign investors to establish companies in Taiwan and allowing Taiwanese citizens to visit their relatives on the mainland for the first time since 1949.

Despite these good reasons to anticipate the dawning of a "new era" in the Taiwanese economy, there still seemed to many observers to be an air of speculative excess to the Taiwan stock market of

1986–87. Volume of trade soared, increasing sevenfold from January to September 1987, to exceed the combined volume of all Asian markets excluding Japan.[3] Price-earnings ratios reached 45, compared with 16 at the beginning of the year.

Taiwan was in the grip of a gambling fever that expressed itself in other venues besides the stock market. An illegal numbers game, called Ta Chia Le or Happiness for All, unknown until 1986, suddenly became a national obsession. It was so popular that "on days when winning numbers are announced, peasants neglect[ed] their fields and workers fail[ed] to report to their factories."[4]

A Taiwanese student of mine at Yale later confided to me that, while he was still a teenager in Taiwan in 1987, his mother had forced him to go regularly to the stock exchange, observe the trading, and report back to her if something significant should happen. It was while carrying out these surveillance missions that he became convinced, he told me, of the utter madness of the speculative situation.

The Taiwan stock market increase was not reversed right away: over the year following the year of most rapid price increase there was yet another increase. But starting a year later, we see the 74.9% decline in the Taiwan stock market, the biggest one-year decline on our list.

The third-largest one-year price increase, of 384.6%, occurred in Venezuela between January 1990 and January 1991. This price surge came on the heels of a severe economic slump that had produced an economic growth rate of –8%, an unemployment rate of 10%, and inflation of 85% in 1989.[5] Then the Iraqi occupation of Kuwait (from August 1990 to February 1991) resulted in an interruption of Persian Gulf oil supplies, a rapid rise in international oil prices, and increased demand for Venezuelan oil. The stage was set for a time of sudden prosperity in Venezuela. The Kuwaiti experience supposedly convinced investors of the importance of Venezuela as an alternate oil supplier outside the unstable Persian Gulf. But this seems unlikely as a rational explanation for the run-up in the Venezuelan stock market, because the potential for disruptions of Persian Gulf oil supplies was already known long before the invasion. President Carlos Andres Perez warned that "Venezuela is living with a totally artificial economy" supported only by the oil price increase; nevertheless the stock market soared.[6] The price increase was not reversed in the subsequent year, but by January 1993 Venezuelan real stock prices had lost 60.3% of their January 1991 value, and by January 1999 they had lost 82.0% of that value.

The fourth-largest one-year price increase, at 360.9%, took place in Peru from August 1992 to August 1993. The increase occurred after a stock market plunge in April 1992, when Alberto Fujimori seized dictatorial powers, dissolving congress and suspending the constitution amid a protracted civil war with the Shining Path guerrillas. But in September 1992 the Shining Path leadership was captured, and by April 1993 democracy had been restored in Peru, ending fourteen years of guerrilla violence that had killed 27,000 people. Inflation had reached 7,000% and economic growth was negative in 1990, but by 1993 inflation was being brought under control and economic growth was positive. A wonderful sense of a "new era" was certainly in evidence—but a quadrupling of stock prices within a year left many wondering if the increase was excessive. The market did go up a bit more the following year, and then it lost a little of its value. By January 1999 the real level of the market was lower, but only by 8%. Of all our examples, the Peruvian stock market increase looks least like a speculative bubble; rather it seems to have been properly motivated by genuinely positive, fundamental news.

The stock market increase in India from April 1991 to April 1992, eleventh on the list in Table 6.1, began just as the assassination of Rajiv Gandhi in May 1991 ended the thirty-eight-year Nehru family dynasty. Gandhi's successor immediately appointed Manmohan Singh, a former professor at the Delhi School of Economics, as finance minister, and the new government announced a deregulation plan that was viewed as a substantial turn away from socialism. Foreign investment was now invited. Singh presented a budget plan that exempted financial assets from the calculation of the wealth tax. Previously, managers had tried to keep their companies' share prices as low as possible to avoid taxation; now they took steps to encourage high prices. The budget plan also reduced regulations on the pricing and timing of new stock issues.

These reforms were certainly plausible reasons for a stock market increase, but the actual increase was widely described as excessive, and authorities warned the nation of the potential for speculative excess. This was also a time of widespread attempts at stock price manipulation. The machinations of Harshad "Big Bull" Mehta, a Mumbai stockbroker, set off a national scandal in 1992, after the market peak had been reached. He was described as creating a "vortex effect" in individual stocks by buying in the market, selling at depressed prices to friendly institutions, and then buying again in the now-diminished pool of available shares, thereby pushing prices up.[7] The 1992 rise in Indian stock prices is now referred to as the "Mehta Peak." It was indeed a peak, since the market fell 50.3% during the following year.

In these examples, there was always some event, or series of events, outside the market itself that suggested the start of a genuine new era. Even if the market was *believed* to be overreacting to the event, it is hard to argue with any certainty that this was the case. In some of the other large price increases, on the other hand, there are no such plausible explanations for the magnitude of the price changes, and media interpretations therefore center on reinterpretations of long-term processes or on market psychology.

For example, in the Italian stock market boom of May 1985 to May 1986, when the market rose 166.4% in real terms, it was noted that economic growth was solid, that inflation remained low, and that the government of Prime Minister Bettino Craxi was stable and well liked. But none of this was really news. One Italian newspaper quoted an analyst as saying, "There are no explanations. . . . Everyone has gone crazy and that's it. This is a collective madness; total. It is useless to try to understand, to stop or to guide."[8] The *Financial Times* of London said, "A fever has gripped Italy: hundreds of first-time small investors are pouring money into the stock market as though they were buying lottery tickets."[9] The real level of the Italian market fell by 15.7% the following year. By September 1992 the Italian market had lost 68.0% of its May 1986 real value.

In France at around the same time, investors' "love affair with the market"[10] surprised observers by its intensity and lack of good explanation, and the French stock market makes our list, increasing

282.6% in real terms from March 1982 to March 1987. The "new era" story that the French government under François Mitterrand was departing from its socialist rigidity seemed inadequate to explain the market surge. Rather, if there was a new era, it seemed to many observers to be only in terms of market psychology, with French investors embracing free markets with renewed ardor. This period of enthusiasm was followed by the worldwide stock market crash of 1987, which set the French stock market back as well, although it still managed to gain another 10.2% over the succeeding five years, March 1987 to March 1992. Curiously, the French market went upward from there, with the growth of French real stock prices between 1992 and the turn of the millennium almost as dramatic, and as mystifying, as that in the United States.[11]

### *Ends of New Eras and Financial Crises*

The sequelae of the extraordinary price increases described in the previous section were highly variable. They were frequently followed by dramatic reversals, but this is by no means always the case. Do the increases carry the seeds of their own destruction, or are the interruptions due to other causes?

Often the ends of bull markets appear to be caused by concrete events unrelated to any irrational exuberance in the stock market. Notable among these are financial crises, such as banking or exchange rate crises. These other events then become the focus of analysis, since their causes appear more definite than those of the stock market crisis. According to such an analysis, the ends of the "new eras" have a narrow technical origin, rather than a psychological or social origin.

The 1994 Mexican crisis appears as the aftermath of the sixth most spectacular five-year stock price increase in Table 6.3. The anatomy of this crisis is a complicated one. Analysts stress an investor run on the peso, followed by investors' refusal to accept again the *tesobono,* the dollar-denominated short-term debt of the Mexican government. The investing public knew that the Mexican government did not have enough dollars in reserve to support the peso exchange rate if many people were to sell pesos, and although this knowledge alone need not have caused a currency devaluation, in combination with a belief that the devaluation of the peso was imminent, it in fact forced the devaluation. A devaluation of the peso, of course, is not itself a bad thing, and in fact it might have been the boost that the Mexican economy needed. But then there was the fact that investors mistrusted and decided not to reinvest in the *tesobono* debt. Since the Mexican government could not sell new debt, as its old debt came due it was unable to repay it. Fortunately, the government was saved by an international loan that enabled it to make good on this debt after all, and an economic crisis was resolved.

However, note—despite having identified the source of the problem as related to the peso, despite the shortness of the Mexican economic crisis, and despite the international loans to Mexico to fix the problem—that the real Mexican stock market was still, as of mid-1999, 50% below its 1994 peak. The period saw a fundamental change in the public's attitude toward the Mexican stock market. Before the 1994 crisis, under the Salinas government, with the advent of the North American Free Trade Agreement and with Mexico's admission into the Organization for Economic Cooperation and Development, there seems to have been an exaggerated "new era" sense of invulnerability and of a great future ahead for Mexico, which faded after the crisis.

The Asian financial crisis of 1997–98 was also much more than a stock market crisis. It included exchange rate and banking crises, and again these tended to attract the attention of analysts. But, as can be seen from Table 6.3, the Asian crisis was preceded by a good number of the largest five-year price increases, and these came substantially before the exchange rate and banking crises. Japan had had a 275.6% five-year real stock price increase from August 1982 to August 1987; Hong Kong a 230.9% stock price increase from October 1982 to October 1987; Korea a 518.3% stock price increase from March 1984 to March 1989; Taiwan a 468.1% stock price increase from May 1986 to May 1991; and Thailand a 430.7% stock price increase over the same period. Most of these price increases came during the period 1982–87, as the world experienced a recovery from the Great Recession of 1981. In all of these countries, the stock market was already down from its peak by December 1996, before there was any hint of the Asian financial crisis. It appears that the collapse of a speculative bubble in these countries preceded the crisis and was part of the ambience that produced the crisis. Yet when the crisis finally came, the stock market stories, as well as stories of public confidence, appeared only vaguely in the background, as attention centered on changes in currency exchange rates, the sudden withdrawal of foreign investors, banking problems, inflation, and labor difficulties.

These financial crisis stories illustrate the complicated factors that sometimes capture the attention of economic and financial analysts. Each of them may seem to be "the" technical story that explains events. Discussions may focus on these factors and pull attention away from the large changes in public opinion that are reflected in speculative prices. Therefore the underlying story of investors overreacting to news and of the feedback of price increases leading to further price increases often tends to get lost.

### *What Went Up (Down) Usually Came Back Down (Up)*

It is impossible to *prove* the assertion that some speculative excesses were behind many of these events. One can always argue that the fundamental reasons offered by investors to justify them were valid in terms of the evidence that was available when the market was going up, and that "new era" stories are never completely without merit as theories of what *might* happen. But one can also ask whether these price movements have tended to be reversed. If the price increases are, on average, reversed, then we have some evidence that the fundamental reasons were not sound.

The data on which these tables are based confirm for countries the result first discovered by Werner De Bondt and Richard Thaler: that winner stocks—if winner status is measured over long intervals of time such as five years—tend to do poorly in subsequent intervals of the same length, and that loser stocks—if loser status is measured over equally long intervals—tend to do well in subsequent intervals of the same length.[12]

From the data used to produce the tables, we find that, for the seventeen countries shown in Table 6.3 for which subsequent five-year data were available, eleven (65%) experienced a decrease, on average, in real stock prices in the five-year periods after large five-year real price increases, and the average price change for the seventeen countries was a decrease of 3.9%.[13] Similarly, for the sixteen countries shown in Table 6.4 for which subsequent five-year data were available, fifteen (94%) experienced an increase in real stock prices in the five-year periods after large five-year real price decreases, and the average price change was an increase of 121.9%. We thus see quite a substantial, though imperfect, tendency for major five-year stock price movements to be reversed in another five years, for both up movements and down movements.

When we look at one-year real price changes, as in Tables 6.1 and 6.2, we find that the tendency toward reversals is less pronounced, as we would expect from past literature on prices of individual stocks. We find that, for the eighteen countries shown in Table 6.1 for which subsequent twelve-month data were available, nine (50%) experienced a decrease in real stock prices in the twelve-month periods after large twelve-month price increases, so that the direction of the change was equally split between up and down, and the average change was an increase of 11.4%. For the twenty-one countries shown in Table 6.2, fourteen (67%) experienced an increase in real stock prices in the twelve-month periods after large twelve-month decreases, and the average real price change was an increase of 10.7%. Twelve months does not appear to be enough time to begin to see a tendency for these extreme price movements to reverse themselves.

Quite possibly, the tendency for individual countries' stock market valuations to grow dramatically and then to be reversed will diminish in the future. With freer capital movements than were possible during the periods covered by the examples in the tables, and with more and more global investors seeking profit opportunities buying undervalued countries or shorting overvalued countries, markets may become more stable. Even so, it is unlikely that these forces will soon eliminate the potential for such movements, particularly infrequent and slow large-country events or world-wide events, for which the attendant profit opportunities are slow and hard to diversify. The possibility of major speculative bubbles, now and in the future, cannot be ignored.

In this section on cultural factors, we have explored the justifications people have given, at various points in history, for changing market valuations, and we have seen evidence of the transitory nature of these cultural factors. Ultimately, however, the conclusions we draw from such evidence depend on our view of human nature and the extent of human abilities to produce consistent and independent judgments. To consolidate our understanding of the argument, we turn, in the next part, to a study of fundamental psychological factors—human tendencies to act independently or to acquiesce, to believe others or to disbelieve them, to feel confidence or self-doubt, to be attentive or inattentive. These tendencies bear on the plausibility of our view of speculative bubbles.

*Part Three*

# *Psychological Factors*

# Seven

## *Psychological Anchors for the Market*

We have seen that the market is not well anchored by fundamentals. People do not even know to any degree of accuracy what the "right" level of the market is: not many of them spend much time thinking about what its level should be or whether it is over- or underpriced today. So what is it that ties down the market's level on any given day? What anchors the market? What is it that determines whether the Dow Jones Industrial Average is at 4,000 or 14,000? What ultimately limits the feedback from price changes to further price changes that amplifies speculative price movements? Why does the market stay within a certain region for days at a time, only to break out suddenly? We have already seen some partial answers to these questions, but to understand the true nature of the anchors at work here, we must also turn to psychology.

In considering lessons from psychology, it must be noted that many popular accounts of the psychology of investing are simply not credible. Investors are said to be euphoric or frenzied during booms or panic-stricken during market crashes. In both booms and crashes, investors are described as blindly following the herd like so many sheep, with no minds of their own. Belief in the rationality of markets starts to sound a lot better when the only alternatives are such pop-psychological theories.

We all know that most people are more sensible during such financial episodes than these accounts suggest. Financial booms and crashes are, for most of us, not emotion-laden events on a par with victories in battle or volcanic eruptions. In fact, during the most significant financial events, most people are preoccupied with other personal matters, not with the financial markets at all. So it is hard to imagine that the market as a whole reflects the emotions described by these psychological theories.

However, solid psychological research does show that there are patterns of human behavior that suggest anchors for the market that would not be expected if markets worked entirely rationally. These patterns of human behavior are not the result of extreme human ignorance, but rather of the character of human intelligence, reflecting its limitations as well as its strengths. Investors are striving to do the right thing, but they have limited abilities and certain natural modes of behavior that decide their actions when an unambiguous prescription for action is lacking.[1]

Two kinds of psychological anchors will be considered here: *quantitative anchors,* which themselves give indications for the appropriate levels of the market that some people use as indications of whether the market is over- or underpriced and whether it is a good time to buy, and *moral anchors,* which operate by determining the strength of the reason that compels people to buy stocks, a reason that they must weigh against their other uses for the wealth they already have (or could have) invested in the market. With quantitative anchors, people are weighing numbers against prices when they decide whether stocks (or other assets) are priced right. With moral anchors, people compare the intuitive or emotional strength of the argument for investing in the market against their wealth and their perceived need for money to spend now.

### Quantitative Anchors for the Market

Designers of questionnaires have learned that the answers people give can be heavily influenced by suggestions that are given on the questionnaires themselves. For example, when people are asked to state within which of a number of ranges their income falls, their answers are influenced by the ranges given. The ranges serve as "anchors" to which they make their answers conform.

Psychologists have shown that people's decisions in ambiguous situations are influenced by whatever available anchor is at hand. When you must come up with an estimate, and you are unsure what to say, you take whatever number is before you. Psychologists Amos Tversky and Daniel Kahneman demonstrated this tendency clearly in an experiment involving a wheel of fortune: a large wheel with the numbers from 1 to 100 on it, similar to those used in television game shows, that is designed to stop at a random number when it is spun. Subjects were asked questions whose answers were numbers between 1 and 100, difficult questions such as the percentage of African nations in the United Nations. They were asked first to say whether the answer they would give was above or below the number just produced by the wheel of fortune. Then they were asked to give their answer. The experimenters found that the answer was quite substantially influenced by the random number on the wheel. For example, if the wheel stopped at 10, the median percentage of African nations according to their subjects was 25, whereas if the wheel stopped at 65, the median percentage was 45. This experiment was particularly interesting because it was designed so that the subject clearly knew that the number produced by the wheel was purely random and, moreover, because the number produced by the wheel should have had no emotional significance for the subject.[2]

In making judgments about the level of stock prices, the most likely anchor is the most recently remembered price. The tendency of investors to use this anchor enforces the similarity of stock prices from one day to the next. Other possible anchors are remembered past prices, and the tendency of past prices to serve as anchors may be part of the reason for the observed tendency for trends in individual stock prices to be reversed. Another anchor may be the nearest milestone of a prominent index such as the Dow, the nearest round-number level, and investors' use of this anchor may help explain unusual market behavior surrounding such levels. Past price *changes* may also provide an anchor, if attention is suitably drawn to them. Recall from Chapter 4 that the drop in the market in the October 19, 1987, crash was nearly the same in percentage terms as that in the October 28–29, 1929, crash that was so much discussed at the time of the 1987 crash.

For individual stocks, price changes may tend to be anchored to the price changes of other stocks, and price-earnings ratios may be anchored to other firms' price-earnings levels. This kind of anchoring may help to explain why individual stock prices move together as much as they do, and thus ultimately why stock price indexes are as volatile as they are—why the averaging across stocks that is inherent in the construction of the index doesn't more solidly dampen its volatility.[3] It may also explain why stocks of companies that are in different industries but are headquartered in the same country tend to have more similar price movements than stocks of companies that are in the same industry but are headquartered in different countries, contrary to one's expectation that the industry would define the fundamentals of the company better than the location of its headquarters.[4] And it may explain why real estate investment trusts traded on stock exchanges tend to behave more like stocks than like the appraised value of their underlying commercial real estate.[5] Indeed all of these anomalies noted in financial markets have a simple explanation in terms of quantitative anchoring to convenient numbers.

### *Moral Anchors for the Market*

With moral anchoring, the market is tied down by people's comparisons of the intuitive force of stories and reasons to hold their investments against their perceived need to consume the wealth that these investments represent. The market is not prevented from going up to arbitrarily high levels because people have any idea what its intrinsically "right" level is or what level would be too high. Rather, if the market were to get too high, the discrepancy between the wealth many people would then have in the market and their current living standards would, when compared with their reasons for holding stocks, encourage them to sell. One can appreciate the nature of this anchor with an extreme example. Suppose, counterfactually, that the psychology of the market caused the level of the stock market to rise so as to make most holders of stocks multimillionaires—on paper. Then, unless the reason these people have to continue holding every single share is perceived to be extremely strong, they would want to start *living* a little more like multimillionaires and sell some of their stocks to be able to spend the money. Such selling would obviously bring stock prices down, since there would be no buyers, and obviously there just isn't sufficient current national income available to sustain anything like this many multimillionaires. The stock market can reach fantastic levels only if people think that they have good reasons not to test it by trying to enjoy their newfound wealth.

Underlying this notion of moral anchors is the psychological principle that much of the human thinking that results in action is not quantitative, but instead takes the form of *storytelling* and *justification.* That is why, in the case of moral anchors, people are weighing a story, which has no quantitative dimension, against the observed quantity of financial wealth that they have available for consumption. Such reasoning is not well described by the usual kind of economic theory, but there is a large amount of evidence in support of the assertion that investor reasoning does take this form.

Psychologists Nancy Pennington and Reid Hastie have shown the importance of stories in decision making by studying how jurors reached decisions in difficult cases. They found that jurors' approach to reasoning through the complicated issues of the trial tended to take the form of constructing a story, filling out the details that were provided to them about the case into a coherent narrative of the chain of events. In describing their verdict, they tended not to speak of quantities or probabilities, or of summing up the weight of the evidence, but rather merely to tell a story of the case, typically a chronology of events, and to remark how well their story fit together and how internally consistent it was.[6]

By analogy, those who sell stocks to the general public often tend to tell a story about the stock, a vivid story describing the history of the company, the nature of the product, and how the public is using the product. The sales call does not as often engage in discussions of quantities or probabilities, or of whether the price is at the right level in terms of quantitative evidence about future dividends or earnings. These quantitative factors are not as congenial to the narrative-based decision making that comes naturally to people.

There is a basic human interest in gambling, seen in one form or another in all cultures,[7] an interest that also expresses itself in speculative markets. Some of the attraction to gambling, despite odds that are often openly stacked against gamblers, apparently has to do with narrative-based thinking. When gamblers are heard talking, they are usually telling stories, not evaluating probabilities, and the possibilities suggested by the stories often seem to have more substantive reality than any quantitative concepts. In these stories, gamblers use a different vocabulary than do probability theorists, preferring the words *luck* or *lucky day,* and rarely uttering the words *probability* or *likelihood.* There are stories of their winnings and losses, of the chains of events that preceded their best or worst luck, of the strength of their intuition that yielded good bets. These stories can convey a sense of meaning and significance to events that are in fact purely random.[8]

It has been noted that employees have a tendency to invest in company stock (that is, stock issued by the firm that employs them), even though it would appear to be more in their interest to diversify away from the source of their own livelihood. About a third of assets in large retirement savings plans are invested in company stock, and in some companies, such as Coca-Cola, company stock reaches 90% of assets.[9] This tendency to invest in company stock can be interpreted as consistent with investors' being influenced by stories: they know many more stories about their own companies and so invest in those companies' stocks.

People also appear to want to construct simple reasons for their decisions, as if they feel the need to justify those decisions in simple terms—if not to others, then to themselves. The need to have a simple reason to explain a decision is similar to the need to have a story behind a decision; both the stories and the reasons are simple rationales that can be conveyed verbally to others.

Psychologists Eldar Shafir, Itamar Simonson, and Amos Tversky demonstrated experimentally an effect that appears to represent decision biases caused by people's search for simple reasons to justify decisions. They presented their subjects with a simple choice between two options: one option was "impoverished," with no striking positive or negative features. The other was "enriched," displaying both distinctly positive and distinctly negative features. In one of their experiments, subjects were asked to choose to which parent they would award sole custody of a child. Parent A, the impoverished option, was described with the words "average income, average health, average working hours, reasonable rapport with the child, and relatively stable social life." Parent B, the enriched option, was described with the words "above-average income, very close relationship with the child, extremely active social life, lots of work-related travel, minor health problems." The experimenters found that the subjects' choices depended on how they were asked about the two choices. When a group of subjects was asked to select the parent to whom they would award custody, 64% chose Parent B. When a second group was asked to pick the parent to whom they would *deny* custody, 55% again chose Parent B. The predominant answers given by the two groups are logically inconsistent, but they are consistent with a feeling that one must have a solid reason to justify a decision. The psychologists found that the same tendency occurs even for purely personal decisions that will never need to be explained to others.[10]

Reasons to hold stocks or other investments can take on ethical as well as practical dimensions. Our culture may supply reasons to hold stocks and other savings vehicles that are related to our sense of identity as responsible people, as good or levelheaded people. *The Millionaire Next Door,* a best-seller since 1996, makes the point that most millionaires in the United States are not exceptional income earners, but merely frugal savers: average folks who are not enticed by a new car every year, an extravagant house, or other such money pits.[11] This book is not only an interesting study of millionaires; it also projects a subtle message suggesting the moral superiority of those who hold and gradually accumulate wealth over a lifetime. It therefore provides an attractive reason to save and invest. The book offers no analyses of price-earnings ratios or anything remotely like specific investment advice, thus subtly reinforcing the impression that these are irrelevant. Instead, it offers lots of stories of successful, frugal people, many of whom prospered during the recent bull market—stories with vivid details and great immediacy for readers. The book's enticing story about investing millionaires who do not test the market by trying to cash out and consume their wealth is just the kind of moral anchor needed to help sustain an unusual bull market.

### *Overconfidence and Intuitive Judgment*

In judging the significance of these psychological anchors for the market, it is important to bear in mind that there appears to be a pervasive human tendency toward *overconfidence* in one's beliefs. People are ready to act on stories or reasons that one might think they should have little confidence in.

People think they know more than they do. They like to express opinions on matters they know little about, and they often act on these opinions. We have all observed at one time or another that there are a lot of know-it-alls out there. But psychologists have described the tendency toward overconfidence with some care and indications of its generality.

Psychologists Baruch Fischhof, Paul Slovic, and Sarah Lichtenstein showed that if people are asked simple factual questions (such as which of two popular magazines has the higher circulation or which of two common causes of death is the more frequent) and are then asked to give the probability that their answer is right, they tend to overestimate the probability that they are right. In fact, when people said they were certain they were right they were in fact right only about 80% of the time.[12]

This result has been the subject of controversy among psychologists, and the overconfidence phenomenon has not been found to be universal. It has been shown that people can sometimes be trained out of their overconfidence in the experimental setting.[13] Yet some basic tendency toward overconfidence appears to be a robust human character trait: the bias is definitely toward overconfidence rather than underconfidence. I find that overconfidence is apparent when I interview investors; they seem to express overly strong opinions and rush to summary judgments.

Psychologists have long wondered why it is that people seem to be overconfident. One theory has been that, in evaluating the soundness of their conclusions, people tend to evaluate the probability that they are right on only the last step of their reasoning, forgetting how many other elements of their reasoning could be wrong.[14] Another theory is that people make probability judgments by looking for similarities to other known observations, and they forget that there are many other possible observations with which they could compare.[15] The reason for overconfidence may also have to do with hindsight bias, a tendency to think that one would have known actual events were coming before they happened, had one been present then or had reason to pay attention.[16] Hindsight bias encourages a view of the world as more predictable than it really is.

Another factor in overconfidence as it relates to speculative markets is *magical thinking*. When we speak of people's intuition about the likelihood that investments will do well or poorly and their own decisions to invest, we are speaking of their innermost thoughts—thoughts that they do not have to explain or justify to others. Patterns of thought referred to as "magical thinking" or "quasi-magical thinking" by psychologists are likely to play a role. People have occasional feelings that certain actions will make them lucky even if they know logically that the actions cannot have an effect on their fortunes.

People will make serious decisions based on thinking that they would, if pressed, admit was illogical. It has been shown that people will place larger bets on a coin that has not yet been tossed than on a coin that has already been tossed (and for which the outcome has been concealed). And people will, if asked how much money they would demand to part with a lottery ticket they already hold, give a figure over four times greater if they themselves chose the lottery number on the ticket. Apparently, at some magical level people think that they can influence a coin that has not yet been tossed and influence the likelihood of winning the lottery by choosing the number.[17]

Based on such experimental results, it seems clear that people are capable of thinking, at least at some intuitive level, "If I buy a stock, then it will go up afterwards" or "If I buy a stock, then others will probably want to buy the stock, too, because they are like me" or "I have a hot hand lately; my luck is with me." Such thinking is likely, in a subtle way, to contribute to the overconfidence that may help the propagation of speculative bubbles.

Another aspect of overconfidence is that people tend to make judgments in uncertain situations by looking for familiar patterns and assuming that future patterns will resemble past ones, often without sufficient consideration of the reasons for the pattern or the probability of the pattern repeating itself. This anomaly of human judgment, called the *representativeness heuristic,* was demonstrated in a number of experiments by psychologists Tversky and Kahneman.

For example, these researchers asked people to guess the occupation, from a list of occupations, of people with a given personality description. If the description given was that the person was artistic and sensitive, they tended to choose conductor or sculptress, rather than laborer or secretary, disregarding entirely the fact that the former occupations are extremely rare and thus that the answers are much less likely to be right.[18] It would be wiser, in answering such questions, almost never to guess the occupation conductor or sculptress, since the base rate probabilities are so low. But people look for the best-fit occupation, disregarding the base rate probabilities.

Economists Nicholas Barberis, Andrei Shleifer, and Robert Vishny have developed the representativeness heuristic into a theory of investors' selective overconfidence and into a psychological theory of an expectational feedback loop. These authors argue that investors, when they see stock prices move in the same direction for a while, gradually begin to assume that the trend is representative of many trends that they have seen in other economic data. According to a psychological principle of conservatism, people are slow to change their opinions. For this reason, it takes some time before investors begin to conclude that the trend will continue. The interplay between the representativeness heuristic and the principle of conservatism determines the speed at which the speculative feedback progresses.[19]

Overconfidence, however generated, appears to be a fundamental factor promoting the high volume of trade we observe in speculative markets. Without such overconfidence, one would think that there would be little trading in financial markets. If people were completely rational, then half the investors should think that they are below average in their trading ability and should therefore be unwilling to do speculative trades with the other half, who they think will probably dominate them in trading. Thus the above-average half would have no one to trade with, and there should ideally be no trading for speculative reasons.[20]

Overconfidence in judgments can at times influence people to believe that they know when a market move will take place, even if they generally believe as an intellectual matter that stock prices are not forecastable. In the survey that I carried out of investors right after the crash of October 19, 1987, I asked them, "Did you think at any point on October 19, 1987, that you had a pretty good idea when a rebound was to occur?" Of individual investors who had bought on that day, 47.1% said yes; of institutional investors, 47.9% said yes. Thus nearly half of those trading that day thought they knew what the market would do that day. I find this remarkable. Even among all individual investors, most of whom did not buy or sell at all on that day, 29.2% answered yes to this question; among all institutional investors, 28.0% answered yes.

Why would anyone think that they knew what the market would do on any given day, and especially on such a tumultuous day? The idea that one would know such things stands contrary to the most elementary observations about markets' forecastability, and contrary to the conventional wisdom that accurate market timing is very difficult. Quite a few people apparently do not consistently believe that the market is never very forecastable.

The next question on the questionnaire was, "If yes, what made you think you knew when a rebound would occur?" There was a striking absence of solid grounding for the answers. References were made to "intuition," "gut feeling," "historical evidence and common sense," or "market psychology." Mentions of concrete facts or references to explicit theories were rare, even among the institutional investors.

These intuitive feelings about the future course of the market were extremely important for the course of the stock market crash, for apparently it was these intuitive judgments that set the anchors that stopped the price decline. To understand speculative bubbles, positive or negative, we must appreciate that overconfidence in one's own intuitive judgments plays a fundamental role.

### *The Fragility of Anchors: Difficulty Thinking Ahead to Contingent Future Decisions*

The anchors discussed here account for the stability of the market from day to day, but we must also account for the ability of these anchors to let loose occasionally—sometimes suddenly. Markets do make dramatic shifts. Part of the reason for the surprises the market hands us from time to time is that news events have an effect on people's reasons that even they could not have expected.

Psychologists Shafir and Tversky have described a phenomenon they call *nonconsequentialist reasoning:* reasoning that is characterized by an inability to think through the elementary conclusions one would draw in the future if hypothetical events were to occur. According to Shafir and Tversky, people cannot decide until the events actually occur. When we learn to play games of logic, for example chess, we must practice thinking ahead to the decisions we will make in the future in response to the other player's decisions. One learns to think, "If I move here, then she might move either here or there, and if she moves here I will be fine, but if she moves there I will be faced with a difficult situation. . . ." That is, one learns to think through the ramifications of all relevant branches of a decision tree. In everyday life we to some extent practice the same modes of thinking that we learned in playing these games. But real-world decisions are clouded by emotions and a lack of clearly defined objectives, and people do not generally behave as if they have thought things through well in advance.

Shafir and Tversky give an example of students' decision making about whether to take a vacation in Hawaii after learning whether they had passed or failed an important exam. Faced with such a choice, they look into their own minds for their feelings about the choice. Some students who have passed the exam will think, "I should take the vacation as a celebration and a reward." Some students who have failed the exam will think, "I should take the vacation as a consolation, to improve my mood after having failed." Some students will decide to take a vacation whether or not they pass the exam. Those students who would take the vacation in either case should be able, if they were fully logical, to book the vacation well in advance of the exam, knowing that the information about the outcome of the exam is not really relevant to their decision. But these people sometimes have great difficulty making such a choice before they know the outcome of the exam. Before the exam, they cannot fully anticipate the emotional reason for taking the vacation, and so they cannot feel good about committing themselves to it.[21]

Although this example presents a situation in which the difficulty people face is in deciding how they themselves will feel in the future, rather than in deciding on questions of simple fact as in the game of chess, in reality decisions about investments are likely to have as much of an emotional component as decisions about whether to go on a vacation.

For this reason, the effects of news stories on the stock market sometimes have more to do with discovery of how we *feel* about the news than with any logical reaction to the news. We can make decisions then that would have been impossible before the news was known. It is partly for this reason that the breaking off of a psychological anchor can be so unpredictable: people discover things about themselves, about their own emotions and inclinations, only *after* price changes occur.

Psychological anchors for the market hook themselves on the strangest things along the muddy bottom of our consciousness. The anchor can skip and drag, only to snag again on some object whose strength would surprise us if we saw it at the surface. We have considered in this chapter some of the psychological factors that explain the nature of such anchors. But the anchors can have significance for the market as a whole only if the same thoughts enter the minds of many. In the next chapter, we turn to the social basis of thinking: the tendencies toward herd behavior and the contagion of ideas.

# Eight

# *Herd Behavior and Epidemics*

A fundamental observation about human society is that people who communicate regularly with one another think similarly. There is at any place and in any time a *Zeitgeist*, a spirit of the times. It is important to understand the origins of this similar thinking, so that we can judge the plausibility of theories of speculative fluctuations that ascribe price changes to faulty thinking. If the millions of people who invest were all truly independent of each other, any faulty thinking would tend to average out, and such thinking would have no effect on prices. But if less-than-mechanistic or irrational thinking is in fact similar over large numbers of people, then such thinking can indeed be the source of stock market booms and busts.

Part of the reason people's judgments are similar at similar times is that they are reacting to the same information—the information that was publicly available at that time. But, as we shall see in this chapter, rational response to public information is not the only reason that people think similarly, nor is the use of that public information always appropriate or well reasoned.

### *Social Influence and Information*

Acclaimed social psychologist Solomon Asch reported an experiment in 1952 that he interpreted—and that was widely interpreted by others—as showing the immense power of social pressure on individual judgment. His paper was published at a time of widespread public concern with the effects of Communist propaganda, alarm at the apparently successful brainwashing techniques of Chinese Communists, and continuing puzzlement over the ability of the Nazis in Germany to obtain an obedient response when ordering mass exterminations of Jews and other "undesirables." Asch's findings were widely cited in the media as providing a scientific basis for claims that people do not have fully independent judgment. His results are still cited today; those who found serious flaws in his interpretation of those results are not nearly as well remembered.

In his famous experiment, Asch placed the subject into a group of seven to nine other people who were, unbeknownst to the subject, confederates who had been coached by Asch. The entire group was asked to answer a sequence of twelve questions about the lengths of line segments shown to them on cards, and the subject would hear most of the others' answers before giving his own answer before the group. The correct answers to the questions were obvious, but the confederates deliberately gave wrong answers to seven of the twelve questions. Faced with a group of people who were unanimously giving what seemed to be obviously wrong answers to the questions, a third of the time the subjects caved in and gave the same wrong answers as had been given by the confederates. Furthermore the subjects often showed signs of anxiety or distress, suggesting that fear of being seen as different or foolish before the group had swayed their judgment.[1]

Asch explained his results as due to social pressure. There is probably some validity to this interpretation, but it turns out that the subjects' wrong answers were not primarily due to such pressure. Three years after Asch published his findings, psychologists Morton Deutsch and Harold Gerard reported a variant of Asch's experiment in which the subjects were told that they had been placed *anonymously* into a group of people, people that they never saw and never would see, and whose answers they could observe only indirectly through an electronic signal. (In fact there was really no group at all.) Subjects could give their answers to the questions merely by pressing a button, unobserved by others, so that there was no need to stand up to a group face to face. Otherwise, the experiment proceeded as it had under Asch. And the subjects gave nearly as many wrong answers as they had before.[2]

Deutsch and Gerard concluded that the wrong answers in the Asch experiment had been given in large part because people simply thought that all the other people could not be wrong. They were reacting to the *information that a large group of people had reached a judgment different from theirs,* rather than merely the fear of expressing a contrary opinion in front of a group. This behavior is a matter of rational calculation: in everyday living we have learned that when a large group of people is unanimous in its judgment on a question of simple fact, the members of that group are almost certainly right. The anxiety and distress that Asch's subjects expressed may have come partly from their conclusion that their own senses were somehow not reliable.

Another widely cited series of experiments relevant to herd behavior is Stanley Milgram's investigations of the power of authority. In Milgram's experiments, the subject was asked to administer electric shocks to another person sitting close by, who was, again unbeknownst to the subject, a confederate. There really were no electric shocks, but the confederate pretended to be experiencing them, feigning pain and suffering. The confederate asserted that he was in great distress and asked that the experiment be stopped. But when the experimenter told the subjects to continue administering the shocks, insisting that the shocks would cause no permanent tissue damage, many did so.[3]

These results were widely interpreted as demonstrating the enormous power of authority over the human mind. Indeed the results may be understood partly on those terms. But there is another interpretation: that people have learned that when experts tell them something is all right, it probably is, even if it does not seem so. (In fact, it is worth noting that in this case the experimenter was indeed correct: it *was* all right to continue giving the "shocks"—even though most of the subjects did not suspect the reason.) Thus the results of Milgram's experiment can also be interpreted as springing from people's past learning about the reliability of authorities.[4]

Asch's and Milgram's studies are as interesting as ever when viewed from the standpoint of this information-based interpretation. The experiments demonstrate that people are ready to believe the majority view or to believe authorities even when they plainly contradict matter-of-fact judgment. And their behavior is in fact largely rational and intelligent. Most people have had many prior experiences of making errors when they contradicted the judgments of a larger group or of an authority figure, and they have learned from these experiences. Thus the Asch and Milgram experiments give us a different perspective on the overconfidence phenomenon: people are respectful of authorities in formulating the opinions about which they will later be so overconfident, transferring their confidence in authorities to their own judgments based upon them.

Given the kind of behavior observed by Asch and Milgram, it is not at all surprising that many people are accepting of the perceived authority of others on such matters as stock market valuation. Most must certainly trust their own judgment in this area even less than the experimental subjects trusted the evidence of their own eyes about the lengths of lines on cards or the pain and suffering that a person sitting next to them was experiencing.

## *Economic Theories of Herd Behavior and Information Cascades*

Even completely rational people can participate in herd behavior when they take into account the judgments of others, and even if they know that everyone else is behaving in a herdlike manner. The behavior, although individually rational, produces group behavior that is, in a well-defined sense, irrational. This herdlike behavior is said to arise from an *information cascade*.[5]

A simple story will illustrate how such an information cascade could get started. Suppose two restaurants open next door to each other. Each potential customer must choose between the two. Would-be customers may be able to make some judgments about the quality of each of the restaurants when viewing it through the front window, but such judgments will not be very accurate. The first customer who arrives must choose based only on viewing the two empty restaurants and makes a choice. However, the next potential customer can rely not only on his or her own information, based on the appearance of the restaurants, but also—by seeing the first customer eating in one or the other of the restaurants—information about the choice made by the first customer. If the second customer chooses to go to the same restaurant as the first, the third customer will see two people eating in that restaurant. The end result may be that all customers may wind up eating at the same restaurant—and it could well be the poorer restaurant, since there was no real consideration of the combined evidence inherent in all their observations about the two restaurants. If all of them had been able to pool their first impressions and discuss these as a group, they might have been able to deduce which restaurant was likely to be the better one. But in this scenario they cannot make use of each other's information, since they do not reveal their own information to others when they merely follow them.

The restaurant story, and the economic theory that underlies it, is not in itself a theory of stock market bubbles. However, it has clear relevance to stock market behavior, and it can provide a foundation for a theory about how rational investors may be led astray.[6] According to such a theory, the popular notion that the level of market prices is the outcome of a sort of vote by all investors about the true value of the market is just plain wrong. Hardly anyone is really voting. Instead people are rationally choosing not to, as they see it, waste their time and effort in exercising their judgment about the market, and thus choosing not to exert any independent impact on the market. Ultimately, all such information cascade theories are theories of *the failure of information about true fundamental value to be disseminated and evaluated.*

It is important to emphasize that this failure to disseminate information to others can be modeled in economic theory in terms of purely rational behavior with no limitations of intelligence, only limitations of revealed information. But to achieve a better understanding of the issues relevant to financial market mispricing, one must also understand some parameters of human behavior, of limitations of human information processing, that are relevant to the transmission of information and the potential for speculative bubbles.

### *Human Information Processing and Word of Mouth*

The human mind is the product of evolution almost entirely in the absence of the printed word, e-mail, the Internet, or any other artificial means of communication. Human society has been able to conquer almost all habitats of this planet primarily because of its own innate information processing ability. A fundamental component of this information processing ability is effective communication of important facts from one person to another.

This superior ability to communicate knowledge has been made possible over the past few million years by evolutionary changes within the human brain that have optimized the channels of communication and created an emotional drive to communicate effectively. It is because of this emotional drive that most people's favorite activity is conversation. Look around you. Everywhere you go, when two or more people are not working or playing or sleeping (and, in some cases, even when they are doing these things), they are talking. The incessant exchange of information is a fundamental characteristic of our species. The information that tends to flow most rapidly is the kind that would have helped society in centuries past in its everyday living: information about such things as food sources, dangers, or other members of society.

For this reason, in modern society there is likely to be rapidly spreading conversation about a buying opportunity for a hot stock, or about immediate threats to personal wealth, or about the story of the people who run a company. These topics resemble the kinds of things our ancestors have talked about since time immemorial. But conversation seems to flow less well about abstract topics, such as the mathematics of finance, or statistics about asset returns, or optimal levels of saving for retirement. Transmission of such knowledge is of course effortful, infrequent, and imperfect.

### *Face-to-Face Communications versus Media Communications*

The conventional media—print media, television, and radio—have a profound capability for spreading ideas, but their ability to generate active behaviors is still limited. Interpersonal and interactive communications, particularly face-to-face or word-of-mouth communications, still have the most powerful impact on our behavior.

In a 1986 study of individual investors, John Pound and I sought to determine how their attention was first drawn to a stock. We mailed a questionnaire to a random sample of individual investors and asked them to consider the company whose stock they had purchased most recently. We asked, "What first drew your attention to the company?" Only 6% specified periodicals or newspapers. The majority of the answers named sources that would involve direct interpersonal communication.[7] Even if people read a lot, their attention and actions appear to be more stimulated by interpersonal communications.

The power of interpersonal, word-of-mouth communication about investments has been amply illustrated by the work of the market surveillance units at the exchanges and within the Securities and Exchange Commission. Their brief is to detect insider trading, and to that end they carefully follow the trail of communications among individual investors. Court documents reveal, for example, that a sequence of word-of-mouth communications was touched off in May 1995, when a secretary at IBM was asked to photocopy documents that included references to IBM's top-secret takeover of Lotus Development Corporation, a deal scheduled to be announced on June 5 of that year. She apparently told only her husband, a beeper salesman. On June 2, he told another person, a co-worker, who bought shares eighteen minutes later, and another friend, a computer technician, who initiated a sequence of phone calls. By the time of the June 5 announcement, twenty-five people connected to this core group had spent half a million dollars on the investment based on this tip. They included a pizza chef, an electrical engineer, a bank executive, a dairy wholesaler, a former schoolteacher, a gynecologist, an attorney, and four stockbrokers.[8] Clearly word-of-mouth communication can proceed with great speed and across disparate social groups.

Word-of-mouth transmission of ideas appears to be an important contributor to day-to-day or hour-to-hour stock market fluctuations, even though direct word-of-mouth transmission cannot proceed across the nation quite as fast as markets move. In the questionnaire survey of investors that I sent out during the week of the stock market crash of 1987 (described in detail in Chapter 4), I asked them about word-of-mouth communications. Of the individual investor respondents, 81.6% said that they had learned of the crash before 5 P.M. on the same day. Thus they had learned of the crash from sources other than the next day's morning newspaper or that day's evening news. The average time of day that these investors heard of the crash was 1:56 P.M. Eastern Daylight Time (EDT). For institutional investors, the average time that they heard of the crash was 10:32 A.M. EDT. Individual investors reported talking on average to 7.4 other people about the market situation on the day of the crash; institutional investors reported talking on average to 19.7 other people.

The channels of human communication that we know today seem to favor the interpersonal face-to-face and word-of-mouth communication that developed over millions of years of evolution, during times when such communication was virtually the only form of interpersonal communication. The patterns of communication hard-wired into our brains rely on there being another person's voice, another person's facial expressions, another person's emotions, and an associated environment of trust, loyalty, and cooperation. Because these elements are missing from the written or electronic word, people find it somewhat more difficult to react to these sources of information. They cannot give these other sources the same emotional weight, nor can they remember or use information from these other sources as well. This is an important reason why we still have teachers—why we cannot tell our children to simply sit down and read books or rely on computer-aided instruction.

It is also for this reason that television is such a powerful medium, in that it mimics much of the appearance of direct interpersonal conversation. Watching television simulates the very action—the voices, faces, and emotions—that we experience in conversation. Indeed, television advertisers often recreate images of everyday conversation about their products. But television today is still not interactive; the communication it offers is only one-way, and so it is still not as effective as direct person-to-person communication.

The telephone, invented well over a hundred years ago, may still be the most important artificial medium for interpersonal communication today, because it so closely simulates face-to-face communications, lacking only the visual stimuli. Studies by sociologists and communications researchers have found that telephone conversations come very close to face-to-face communications in information transmission and problem-solving functions, though they still fall somewhat short in conflict-resolution and person-perception functions.[9]

The impact of the telephone appears to have been a factor behind the volatile stock market of the 1920s. Although the telephone was invented in 1876, it did not become economical, effective, and widely used until a number of improvements had been made, such as the invention in 1915 of vacuum tube amplification of longer-distance telephone calls. By the mid-1920s the average person was making over two hundred telephone calls per year in the United States. The 1920s saw the spread of "boiler rooms" and "bucket shops" that actively sold stocks to the public using the telephone, employing questionable tactics that easily slipped past ineffective "blue-sky" legislation at the level of the states. The proliferation of telephones undoubtedly made it easier to sell stocks to the public, and the resulting impetus to fraud helped bring the country to the point of enacting the Securities Act of 1933 and the Securities Exchange Act of 1934, which created the Securities and Exchange Commission.[10]

Today we are witnessing another explosion of technological innovations that facilitate interpersonal communication, consisting of e-mail, chat rooms, and interactive Web sites. These new and effective media for interactive (if not face-to-face) communication may have the effect of expanding yet again the interpersonal contagion of ideas. They may have allowed enthusiasm for the market to spread much more widely in the 1990s than it would otherwise have. Certainly we are still learning how to regulate the use of these new media in the public interest.

Although e-mail and chat rooms are significant changes in the technology of communications, it is not clear that their advent is more significant than that of the telephone many decades ago. Because the telephone allows communication of emotions as expressed vocally, it may yet be a better simulator of effective communication than e-mail or chat rooms in their usual configuration.

Continued technological progress in those computer-based communications media that allow better simulation of face-to-face communication will undoubtedly make the transmissibility of ideas more effective in the future. For example, according to the market research firm International Data Corporation, desktop and compact videoconferencing systems, which allow users to see the faces of others during a conversation over a distance, are just now becoming economical enough for wide use; the installed base worldwide is expected to climb from 622,000 endpoints in 1998 to 4.2 million by 2003.[11]

### *Epidemic Models Applied to Word-of-Mouth Communication*

The mathematical theory of the spread of disease has been used by epidemiologists to predict the course of infection and mortality.[12] These models can be used to better understand the transmission of attitudes and the nature of the feedback mechanism supporting speculative bubbles.

In the simplest epidemic model, it is assumed that the disease has a given *infection rate* (the rate at which the disease spreads from contagious people to susceptible people) and a given *removal rate* (the rate at which infected people become no longer contagious, through recovery or death).

If the removal rate is zero, the graphical plot of the number of infected people after the introduction of one contagious person follows a mathematical curve called the *logistic curve.*[13] With the logistic curve, the percent of the population that is infected rises initially at the infection rate. Although the rate of increase is nearly constant at first, the absolute number of people recorded as contracting the disease rises faster and faster: as more and more people become contagious, more and more people become infected and are seen in doctors' offices complaining of the first symptoms of the disease. But the rate of increase starts to decline as the pool of yet-to-be-infected susceptibles begins to be depleted. Even though the intrinsic infection rate of the disease is unchanged, the rate at which new infected people are being produced declines because those who are infected meet fewer people who have yet to become infected. Eventually the entire population is infected and the logistic curve becomes flat, at 100%; then of course there are no new cases.

If the removal rate is greater than zero, but less than the infection rate, the model predicts instead that the course of the epidemic will be bell shaped: the number of infectives will at first rise from zero, peak, and then drop back to zero. The peak can occur before 100% of the population is ever infected.

If the removal rate is greater than the infection rate, then the epidemic will never get started and never even be observed.

Epidemiologists use these models constructively to understand the pattern of disease outbreaks. Using such models they can infer, for example, that if the removal rate is just above the infection rate, then a nearly healthy population is in danger of an epidemic, for any small uptick in the infection rate or downtick in the removal rate can tip the balance toward a new epidemic. Thus epidemiologists can infer that a change in weather patterns that will tend to keep people indoors together (where they are more likely to infect each other) may cause the infection rate to increase above the removal rate. The epidemic will then begin, but the absolute number of infectives will grow slowly at first. If, in this example, the weather changes fairly soon again in such a way that the infection rate is brought back down, so that the number of infectives never becomes very large, then the epidemic will fail to be noticed by the general public. But if the bad weather lingers long enough relative to the difference between the bad-weather-infection rate and the removal rate, then the epidemic will become large and noticeable in the population at large. Epidemiologists can use this model to predict, according to this example, how long a spell of bad weather is necessary to produce a serious epidemic.

The same kind of epidemic models have been applied to other biological phenomena that may have relevance to financial markets. Economist Alan Kirman has used them to model the behavior of ants in exploiting food sources, and he notes that the models also seem relevant to stock market price changes.[14] It has been found experimentally that ants, when presented with two identical food sources near their nest, tend to exploit both sources, but one more intensively than another. Over time (and as the experimenter constantly replenishes the food sources so that they remain exactly equal), the primary attention of the ants may switch from one source to the other. Why should they not exploit the two equally, and what causes them to switch their attention? Kirman notes that ants *individually* recruit other ants to food sources; there is no central direction for the nest as a whole. Recruitment is done by contact and following (tandem recruitment) or by laying a chemical trail (pheromone recruitment). Both of these processes are the ant equivalent of word-of-mouth communication. Kirman shows that if there is randomness in the recruitment process, the experimentally observed phenomena can be explained in terms of a simple epidemic model.

Although disease spread and ant behavior are of theoretical interest in our consideration of stock market bubbles, of greatest practical relevance is the fact that epidemic models have been applied by sociologists to predict the course of word-of-mouth transmission of ideas.[15] The dynamics of such transmission may mimic that of disease. The formal mathematical theory of epidemics appears, however, to be less accurate for modeling social processes than for modeling disease spread or ant behavior, and it has yet to spawn an influential and successful literature by social scientists. This lack of success may be explained by the fact that the basic parameters of these models are not as constant in the social sciences as in biological applications.

One reason for the lack of success in applying epidemic models to the spread of ideas may be that the mutation rate, the rate of transmission errors, is much higher for ideas than for disease or other biological processes. Many of us recall the children's game of telephone, in which the first person selects a simple story and whispers it into the ear of the second person, who then whispers it into the ear of the third, and so on. When the story is finally told to the group by the last person in the chain, the distortion of the original story is often so dramatic as to provoke laughter. The person-to-person transmission of stories of any complexity is just not very reliable.

For this reason, pure word-of-mouth transmission of ideas, even if abetted by the telephone, is not likely to extend widely enough to infect an entire nation all by itself. The accuracy of transmission will falter long before that happens. In contrast, computer-to-computer transmission is unerring. Computer viruses can spread nationally and internationally with no alteration whatsoever. But viruses do not have the ability to change people's thinking; they do not get beyond the machine. The ability of users of e-mail to forward others' messages or to provide Web links effectively permits word of mouth to spread unerringly. And new technology that makes it possible and natural to forward word-of-mouth messages from others as part of a telephone conversation or a video conference would again dramatically improve the accuracy and persistence of interpersonal communications.

Although the imprecision and variability of interpersonal communications as they currently occur prevent formal mathematics from predicting with any reliability how ideas spread, epidemic models are still helpful in understanding the kinds of things that can bring about changes in market prices. For example, it is useful to consider that any change in the infection rate or removal rate will change the rate of spread of new ideas.

Thus, for example, a major national news story unrelated to financial markets may lower the infection rate of ideas related to speculative markets by deflecting attention from them. This phenomenon may help explain why, as noted in Chapter 4, stock price movements are not notoriously volatile at times of national crisis despite the potential importance of such crises for the nation's businesses and why most large stock market movements occur when there is not much other news. On the other hand, national news that ties in with or encourages discussion of the stock market may raise the infection rate. This may be part of the explanation for the Internet's apparently exaggerated effect on the stock market: attention being paid to the Net promotes conversation about technology stocks in general, thereby raising the infection rate for theories about these stocks.

The word-of-mouth transmission of ideas does not have to infect the entire nation to affect national stock prices. Moreover, word of mouth may function to amplify public reaction to news events or to media accounts of such events. It is still necessary to consider the infection rate relative to the removal rate in order to understand the public impact of any new idea or concept, since most people's awareness of any of these is still socially mediated. Thus the likelihood of any event affecting market prices is enhanced if there is a good, vivid, *tellable* story about the event.

The importance of a tellable story for keeping the infection rate of ideas high can be seen in many examples drawn from new-product marketing, such as the promotion of motion pictures. Marketers launch an ad campaign as the movie is first screened, to attract the attention of especially receptive people. Only a small fraction of the population responds directly to the initial advertisements. Yet the success of the movie ultimately depends on the reaction of these people to the film—and the opinions they pass on to others. It is well known that the advice of movie critics has less impact than the mass effect of such word of mouth. Producers have learned over the years the importance of including set pieces in movies. These are scenes that in and of themselves have story quality, scenes that, either during a screening or even as part of a trailer, pack word-of-mouth potential analogous to that of popular jokes or tall tales—or stories linked to high-flying companies on the nation's exchanges.

By analogy, news events that are more likely to be transmitted in informal conversations are in turn more likely to contribute to the contagion of ideas. The dry, analytical outlook an expert may offer for the nation's economy is very unlikely to be transmitted by word of mouth. In contrast, news that the market has made a sudden move is vastly more likely to be communicated. To be sure, experts' opinions sometimes tag along with news stories about price movements, but they are seldom vivid enough to become the focus of word-of-mouth communications by themselves.

Word-of-mouth communications, either positive or negative, are an essential part of the propagation of speculative bubbles, and the word-of-mouth potential of any event must be weighed in judging the likelihood of that event to lead to a speculative bubble. Thus, for example, the predictions of widespread computer problems due to the so-called Y2K bug was a classic word-of-mouth story because of its association with both the nation's fascination with computers and the new millennium. Thus—although fears ultimately provided groundless—it was likely to have an exaggerated impact on the market when compared with other less vivid stories.

### *A Pool of Conflicting Ideas Coexisting in the Human Mind*

One reason why the contagion of ideas can sometimes happen rapidly, and why public thinking can experience such abrupt turnarounds, is that the ideas in question are already in our minds. Even conflicting ideas can coexist at the same time in our minds, and a shift in supporting facts or public attentions may suddenly bring to the fore an apparent belief that contradicts formerly stated beliefs.

For example, people widely believe that the stock market is unforecastable and that market timing is futile. But they also believe (as we saw in Chapter 3) that if the stock market were to crash, it would surely come back up. Such views are clearly inconsistent.

One explanation for the fact that people are able to hold such conflicting views simultaneously is that they *think* they have heard both views endorsed by experts. The culture transmits a number of supposed facts, often attributed only to "them," as in "They say that. . . ." When stories are casually accepted on some imagined authority, conflicts are likely.

Sometimes, stories achieve currency even though they can be traced to no competent authority whatsoever. One hears again and again, for example, that "they say" that only 10% of the human brain is actually used by most people—a myth that extends back to the nineteenth century, when neurological science was clearly incapable of either establishing or disproving such a fact. "They say" also that the birth rate in New York City jumped nine months after a 1965 power blackout left New Yorkers with nothing to do for a while: but there was no jump in the birth rate.[16] And, more apropos, "they say" that there were an unusually high number of suicides at the time of the crash of 1929, but there were not.[17] Stories that are useful in conversations, and in media presentations, have a currency often unrelated to the facts.

Given this tendency to attribute views to real or imagined experts, people do not worry much about apparent contradictions among the views they hold. There is a willingness to free ride here—to suppose that the experts have thought through the apparent contradictions and therefore to assume that the experts know why they are not in fact contradictions at all. It is certainly true that sometimes theories that appear to be contradictory really are not. And from there it is but a short step to the supposition that the experts could explain away most apparent contradictions—if one asked.

People's thinking about the arcane field of investments is surely clouded with many half-thought-through ideas that may be mutually contradictory, or at least have not been put into any coherent analytical framework. It is a real challenge to try to infer what these ideas will mean for concrete investment decisions.

The significance of the fact that contradictory views are held simultaneously is that people may have no clear attachment to many of their views. Therefore we cannot attach too much credence to investors' stated belief that the market will surely come back up after a crash, for the circumstances of the actual crash could bring to the forefront other, contradictory views that would explain away a lack of market resilience. Investors would then react in ways that could not have been foreseen based on their previously expressed confidence.

### *Socially Based Variations in Attention*

The human brain is structured to have essentially a single focus of conscious attention at a time, and to move rapidly from one focus to another. The sensory experience that comes to us from our environment is vastly complicated, and the brain manages to filter out almost all of this complexity to produce a sense of the here and now—an interpretation of what is most important at present—and a sequence of thoughts that weave in this interpretation. Thus, for example, when one is sitting in an airport waiting to board one's plane, one's attention constantly returns to the theme "waiting to board" and organizes many thoughts and observations around it, as if it were the essence of current reality. One usually does not study the weave of the carpet or the smudges of dirt on the windows, or ponder the shape of the letters on the information screen, though in principle one could. These details are typically beyond our consciousness, even though we are receiving, and processing, sensory information about them.

The ability to focus attention on important things is one of the defining characteristics of intelligence, and no one really understands how the brain does it. Failure to focus attention on the proper things is also one of the most characteristic of human judgment errors. The mechanism for focusing attention that has evolved in the human brain, although remarkable, is still far from perfect.

If one looks back on some of the most significant errors one has made in life, one is likely to find that these often arose from a failure to pay attention to details. One would have responded instantly and changed one's actions had someone repeatedly demanded attention and pointed out certain key facts. Thus, in understanding errors that people have made in the past, it is important to consider what it was that they were *not* paying attention to.

One of the mechanisms that the brain has evolved to direct attention properly is a socially based selectivity. We pay attention to many of the same things that others around us are paying attention to. This social basis for attention allows individuals who recognize the importance of some information to bring it to the attention of other members of the community, and it creates a view of the world and an information set that are common to the community. Such a view and information set allow the community to act well in concert. At the same time, the social component of attention does not work perfectly, and it may cause errors to be made in common by the entire group because the common focus of attention pushes aside attention to details that individuals might otherwise notice. As with individual attention, the phenomenon of social attention is one of the great creations of behavioral evolution and is critical for the functioning of human society, but it is also an imperfect creation.

The social attention mechanism generates a sudden focus of the attention of the entire community on matters that appear to be emergencies. Thus, to return to the epidemic model, the infection rate may suddenly and dramatically increase. A sudden major move in the stock market is one of those events that pushes aside all other conversation.

This social basis for attention, operating by word of mouth and facilitated by media transmission of ideas, can generate attention focuses that spread rapidly across much of the world. With a substantial fraction of the human minds on the planet suddenly grabbed by the market, it should not be at all surprising that markets on opposite sides of the globe move together, even if the fundamentals in different countries do not suggest any reason for such co-movement.

### *People Cannot Explain Changes in Their Attention*

Furthermore, people often find it very difficult to explain what made them decide to take a certain course of action; the original attentional trigger may not be remembered. This is a principal reason why changes in speculative asset prices, which very quickly reflect changes in attention, often seem so inexplicable.

Price changes themselves may be an attention grabber, even among professional investors. In a study of institutional investors' choice of individual stocks, John Pound and I produced a list of stocks whose prices had increased rapidly within the preceding year and that also had high price-earnings ratios. We then obtained a list of institutional investors who had reported to the Securities and Exchange Commission that they had bought one of the stocks (the experimental group) and compared these with a list of institutional investors in a random sample of stocks (the control group). We asked respondents on both lists if they agreed with the following statement regarding their stock (the rapid-price-increase stock for the experimental group or the random stock for the control group): "My initial interest was the result of my, or someone else's, systematic search over a large number of stocks (using a computerized or similar search procedure) for a stock with certain characteristics."[18] Since these were investment professionals, it is perhaps not surprising that 67% of the random sample, the control group, said they agreed with this statement. But, among the experimental group, the investors in the rapid-price-increase stocks, only 25% agreed. Since attentional triggers are often poorly remembered, we cannot *expect* them to tell us that the price increase stimulated their interest, but our experimental design shows that the price increase, or associated events, did play a role in attracting their attention. The important point is that most of the investors in rapid-price-increase stocks themselves say that they were unsystematic in their decision making.

When variations in attention are important causes of changing behavior, we cannot expect people to tell us the reasons for their changed behavior. People usually cannot easily explain what drew their attention to something, and so they cannot explain their own behavior. A 1931 experiment by psychologist N. R. F. Maier will illustrate. Maier presented his subjects with the problem of tying two cords together: cords that were suspended from the ceiling far enough apart that one could not reach them both at the same time unless they were somehow brought together. Subjects were given a number of tools with which to attempt this task and were asked to see how many different ways they could invent to tie the two cords together. One way to complete the task was to tie a weight to the end of one of the cords, set it swinging like a pendulum, grab the end of the other cord with one hand, and then catch the swinging cord with the other hand. When the experimenter himself set one of the cords swinging, many subjects quickly came up with this idea. But when asked how they had hit upon the idea, only a third of them mentioned having seen the swinging cord. The swinging cord merely changed the focus of their attention, and most subjects could not see the connection between their actions and the stimulus that had given them the idea.[19]

By analogy, a stock market boom can start for no better reason than that some factor, like the swinging cord, calls attention to the market. In the context of the present stock market situation, such events as spotting an ad for a mutual fund or the receipt of election forms for an employer's 401(k) plan may be the swinging cord. But we will never learn about the importance of these stimuli from most of our subjects by simply asking them. Even if people recall the stimuli, they will not be able to tell us *how* they affected them.

## The Story So Far

This chapter concludes the essence of my argument that *irrational exuberance* is at work in producing the elevated stock market levels we have seen recently. We began in Part I with a list of twelve precipitating factors, whose effect is sometimes amplified via feedback loops and naturally occurring Ponzi schemes, aided by the lubricant of the news media as sometime promoter of market exuberance. We saw evidence of strangely high investor confidence and undiminished expectations for the market.

We then considered, in Part II, the cultural components of exuberance, the varying degrees of social attention to new era theories, and the tendencies of these new era theories both to react to the market and to stimulate it temporarily. In Part III we have stepped back and examined some of the basic psychological factors that allowed the changes described in the earlier parts to exert their effects. Chapter 7 showed how trivial and barely visible psychological anchors may ultimately determine market levels, and how investor overconfidence can strengthen the pull of these anchors. The present chapter has attempted to resolve the essential puzzle of the current market situation: that we see newly high valuations but cannot detect a cause for those valuations that is associated with rational public thinking.

In the remainder of the book, I place the theory of irrational exuberance into a broader context. In the next part, I consider some influential arguments against the notion that anything irrational is going on. In the concluding chapter, I turn to the ultimate questions that this exuberance poses for policy: individual, institutional, and governmental.

# *Part Four*

# *Attempts to Rationalize Exuberance*

## *Nine*

# *Efficient Markets, Random Walks, and Bubbles*

The theory that financial markets are very efficient, and the extensive research investigating this theory, form the leading intellectual basis for arguments against the idea that markets are vulnerable to excessive exuberance or bubbles. The *efficient markets theory* asserts that all financial prices accurately reflect all public information at all times. In other words, financial assets are always priced correctly, given what is publicly known, at all times. Price may *appear* to be too high or too low at times, but, according to the efficient markets theory, this appearance must be an illusion.

Stock prices, by this theory, approximately describe "random walks" through time: the price changes are unpredictable since they occur only in response to genuinely new information, which by the very fact that is new is unpredictable. The efficient markets theory and the random walk hypothesis have been subjected to many tests using data on stock markets, in studies published in scholarly journals of finance and economics. Although the theory has been statistically rejected many times in these publications, by some interpretations it may nevertheless be described as approximately true. The literature on the evidence for this theory is well developed and includes work of the highest quality. Therefore, whether or not we ultimately agree with it, we must at least take the efficient markets theory seriously.

### *Basic Arguments That Markets Are Efficient and That Prices Are Random Walks*

The idea of efficient markets is so natural that it has probably been with us for centuries. Although the term *efficient markets* apparently first became widely known through the work of University of Chicago professor Eugene Fama and his colleagues in the late 1960s, the theory itself preceded this name by many years.[1] It was clearly mentioned in 1889 in a book by George Gibson entitled *The Stock Markets of London, Paris and New York.* Gibson wrote that when "shares become publicly known in an open market, the value which they acquire may be regarded as the judgment of the best intelligence concerning them."[2] In this century, the efficient markets theory has long been a fixture in university economics and finance departments. The theory has commonly been offered to justify what seem to be elevated market valuations, for example, the 1929 stock market peak. Prof. Joseph Lawrence of Princeton concluded in 1929 that "the consensus of judgment of the millions whose valuations function on that admirable market, the Stock Exchange, is that stocks are not at present over-valued. . . . Where is that group of men with all-embracing wisdom which will entitle them to veto the judgment of the intelligent multitude?"[3]

The most simple and direct argument for efficient markets theory comes from the observation that it seems to be difficult to make a lot of money by buying low and selling high in the stock market. Many seemingly capable people try but fail to do this with any consistent degree of success. Moreover, one observes that in order to make money one must compete against some of the smartest investors, the so-called "smart money," who trade in financial markets looking for the same opportunities. If one thinks that an asset is either under- or overpriced, one must then reflect on why it remains so despite the efforts of the smart money to make a profitable trade.

If the smart money were able to find ways to make profits by buying low and selling high, then the effect of such smart money would be, according to the efficient markets theory, to drive asset prices to their true values. They would be buying underpriced stocks and thereby tending to bid their prices up. They would be selling overpriced stocks and thereby tending to bid their prices down. Moreover, if there were substantial mispricing of securities, then their profits doing this trading would tend to make the smart money into rich people, thereby increasing their influence on the market and increasing their power to eliminate mispricing.

Unfortunately, this argument for the efficient markets hypothesis does not tell us that the stock market cannot go through periods of significant mispricing lasting years or even decades. The smart money could not make money rapidly by exploiting such a profit opportunity, and there would be considerable uncertainty about when the mispricing would end. If indeed one knew today that the market would do poorly over the next ten or twenty years, but did not know exactly *when* it would begin do poorly and could not prove one's knowledge to a broad audience, then there would be no way to profit significantly from this knowledge. There is thus no substantial reason to think that the smart money must necessarily eliminate such stock mispricing.

But this limitation of the efficient markets theory is often overlooked. The assumption is made that the same efficient markets theory that says that it is difficult to predict day-to-day changes implies that one cannot predict *any* changes.

### *Reflections on "Smart Money"*

At its root, the efficient markets theory holds that differing abilities do not produce differing investment performance. The theory claims that the smartest people will not be able to do better than the least intelligent people in terms of investment performance. They can do no better because their superior understanding is already completely incorporated into share prices.

If we accept the premise of efficient markets, not only is being smart no advantage, but it also follows immediately that being *not so smart* is not a *disadvantage* either. If not-so-smart people could lose money systematically in their trades, then this would suggest a profit opportunity for the smart money: just do the opposite of what the not-so-smart money does. Yet according to the efficient markets theory, there can be no such profit opportunity for the smart money.

Thus according to this theory, effort and intelligence mean nothing in investing. In terms of expected investment returns, one might as well pick stocks at random—the common metaphor of throwing darts at the stock market listings to choose investments. It is ultimately for this reason that so many people think that they do not need to pay attention to whether any given stock is or is not overpriced, and why they feel they can ignore the unusual valuation of the market today.

But why should the smartest people set all prices? Many apparently less-intelligent or less well-informed people are buying and selling—why should they not have an impact on prices?

One notion, referred to previously, is that the smartest money has already mostly taken over the market through its profitable trading and has now set prices correctly; the less-intelligent investors are holding so little as to be insignificant forces in the market. This is an easy argument to dismiss. First of all, if this is the reason why the smart money dominates, then it must have been the case that there *were* profitable trades for them, otherwise they could not have used their intelligence to take over the market. But if there *were* profitable trades, then there must *still be* profitable trades, since smart money investors retire from the business and must be replaced. One cannot argue that smart money took over the market a hundred years ago and that ever since they have dominated the market, since those smart traders of yore are all dead now.

Another piece of evidence that has been offered in support of the efficient markets theory is that professional investors, institutional money managers, or securities analysts do not seem to have any reliable ability to outperform the market as a whole, and indeed they often seem to underperform the market once account is taken of transactions costs and management fees. This result may seem puzzling, since one would think that professional investors are more educated about investing, more systematic than individual investors. But perhaps the result is not as puzzling as it at first seems. Individual investors get advice from professional investors, and they can also observe (albeit with some time lag) what professional investors are doing. So there may be no significant difference between the success of professional investors and the market as a whole, even if their analysis is very valuable to others. Individual investors with substantial resources tend to be educated and intelligent people, too. Moreover, some recent studies have documented that professional analysts' advice is indeed worth something, if it is acted upon swiftly enough.[4]

Ultimately the reason that studies have not found stronger evidence that people who are smarter tend to make more money is that there is no good way to measure how smart investors are. We do not have databases giving the IQ scores of investment managers, to enable us to compare their performances with their scores, and even if we did, it is not clear that the available intelligence tests would measure the right abilities.

One study, by Judith Chevalier and Glenn Ellison, did come close to acquiring data about investment managers' intelligence, by tabulating the average Scholastic Aptitude Test (SAT) scores of the colleges the investment managers attended. They did indeed find some evidence that firms whose managers attended higher-SAT colleges performed somewhat better, even after controlling for other factors.[5] Certainly their one study does not settle the issue of intelligence and investing success. Yet, from the available evidence, I see no reason to doubt the thesis that smarter people will, in the long run, tend to do better at investing.

### *Examples of "Obvious" Mispricing*

Despite the general authority of the efficient markets theory in popular thinking, one often hears examples that seem to offer flagrant evidence against it. There are in fact many examples of financial prices that, it seems, cannot possibly be right. They are regularly reported in the media. Recently, many of these examples have been Internet stocks: judging from their prices, the public appears to have an exaggerated view of their potential.

Consider, for example, eToys, a firm established in 1997 to sell toys over the Internet. Shortly after its initial public offering in 1999, eToys' stock value was $8 billion, exceeding the $6 billion value of the long-established "brick and mortar" retailer Toys "R" Us. And yet in fiscal 1998 eToys sales were $30 million, while Toys "R" Us sales were $11.2 billion, almost 400 times larger. And eToys profits were a negative $28.6 million, while Toys "R" Us profits were a positive $376 million.[6] In fact, Toys "R" Us, like other established toy retailers, has now created its own Web site. Despite some initial difficulties getting its site launched, it has a longer-run advantage over eToys in that dissatisfied purchasers of toys on the Internet can go to one of its numerous retail outlets for returns or advice. In addition, customers who are already shopping at one of those outlets may naturally gravitate to the Toys "R" Us Web site when they make Web purchases.

The valuation the market places on stocks such as eToys appears absurd to many observers, and yet the influence of these observers on market prices does not seem to correct the mispricing. What could they do that would have the effect of correcting it? Those who doubt the value of these stocks could try to sell them short, and some will, but their willingness to do so is limited since there is always a possibility that the stock will be bid up even further by enthusiastic investors. Absurd prices sometimes last a long time.

It seems obvious that investors in these stocks are not thinking very clearly about long-run investment potential, and also that there are no forces in the market to prevent these investors from causing substantial overpricing. Doesn't such evidence clearly speak against market efficiency, at least for some stocks? And if some stocks can be overpriced, then does it not follow that the market as a whole can be overpriced, given that those stocks are part of the market?

### *Questioning the Examples of Obvious Mispricing*

Still, despite the apparent obviousness of some examples of mispricing, there are those who question the examples. Jeremy Siegel, in his book *Stocks for the Long Run,* points out that some of the most widely cited examples of mispricings in years gone by really made sense in the long run. Siegel cites a list of fifty stocks that were apparently called the "Nifty Fifty" as early as 1970 or 1972: glamorous stocks for which people had high expectations and that traded at very high price-earnings ratios. The list includes some high-tech firms, such as IBM and Xerox, as well as some high-profile consumer products firms, such as Coca-Cola and McDonald's. These stocks were cited in a 1977 *Forbes* magazine article as examples of investors' folly after the values of the Nifty Fifty plummeted following the 1973–74 stock market debacle.[7]

Siegel showed that, as a group, the Nifty Fifty stocks really were not overpriced in 1970 for the long run. If you had bought and held an equally weighted portfolio of these stocks from 1970 until 1996, you would have done as well as the Standard & Poor's 500 Index.[8] This example appears to provide evidence that clearly refutes the claim that there are times when stock prices are just plain wrong. If the Nifty Fifty are examples of absurdly overpriced stocks, then it seems that we have failed to make our case that such examples are proof of market irrationality.

Peter Garber, in his book *Famous First Bubbles,* argues that the most famous bubble of all, the seventeenth-century tulip mania in Holland, was not a clear example of irrational mispricing either. The story of the tulip mania, popularized in a book by Charles Mackay in 1841, is so well known today as to be part of our popular culture, and it is widely cited as an example of a speculative bubble. The term refers to a time when prices of tulip bulbs reached what seemed like absurd levels and then crashed. In 1636, for example, a single tulip bulb was sold in exchange for twelve acres of building land. In his book Mackay claimed that people were "insensibly attached" to the tulip trade and that "the rage among the Dutch to possess them [tulips] was so great that the ordinary industry of the country was neglected."[9]

But Mackay offered no concrete evidence that people were behaving insensibly and moreover could not show that the rage had anything to do with any speculative mispricing. Garber points out that the really high prices were for rare varieties of tulips that had unusual patterns of coloration due, we now know, to infection by a mosaic virus. These tulips could not be readily propagated and were genuinely rare. People in Holland at the time highly valued these unusual tulips, which had great significance in their culture.[10] Thus there is nothing more foolish about their high tulip prices than about the high prices that rare art objects or other collectibles often fetch today. Moreover, the price behavior of the tulip bulbs looks rather like that of the prices of many other speculative assets; they did not boom once, crash once, and then stay down as some simple stories suggest. Prices of tulips went up and down numerous times, just as stock prices do all the time. These price changes could well have had some rational basis in new information about public demand for rare flowers becoming known to investors over time.

These analyses by Siegel and Garber impugn some of the favorite examples of irrational prices in speculative markets. But there is actually little evidence in favor of efficient markets theory to be found in their analyses.

Although it is true that investors who held for the really long run did all right in the Nifty Fifty, almost all of the investors who held them in 1970 probably sold long before 1996, at a loss. We cannot really believe that all those investors in 1970 knew that the prices would come back up by the 1990s and would wait until then to redeem them.

Moreover, these fifty stocks are not fifty independent pieces of evidence that add up to strong evidence; they are firms in similar industries at similar times. And, as Siegel himself notes, if one considers the top twenty-five firms in the Nifty Fifty when ranked by price-earnings ratio, these firms are still far underperforming the market.

Consider the firm with the highest price-earnings ratio of the Nifty Fifty in 1972: Polaroid Corporation, the ultimate "story" stock, which was then priced at 94.8 times earnings. Its founder, Edwin Land, had dropped out of Harvard as a freshman, much as Bill Gates did decades later, to develop an idea for polarized light filters. He founded Polaroid to produce the filters and market them in a number of applications, including not only scientific devices but also sunglasses and 3-D movies. Over the course of his career

Land produced hundreds of inventions, including the celebrated Polaroid camera that developed photographs instantly. Some of his inventions and applications were intriguing novelties that were readily visible to the general public. His youthful move to establish what was then a novel high-tech firm provided a sensational story that makes its subsequent overpricing by the general public unsurprising. Polaroid Corporation was the 1970s version of a glamorous Internet stock, and it has indeed turned out badly since then: between 1972 and 1997 it underperformed the market by 11.2% a year.[11]

Thus, even after Siegel's evidence we still have many firms that look like examples of wild mispricing when 1970 prices are examined even decades later. Moreover, Siegel himself does not claim that his evidence suggests that all prices are right, and he argues that today many Internet stocks have indeed been overpriced.[12]

Likewise, Peter Garber, in his analysis of the tulip mania, also stops short of a complete rejection of the evidence for mispricing. Noting that in January 1636 even common tulip bulbs, not only those infected with the mosaic virus, increased twentyfold in price and then underwent a precipitous decline, he confesses that he is "hard pressed to find a market fundamental explanation" for this event.[13]

### *Statistical Evidence of Mispricings*

It is difficult to make any solid judgments about market efficiency based on a few anecdotes about alleged extreme mispricing of assets. But in fact there is no shortage of systematic evidence that firms that are "overpriced" by conventional measures have indeed tended to do poorly afterward. Many articles in academic finance journals show this, not by colorful examples but by systematic evaluation of large amounts of data on many firms. For example, Sanjoy Basu found in 1977 that firms with high price-earnings ratios tend to do poorly subsequently, and Eugene Fama and Kenneth French in 1992 found the same for stocks with high price-to-book value.[14] Werner De Bondt and Richard Thaler reported in 1985 that firms whose price has risen a great deal over five years tend to go down in price in the next five years, and that firms whose price has declined a great deal over five years tend to go up in price in the succeeding five years.[15] (In Chapter 6 we saw that a similar tendency has held for national stock markets around the world.) Jay Ritter found in 1991 that initial public offerings tend to occur at the peak of industry-specific investor fads and then to show gradual but substantial price declines relative to the market over the subsequent three years.[16] Thus there is a sort of regression to the mean (or to longer-run past values) for stock prices: what goes up a lot tends to come back down, and what goes down a lot tends to come back up.

These findings, and similar findings by many other researchers, have encouraged an approach to the market called *value investing,* that of picking portfolios of stocks that are underpriced by conventional measures, on the theory that they have been overlooked only temporarily by investors and will appreciate eventually. The other side of this strategy is to sell overpriced stocks short. One might think that the effect on the market of so many value investors would be to reduce, and even possibly eliminate for a time, the relation across stocks between value and subsequent returns. Value investors are after all buying the underpriced assets and bidding up their prices, and also diverting demand away from overpriced assets.

Many value investing strategies will probably cease to work as investors flock to exploit them, yet it certainly does not follow that value investing as a whole will ever be out for good. There are many different ways to define value, and the market as a whole is not going to find it easy to eliminate all such profit opportunities.

Moreover, even if the effect of value on return *across stocks* disappears, it does not follow that the effect of value on return *over time for the market as a whole* must also disappear. The characteristic strategy of value investors is to pull out of overvalued individual stocks, but not to pull out of the market as a whole when it appears to be overvalued.

### *Earnings Changes and Price Changes*

Another argument that markets are basically efficient, in the most global sense, is merely that stock prices roughly track earnings over time—that despite great fluctuations in earnings, price-earnings ratios have stayed within a comparatively narrow range.

Peter Lynch, an investment analyst appearing frequently in the media these days, in an advertisement for Fidelity Investments that features a full-page photograph of him, is quoted in banner red letters: "Despite 9 recessions since WWII, the stock market's up 63-fold because earnings are up 54-fold. Earnings drive the market." The ad appears to be designed to convince readers that price growth is approximately justified by earnings growth. But in fact the numbers are deceptive. When such a long time interval is chosen for comparison, when no inflation correction is made, and since earnings were very low right after World War II, it is not surprising that Lynch can find such a correspondence. But if other examples are chosen, price changes may seem far less justified by earnings growth.[17] Lynch's statement is indicative of a common view that stock price changes are generally justified by earnings changes, and that this proves that stock market price movements are not due to any irrational behavior on the part of investors.

As we have noted, there have been only three great bull markets, periods of sustained and dramatic stock price increase, in U.S. history: the bull market of the 1920s, culminating in 1929; the bull market of the 1950s and 1960s, followed by the 1973–74 market debacle; and the bull market running from 1982 to the present. (One might also add the bull market leading to the peak in 1901, but it was not so dramatic.)

The first great bull market, from 1920 to 1929, was a period of rapid earnings growth. Real S&P Composite earnings tripled over this period, and real stock prices increased almost sevenfold. The market change might be viewed as a reaction to the earnings change, albeit an overreaction.

But in the second great bull market, the correspondence between price growth and earnings growth is not so clear. Most of the price growth then occurred in the 1950s, and from January 1950 to December 1959 the real S&P Composite Index almost tripled. But real S&P earnings grew only 16% in total over this entire decade, an earnings performance that was below average by historical standards. In terms of overall economic growth, the 1950s are a little above average, though not as strong as either the 1940s or the 1960s: average real gross domestic product growth was 3.3% a year from 1950 to 1960.

In the third great bull market, real stock prices have risen more or less continually from 1982 to 1999, but earnings have not grown at all uniformly. Real S&P Composite earnings were actually lower at the bottom of the recession of 1991 than they were at the bottom of the recession of 1982, but the real S&P Composite Index was almost two and a half times as high. So, in this bull market, price increases cannot be viewed as a simple reaction to earnings increases.

These examples show that earnings growth and price growth do not correspond well at all. One cannot criticize bubble theories by claiming that they do.

### *Dividend Changes and Price Changes*

If stock prices show no clear relation to earnings, there is still the question of dividends. It has been claimed by some economists that there is a good relation between real stock price movements and real dividend movements. Economists Robert Barsky and Brad De Long have argued that stock price movements cannot be considered to have been caused largely by the speculative behavior of investors if they correspond to dividend movements.[18] They suggest that perhaps people were rational to suppose that the recent growth of dividends would continue indefinitely into the future—even though in fact this growth rate has never continued for very long in actual historical data.

Kenneth Froot and Maurice Obstfeld, reacting to the same appearance of co-movement between prices and dividends, postulated an "intrinsic bubble" model in which prices respond in an apparently exaggerated fashion, but in fact rationally, to dividend movements. In their theory, stock prices overreact, in a certain sense, to dividends, but yet there are no profit opportunities to trading to take advantage of this overreaction.[19]

I think that these authors overstate their case for co-movements between dividends and prices. The wiggles in stock prices do not in fact correspond very closely to wiggles in dividends. Recall that between the stock market peak in September 1929 and the bottom in June 1932, when the stock market fell 81% as measured by the real S&P Index, real dividends fell only 11%. Between the stock market peak in January 1973 and the bottom in December 1974, when the stock market fell 54% as measured by the real S&P Index, real dividends fell only 6%. And there are many other such examples.

It is also likely that part of the reason for the observed comovement between real prices and real dividends is the response of dividends to the same factors—possibly including speculative bubbles—that irrationally influence price. Managers set dividends, and in so doing may vary over time the dividend-earnings ratio, that is, the payout rate. The managers are part of the same culture as the investing public, and are therefore probably influenced often enough by the same varying sense of optimism and pessimism that infects the public; they may allow this feeling to influence their decisions on how much of a dividend to pay out. Thus the mere fact that prices and dividends show some substantial similarity is not inconsistent with the possibility that they are both influenced by fashions and fads.

In sum, stock prices clearly have a life of their own; they are not simply responding to earnings or dividends. Nor does it appear that they are determined only by information about future earnings or dividends. In seeking explanations of stock price movements, we must look elsewhere.

### *Excess Volatility and the Big Picture*

There is indeed a good deal of evidence about market efficiency in academic finance journals, but it is hard to say that it is evidence *for* efficiency rather than against it. A great many anomalies have been discovered over the years within the efficient markets theory. There are the January effect (stock prices tend to go up between December and January), the small-firm effect (small firms' stocks tend to have higher returns), the day-of-the-week effect (the stock market tends to do poorly on Mondays), and others.[20] How then can we summarize this literature as supporting market efficiency?

One way of arguing that the literature nevertheless supports market efficiency is to claim that many of these have been small effects, not the stuff of bull or bear markets. Another way is to note that many of these effects disappeared after they were discovered, as indeed the January effect and the small-firm effect seem to have disappeared. This makes it tricky to summarize the literature. On the one hand, the fact that these anomalies persisted for a long time shows that markets are inefficient. On the other hand, the fact that many of them have disappeared suggests that there is a basic truth to the theory.[21]

Merton Miller, a leading advocate of efficient markets theory, recognizes that there are indeed many little anomalies, but he argues that they are inconsequential: "That we abstract from all these stories in building our models is not because the stories are uninteresting but because they may be too interesting and thereby distract us from the pervasive market forces that should be our principal concern."[22] But he does not explain his presumption that the pervasive market forces are rational ones.

Abstracting (as Miller urges us to do) from the little details about day-of-the-week effects and the like, what is the basic evidence that stock markets are efficient in the big-picture sense? Do large changes in stock prices over the years really reflect information about important changes in the underlying companies?

The evidence that there is not much short-run momentum or inertia—that there is not much predictability of day-to-day or month-to-month changes in stock price indexes—does not tell us anything about efficiency in the big-picture sense. We already know from simple economic reasoning that day-to-day changes in stock prices cannot be very forecastable, since such forecastability would be too good a profit opportunity to be true.

One method for judging whether there is evidence in support of the basic validity of the efficient markets theory, which I published in an article in the *American Economic Review* in 1981 (at the same time as a similar paper by Stephen LeRoy and Richard Porter appeared), is to see whether the very volatility of speculative prices, such as stock prices, can be justified by the variability of dividends over long intervals of time. If the stock price movements are to be justified in terms of the future dividends that firms pay out, as the basic version of the efficient markets theory would imply, then under efficient markets we cannot have volatile prices without subsequently volatile dividends.[23]

In fact, my article concluded, no movement of U.S. aggregate stock prices beyond the trend growth of prices has ever been subsequently justified by dividend movements, as the dividend present value has shown an extraordinarily smooth growth path. This conclusion, coming at a time when the finance profession was much more attached to the efficient markets theory than it is now, produced a strong reaction. I received more attacks on this work than I could hope to answer. No one questioned the observation that stock prices have been more volatile than the dividend present value—only whether the difference between the two was statistically significant or whether my interpretation of this difference was on target.

Included in my article was a figure showing the real (inflation-corrected) S&P Composite Stock Price Index for 1871–1979 and, on the same figure, the *dividend present value,* the present value for each year of real dividends paid subsequent to that year on the shares making up the index, computed by making an assumption about dividends after the last year. An updated version of that figure, showing both the stock price and the dividend present value through 2000, is shown as Figure 9.1. The curves shown to the left of 1980 are essentially the same as those shown in my 1981 article.[24]

The dividend present value is not known with certainty in the year to which it corresponds, since it is determined entirely by dividends after the year, which have yet to be paid. According to the efficient markets model, the dividend present value subsequent to any given year is the (as yet unknown) true fundamental value of the stock market in that year. The actual level of the real stock market in that same year, the stock price shown in Figure 9.1, is supposed to be the optimal prediction, using information available in that year, of the dividend present value shown for the same year.

Looking at this figure, we can get a sense of the extent of big-picture, important evidence for the efficiency of the aggregate stock market in the United States. If the dividend present value moved

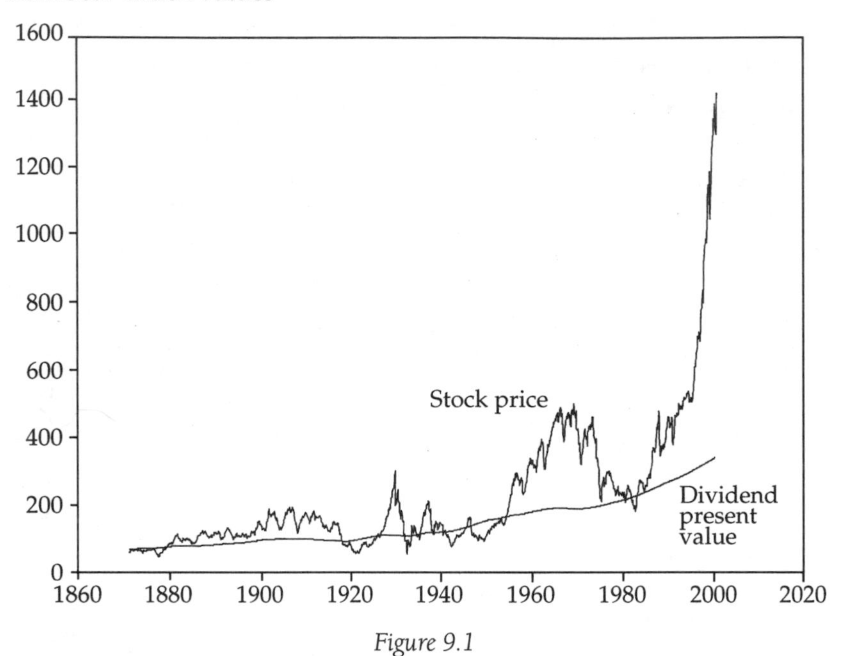


*Figure 9.1*

***Stock Price and Dividend Present Value, 1871–2000***

Real S&P Composite Stock Price Index (irregular curve) and present value of subsequent real dividends (smoother curve). *Source:* Author's calculations using data from sources given in Figure 1.1 and described in Chapter 1, note 2. See text and note 24 of this chapter for a description of the calculations.

up and down massively over time, and if the actual stock price appeared to move with these movements as if it were successfully forecasting the changes in the dividend present value, then we could say that there was evidence that stock prices were behaving in accordance with the tenets of the efficient markets theory. But we see no such tendency of the stock price to forecast the dividend present value: the dividend present value is not doing anything especially dramatic, whereas the price is jumping around a great deal.[25] The dividend present value is extremely steady and trendlike, partly because it extends so far into the future and partly because dividends have not moved very dramatically. Now that one sees it plotted, it seems obvious from what some of us (who have thought about it and have good intuitive grasp of quantities) have always known at gut level: these big stock market movements were not in fact justified by what actually happened to dividends later. One might try to argue that a little over a century is not a long enough time period to be confident that one *would* expect to see such justification, but the fact still remains that there has been no such justification.

Let us concentrate first on the portion of Figure 9.1 to the left of 1980, which was available when I published my findings in 1981. The dividend present value calculation has smoothed out the year-to-year fluctuations in dividends. Dividend fluctuations have had little impact on the dividend present value because these fluctuations have always been temporary.

Look, for example, at the change in the dividend present value over the bull market years of the 1920s, culminating in 1929. The real S&P Composite Index increased 415.4% from its low in December 1920 to its high in September 1929. At the same time, the dividend present value increased by only 16.4%.

Why is there such a discrepancy between the growth of the stock price and the growth of the dividend present value? Real dividends paid on the S&P Composite Index rose 106.7% over this interval, far short of the 415% increase in real stock prices but still much higher than the increase in the dividend present value. If the overall dividends were growing so much during the 1920s, then why was their present value growing so little? The answer is that the dividend increase of the 1920s did not last long; it was confined largely to the 1920s and so did not contribute enormously to the present value of all real future dividends out to infinity. The growing dividends of the 1920s were just a small part of the long-run picture that the market is supposed, according to the efficient markets theory, to price, and that price should not be overly influenced by a few years' fluctuation in dividends.

Look, too, at the movement of the value of real dividends over the years subsequent to 1929, including the Great Depression of the 1930s. While the real S&P Composite Index dropped disastrously, down 80.6% from the peak in September 1929 to the bottom in June 1932, the dividend present value dropped only 3.1%. The reason that the decline in the dividend present value is so small between 1929 and 1932 is that dividends just did not fall dramatically or for very long. Real dividends actually fell little between September 1929 and June 1932, since firms were reluctant to cut their nominal dividends by as much as the deflation in the economywide price level would suggest.

Thus, ex post, we know that the run-up in the stock market from 1920 to 1929 was a colossal mistake and that the drop from 1929 to 1932 was another colossal mistake. Virtually nothing actually happened over either of these intervals to the dividend present value. Of course, people might have *thought* that there really was news that was going to change the longer-run course of dividends, and they might have *thought* there was a reason for a sudden drop in prices. They might even have had plausible-sounding reasons to think so. But in fact no such change occurred.

The point I made in 1981 was that stock prices appear to be too volatile to be considered in accord with efficient markets. If stock prices are supposed to be an optimal predictor of the dividend present value, then they should not jump around erratically when the true fundamental value is growing along a smooth trend.

We learn by considering Figure 9.1 that the common interpretation given in the media for stock market fluctuations in terms of the outlook for the short-run business cycle is generally misguided. The prospect that a temporary recession is on the horizon should have virtually no impact on stock prices, if the efficient markets theory is correct. Fluctuations in stock prices, if they are to be interpretable in terms of the efficient markets theory, must instead be due to new information about the long-run outlook for real dividends. Yet in the entire history of the U.S. stock market we have never seen such fluctuations, since dividends have fairly closely followed a steady growth path. As I argued in my 1981 paper, the only way to reconcile the volatility of stock prices with the efficient markets model is to suppose that, one way or the other, the historical fluctuations of dividends around their growth path are not representative of the *potential* fluctuations. That is, one would have to say that the fluctuations observed in market prices were the result of people's legitimate concerns with possible major and lasting dividend movements that just did not chance to happen in the century of data we observe. For example, people might have been concerned about a big, rare event, such as a complete nationalization and confiscation of the stock market by the government, or an enormous technological breakthrough that would make existing companies able to pay many times more dividends.

As noted earlier, my work invited the attention of an army of critics. Most notable among them was Robert Merton, a brilliant financial theorist who was later to win the Nobel Prize in economics (and also to suffer a major financial loss as a principal in the Long Term Capital Management hedge fund). Merton, with Terry Marsh, wrote an article in the *American Economic Review* in 1986 that argued against my results and concluded, ironically, that speculative markets were not too volatile.[26]

John Campbell and I wrote a number of papers attempting to put these claims of excess volatility on a more secure footing, and we developed statistical models to study the issue and deal with some of the problems emphasized by the critics.[27] We felt that we had established in a fairly convincing way that stock markets do violate the efficient markets model.

Our research has not completely settled the matter, however. There are just too many possible statistical issues that can be raised, and the sample provided by only a little over a century of data cannot prove anything conclusively.

It should also be noted that some substantial fraction of the volatility in financial markets *is* probably justified by news about future dividends or earnings. The very trendlike behavior of U.S. corporate dividends over the past century was probably partly due to luck, not a law saying that dividends must hug a trend. Taking account of uncertainty about the trend, Campbell and I, in interpreting the results of one of our statistical studies, estimated that 27% of the annual return volatility of the U.S. stock market might be justified in terms of genuine information about future dividends.[28] Campbell and John Ammer, using similar methodology and a more recent (postwar) data set, found that 15% of the variability in monthly returns in the U.S. stock market could be attributed to genuine information about future dividends.[29]

I have found less evidence of excess volatility in long-term interest rates and little evidence of excess volatility in the spread between stock price indexes.[30] Excess volatility due to speculative bubbles is probably just one of the factors that drive speculative markets, and the prominence of this factor varies across markets and over time. We are not always in an excess volatility situation.

### *The Graph Updated*

But we do seem to be in such a situation in the stock market now. The data set that I used for my paper on excess volatility of stock prices ended in 1979, over twenty years ago. One can see what has happened to stock prices since then by looking at the curves in Figure 9.1 to the right of 1979. What a transformation twenty years of data has brought! The price series, terminating in 2000, has shot up, relative to dividends, beyond anything seen before.[31]

One interpretation of Figure 9.1 is that the sudden spike represents the "big, rare event" that might finally reconcile the efficient markets theory with these data. But it would have to be a sudden, sharp spike in the *dividend* series, not the price series, to suggest such a reconciliation with the efficient markets theory. The spike in price alone only deepens the excess volatility puzzle and requires that dividends will have to move much farther indeed if their movements are to save the simple efficient markets model.

The invocation of efficient markets theory to imply that the recent upspike in the stock market is a routine and accurate response to genuine news is just not correct. To justify the notion that the stock market is at the appropriate level now, we would have to argue that it was not before. Such an argument would stand in sharp contradiction to efficient markets theory—and yet we cannot dismiss that argument out of hand, given the large number of people advancing it. So we turn to that argument in the next chapter.

## *Ten*

# *Investor Learning—and Unlearning*

Besides the efficient markets–random walk argument, another rationalization for the exuberance in the market is that the public at large has learned that the long-term value of the market is really greater than they had thought it was, and greater than conventional indicators would have suggested it should be. According to this theory, the market is higher today because the public has now learned some simple facts about historical average returns and diversification. This argument differs from the efficient markets argument in supposing that the market was previously priced too low because of public ignorance. The argument is essentially that "The market was not efficient a few years ago; it was too low; but (maybe) it is efficient now."

It is potentially plausible, at least at first look, that society may have learned that the market is much more valuable than it was once thought to be. Society as a whole does learn, and the cumulative effect of such learning is the reason that modern society has made such progress when compared with former centuries. But the question remains whether society has really learned something important about the stock market. Is this really true? If so, what have we learned?

### *"Learning" about Risk*

It is commonly said that people have recently learned that the stock market is much less risky than they once thought it was, and that the stock market has always outperformed other investments. Their "learning" is allegedly the result of widespread media coverage in the past few years of the historical superiority of stocks as investments, and of the publication in 1994 of the first edition of Jeremy Siegel's book *Stocks for the Long Run.* According to this view, people have realized that, in light of historical statistics, they have been too fearful of stocks. Armed with this new knowledge, investors have now bid stock prices up to a higher level, to their rational or true level, where the stocks would have been all along had there not been excessive fear of them. Stocks, selling now at a higher price, will pay a correspondingly lower yield—but that is all right with investors, since they now know that stocks are not all that risky. In other words, the *equity premium,* the extra return that people require to be compensated for the risk of investing in the stock market, has gone down because investors have suddenly come to appreciate the historical record of stock market risk.[1]

It is true that the public does appear to perceive less risk in the stock market than they did ten years ago. In Chapter 3 we saw survey results that showed that people now tend to believe that a large one-day stock market decline will be reversed the next day. We saw that there is now strong popular support for the notion that if there is another stock market crash, the market will surely be back up within a couple of years or so. So it is clear that the possibility of major stock market declines does not worry most people very much anymore. But is this because people have acquired some genuinely new knowledge? Or are the new public opinions caused by something altogether different—and ephemeral?

A problem with this "new learning" theory is that the historical fact that investors have supposedly learned—that the stock market has largely outperformed other investments—is not a new revelation. In fact, a best-selling book in 1924 by Edgar Lawrence Smith made a number of historical comparisons of investments in stocks versus bonds and found that stocks always came out ahead over long holding periods, in both periods of rising general prices (inflation) and periods of declining general prices (deflation).[2] Smith emphasized—as did another author at the time, Kenneth Van Strum—that investing in bonds was risky, too, because, even though the nominal values of bond payments are fixed, their real value fluctuates with the general price level.[3]

According to Prof. Irving Fisher, writing in 1929, "These writings threw a bombshell into the investing world." Fisher thought that the bull market of the 1920s occurred because the public had learned from these books: "It was only as the public came to realize, largely through the writing of Edgar Lawrence Smith, that stocks were to be preferred to bonds during a period of dollar depreciation, that the bull market began in good earnest to cause a proper valuation of common shares."[4]

Others shared Fisher's belief about public learning. Charles Amos Dice wrote in 1929 that "the old prejudice against security markets and the fear of them have been largely dispelled by public education regarding stocks and bonds."[5] A writer for the *New York Herald Tribune* asserted in 1929: "It is gratifying to observe the growth of business. . . . But there is a much larger significance in the growth of understanding among the people who make the growth of business possible. . . . There is nothing to retard the progress of any sound industry when an increasing number of people believe in it, become part owners in the business, and are regularly and reliably informed."[6]

If people did learn in 1929 that stocks dominated bonds at 1920s prices, they seem to have forgotten the information later, or at least changed their feelings about it. The question before us now is: Observing the recent stock market, have they really "learned" this time that stocks always outperform bonds, and will they continue to "know" this in the future?

The "fact" that is widely cited is that in the United States there has been no thirty-year period over which bonds have outperformed stocks. The supposed fact is not really true, since, as Jeremy Siegel himself points out in his book *Stocks for the Long Run,* stocks underperformed bonds in the period 1831–61.[7] That may seem like a long time ago until one realizes that there are not that many nonoverlapping thirty-year periods in U.S. stock market history: only four complete periods since 1861. There are many *overlapping* thirty-year periods, but of course these are not independent pieces of evidence. Given the relatively short history of thirty-year periods of stock market returns, we must recognize that there is little evidence that stocks cannot underperform in the future.

If we take ten-year periods as our standard, then we do get some more recent periods when stocks have underperformed short-term interest rates. I have identified in this book three major peaks of the price-earnings ratio before the recent period: peaks in June 1901, September 1929, and January 1966. In the ten-year period following two of these three peaks (the 1929 and 1966 peaks), the period stock market return underperformed short-term interest rates.[8] If we take twenty-year periods as our standard, then it is true that, of these three time periods, only in the 1901–21 period did stocks really underperform short-term interest rates.[9] But in each of the twenty-year periods following these peaks, the stock market has done badly in real (inflation-corrected) terms. The (geometric) average real return on the S&P Composite Index was –0.2% a year from June 1901 to June 1921, 0.4% a year from September 1929 to September 1949, and 1.9% a year from January 1966 to January 1986. Despite these puny returns, the stock market still outperformed short-term interest rates during 1929–49 and 1966–86 because inflation brought real average short-term interest rates to very low levels, in fact to negative territory in 1929–49. The inflationary periods associated with World War I, World War II, and the Vietnam War all had the effect of wiping out the purchasing power of money earning interest. It is hard to see the relevance to today's situation of the fact that inflation wiped out the real value of short-term interest in those historical periods. Today we have long-term inflation-indexed bonds yielding over 4%, guaranteed against the effects of inflation.

Moreover, the United States may itself be the exception rather than the rule in terms of real returns on the stock market. Philippe

Jorion and William Goetzmann have studied the real stock market appreciation rates (excluding dividends) for thirty-nine countries for the period 1926–96 and found that the median real appreciation rate was only 0.8% per year for these countries (compared to 4.3% per year for the United States).[10] Thus, if we take the experience of other countries as relevant to our own, we might expect a much poorer performance of the stock market in the future.

The evidence that stocks will *always* outperform bonds over long time intervals simply does not exist. Moreover, even if history supported this view, we should recognize (and at some level most people must recognize) that the future will not necessarily be like the past. For example, it could be that, with investors buoyed by past successes in the stock market, there is now widespread over-investment. Companies may have hatched too many ambitious plans and spent too much on product development and promotion; therefore they may not do as well as they have in the past. It could also be that some of the very technological changes that are widely touted as reasons for optimism for existing businesses are in fact reasons why their prospects are more uncertain. New technology may diminish the advantage enjoyed by existing companies and cause them to be replaced by upstart newer companies. Thus these changes could raise, not lower, the probability that stocks will under-perform in the next thirty years. Most important, the future is definitely not like the past in that, given the high price-earnings ratios documented previously, the market is more highly priced than ever before.

So the "fact" of the superiority of stocks over bonds is not a fact at all. The public has not learned a fundamental truth. Instead, their attention has *shifted away* from some fundamental truths. They seem not to be so attentive to at least one genuine fundamental truth about stocks: that they are residual claims on corporate cash flow, available to stockholders only after everyone else has been paid. Stocks are, therefore, by their very definition, risky. Investors have also lost sight of another truth: that no one is *guaranteeing* that stocks will do well. There is no welfare plan for people who lose in the stock market.

## *The "Stocks Have Always Outperformed Bonds" Theme in Investing Culture*

Nine years ago I was already so struck by the ubiquity of the observation that stocks have historically outperformed bonds that I decided to try to learn how common the observation really was. I asked the following in a questionnaire survey of U.S. institutional investors in 1991:

> Consider the following argument:
>
> "Over the past 65 years, stocks have earned much higher returns than bonds and there has been no 20-year period since 1926 that bonds have outperformed stocks. Therefore, anyone with a time horizon of 20 years or more should be investing primarily in stocks."
>
> [Circle one number]
>
> 1. I agree with this statement.
> 2. I disagree with this statement.

Of the 172 respondents, 84% chose 1 and only 16% chose 2—very solid agreement on a strongly worded statement.

The question as worded did not make it clear how often the respondents had heard that stocks have always outperformed bonds. To clarify this, in the fall of 1993 I asked institutional investors a similar but differently worded question:

> Consider the following claim:
>
> "There is no 30-year period since 1860 in which U.S. government bonds have outperformed stocks." Have you heard roughly this claim (even if the details, such as the use of 30 years, are different)?
>
> 1. Yes, often
> 2. Yes, once or twice
> 3. No

Of the 125 respondents, 52% chose "Yes, often," 22% chose "Yes, once or twice," and 26% chose "No." Thus 74% say they remember hearing this statement. Clearly statements like this were already part of our investing culture then.

Knowledge about the long-run historical record, knowledge that dates back at least to 1924 and that clearly was widely remembered in 1991 or 1993, cannot be held directly responsible for the sudden upsurge in stock prices to record levels in the late 1990s. The knowledge was apparently in investors' faces all along. The public confidence that any downturn in the market will be reversed has indeed gained remarkable strength in recent years, but this confidence does not derive from a sudden news flash about the historical record. As I have argued, it derives from such things as a feedback mechanism from past price increases (discussed in Chapter 3), driven ultimately by various precipitating factors (discussed in Chapter 2)—not a sudden discovery of the lessons from long-run historical data.

### *Learning about Mutual Funds, Diversification, and Holding for the Long Run*

James Glassman and Kevin Hassett, in a pair of influential *Wall Street Journal* articles in 1998 and 1999, argued that "investors have become better educated about stocks, thanks in large part to mutual funds and the media. They have learned to hold for the long term and to see price declines as transitory—and as buying opportunities." Thus, they conclude that investors have learned that diversified portfolios of stocks are not risky, that stocks are much more valuable as investments than they had formerly thought. Therefore they are now willing to pay much more for stocks. Because of this increased investor demand for stocks, the stock market will perpetually remain at a higher level in the future.[11]

Glassman and Hassett followed up these articles with a book, *Dow 36,000: The New Strategy for Profiting from the Coming Rise in the Stock Market.* In it they stress that investors have not finished learning that diversified holdings of stocks are not risky and that they will continue to bid up stock prices in coming years as the lesson really sinks in. They claim that "A sensible target date for Dow 36,000 is early 2005, but it could be reached much earlier."[12] If this is true, one has the opportunity to make a *lot* of money between 2000 and 2005, or even sooner, by investing in stocks while investors at large are still learning about the value of stocks. Despite the ostensible theme of the book—that stocks are so riskless that they should be thought of as interchangeable with government bonds—the sales pitch for the book (as can be seen in its title) is actually that one can get rich quick on the transition by investing in stocks now, while *other* people learn later that stocks are riskless.

Glassman and Hassett are right when they say that people are considering the advantages of mutual funds, investing for the long run, and the concept that stock price declines are transitory. But one should not infer from this that people have learned or are in the process of learning some essential truths. We have already seen that stock price declines are not that transitory, that they can persist for decades, and thus that even long-run investors should see risk in stock market investments. There is also reason to believe that much of the enthusiasm for mutual funds is a sort of investor fad that was not caused by any real learning.

Investors show great interest in choosing the right mutual fund, and their interest in mutual funds often takes the form of switching from one to the next. In response to this heightened investor interest, the mutual fund industry has spawned thousands of new funds, with a corresponding proliferation of ads and mailings. Yet studies of mutual fund performance have found that although there is some tendency for mutual funds that have done well to continue to do so, the tendency is weak and short-lived. People appear to believe that it is smart to pore over rankings of mutual fund performance and constantly shift their investments to the current top performers, but in fact they gain relatively little by doing so.[13]

To assess investors' feelings that they can make money in the stock market, and the role that mutual funds play in this process, I included in a 1996 questionnaire survey of individual investors a sequence of questions about their confidence levels for both investing in general and investing in mutual funds. The questions, and the percentage responses for each answer, were as follows:

Trying to time the stock market, to get out before it goes down and to get in before it goes up, is:

| | |
|---|---|
| 1. A smart thing to try to do; I can reasonably expect to be a success at it. | 11% |
| 2. Not a smart thing to try to do; I can't reasonably expect to be a success at it. | 83% |
| 3. No opinion. | 5% |

[Number of respondents: 131]

> Trying to pick individual stocks, trying to predict, for example, if and when Ford Motor stock will go up or IBM stock will go up, is:
>
> 1. A smart thing to try to do; I can reasonably expect to be a success at it. 40%
> 2. Not a smart thing to try to do; I can't reasonably expect to be a success at it. 51%
> 3. No opinion. 8%
>
> [Number of respondents: 131]

> Trying to pick mutual funds, trying to figure out which funds have experts who can themselves pick stocks that will go up, is:
>
> 1. A smart thing to try to do; I can reasonably expect to be a success at it. 50%
> 2. Not a smart thing to try to do; I can't reasonably expect to be a success at it. 27%
> 3. No opinion. 23%
>
> [Number of respondents: 132]

From these results, we see that people effectively believe in the efficiency of the aggregate market and so have given up on timing it; but they often think that they can still pick individual stocks and (particularly) mutual funds. Only 27% will say that trying to pick mutual funds that will do well is not a smart thing to do to, compared with 51% who say that trying to pick individual stocks and 83% who say that trying to time the market are not smart things to do.

If one truly believed in efficient markets, then one would reply "not a smart thing to try to do" to *all* these questions. If stock prices are a random walk, then one cannot pick times to enter the market, one cannot pick individual stocks, and one cannot pick others who will pick them.

Since there is only modest evidence that one can in fact be a success at picking mutual funds, what investors have "learned" has little support in fact. And in any case, should it really be easier to pick managers of mutual funds than managers of individual companies?

It is often said that people have learned about the importance of portfolio diversification and are using mutual funds to achieve this.[14] Given well-managed funds with low management fees, this argument makes some sense. But many funds charge such high fees that investors might be better off trying to achieve diversification themselves, if diversification were the primary investment motive. Moreover, when they are investing outside a tax-free environment, by holding stocks directly investors can avoid capital gains taxes on the gains the mutual fund managers realize when they sell stocks in the funds' portfolios, an important issue with higher-turnover funds. Investors can instead realize, for tax purposes, the losses on the stocks that go down. Mutual funds clearly have their limitations.

### *Learning and Unlearning*

The public is said to have learned that stocks always go right back up after they go down. We have seen evidence that they do largely think this, but that they have gotten their facts wrong. Stocks can go down, and stay down for many years. They can become overpriced and underperform for many years.

The public is said to have learned that stocks must always outperform other investments, such as bonds, over the long run, and so long-run investors will always do better in stocks. We have seen evidence that they do largely think this. But again they have gotten their facts wrong. Stocks have not always outperformed other investments over decades-long intervals, and there is certainly no reason to think they must in the future.

And the public is said to have learned about the wisdom of investing in stocks via mutual funds whose management teams have proven track records. We find that they do largely think this, and once more they are wrong. Picking mutual funds that have done well has much smaller benefits than investors imagine.

When the facts are wrong, it can't be called learning. Someday, investors will "unlearn" these "facts." But before this happens, we must consider what we as individuals and as a society should be doing—a critical issue to which we turn in the final chapter.

# *Part Five*

# ***A Call to Action***

# *Eleven*

# *Speculative Volatility in a Free Society*

The high recent valuations in the stock market have come about for no good reasons. The market level does not, as so many imagine, represent the consensus judgment of experts who have carefully weighed the long-term evidence. The market is high because of the combined effect of indifferent thinking by millions of people, very few of whom feel the need to perform careful research on the long-term investment value of the aggregate stock market, and who are motivated substantially by their own emotions, random attentions, and perceptions of conventional wisdom. Their all-too-human behavior is heavily influenced by news media that are interested in attracting viewers or readers, with limited incentive to discipline their readers with the type of quantitative analysis that might give them a correct impression of the aggregate stock market level.

It is a serious mistake for public figures to acquiesce in the stock market valuations we have seen recently, to remain silent about the implications of such high valuations, and to leave all commentary to the market analysts who specialize in the nearly impossible task of forecasting the market over the short term and who share interests with investment banks or brokerage firms. The valuation of the stock market is an important national—indeed international—issue. All of our plans for the future, as individuals and as a society, hinge on our perceived wealth, and plans can be thrown into disarray if much of that wealth evaporates tomorrow. The tendency for speculative bubbles to grow and then contract can make for very uneven distribution of wealth. It may even cause many of us, at times, to question the very viability of our capitalist and free market institutions. It is for such reasons that we must be clear on the prospect for such contractions and on what should be our individual and national policy regarding this prospect.

Of course, in the current political and economic climate one incurs a substantial risk of embarrassment if one goes on record saying that stock market returns will be low or negative in coming years. We have seen in this book that, although the market appears to have substantial long-term forecastability when it is very overpriced (as it appears to be, based on recent data) or, alternatively, when it is very underpriced, there is always considerable uncertainty about its outlook. But an observer who remains silent about the unjustifiably high values because he or she could be wrong about the outlook is no better than a doctor who, having diagnosed high blood pressure in a patient, says nothing because the patient might be lucky and show no ill effects. (Conversely, whether the stock market falls or continues its upward climb in the opening years of the twenty-first century will neither prove nor disprove this book's essential thesis about irrational exuberance.)

### *The Outlook at the Beginning of the New Millennium*

Let us consider the twelve precipitating factors listed in Chapter 2 as the ultimate causes of the bull market in the closing years of the twentieth century, factors such as the Internet, the decline of foreign economic rivals, and the Baby Boom. Which of these factors are likely not only to persist but to become even stronger—even more supportive of a high market than they have been recently?

If the precipitating factors continue to support the market at its recent record level, and do not increase the market's value further, then returns in the stock market will be confined to dividends. Since the dividend-price ratio in the U.S. stock market has been only a little above 1% recently, given stable market levels, stock market returns would be limited to about 1% per year—a very poor return indeed. We need further growth in these supportive factors to obtain even historically average returns on the market.[1]

A couple of the twelve factors that I listed in Chapter 2 appear likely to grow in importance in the opening years of the twenty-first century. These factors might work in the direction of causing stock prices to increase substantially. In this case, of course—and if, as in the recent past, dividends do not increase apace—then the dividend yield on stocks will sink even lower, making the longer-run sustainability of the market level even more questionable.

Recall that it was argued that the Internet is one of the most visible of humankind's inventions, in that individuals themselves directly participate in it and find it opening new horizons for them. Participation in the Internet gives people a personal sense of technological progress, and this personal participation may give them an exaggerated sense of the promise of the technology—exaggerated at least in terms of the outlook for the existing companies that compose the bulk of the value of the stock market. The Internet is expected to grow quite a bit. According to International Data Corporation, a market research firm, U.S. adult Internet users passed 100 million in late 1999, and the number is predicted to rise to 177 million individuals by 2003. Worldwide, the number of users is expected to grow from 142 million in 1998 to 502 million by 2003.[2] Eventually probably almost everyone will be using the Internet, and thus one might think that the psychological support for high market levels would be strongly enhanced.

However, the effect of further growth in the Internet might be less dramatic than the predictions of millions of new users would at first suggest. Potential new users have already heard about the Internet. It has been advertised everywhere, and so it will not be news to them. As we pass the year 2001 and move into the third millennium, the festive parade of displays and forecasts of futuristic technology will move on, and the Internet will inevitably receive less publicity. In any case, the wealthier people who are more likely to invest in the stock market are already likely to have Internet connections. And the symbolic value of the Net will probably itself fade just because we become accustomed to it. As time goes on, the Internet may seem less and less a symbol of the promise of new technology, and more and more like the phone book. Nevertheless, the future growth of the Internet is still likely to offer some boost to the market.

The enormous growth of opportunities to trade stocks easily and cheaply is also likely to continue, with the expansion of online trading of stocks, the creation of new electronic stock and derivative exchanges, and the implementation of twenty-four-hour trading. According to one forecast, the number of U.S. households with online investing accounts is predicted to increase from 3.1 million in 1999 to 9.7 million in 2003.[3] Such changes, by encouraging increased activity in the market, will no doubt stimulate more and more people to take an interest in the market. As discussed in Chapter 2, this increase in interest may encourage higher market valuations—although the certainty of such an impetus is far from definite.

Other factors I described in Chapter 2 are likely to remain stable, not grow further, in their support of high market value. Such new media institutions as the business channels on cable television and the "Money" sections in newspapers will undoubtedly persist, but it is hard to imagine a doubling in the number of such channels or pages relative to others. The critical question is whether the current level of public attention to them can be sustained over time. It was public response that accounted in part for the expanded media coverage we have already seen. Based on the historical precedents we considered in Chapter 3, the focal point of the news may shift somewhat over time, away from investments. This shift of focus may in turn alter the nature of these media in unpredictable ways. There is a good chance that they may become less supportive of a culture of investing.

There is fundamental uncertainty whether the really low rates of inflation we have seen of late can be expected to continue. By some accounts, the burst of inflation due to the high-pressure economic measures initiated in the 1960s in the United States (as well as other countries) was itself an anomaly, the only sharp peacetime inflation in U.S. history, and is unlikely to be repeated now that we have seen its consequences. However, there has been no fundamental change in our institutions since then, and it is hard to rule out a resurgence of inflation. An oil shortage or a war, to pick just two examples, might have that effect, as they have in the past.

For now, continuation of lower inflation appears a likely prospect, and continuing low inflation will continue to promote low nominal yields on fixed-income investments and thus encourage high valuations on stocks. One thing that is fairly certain is that inflation will not get significantly lower: no monetary authority is likely to permit substantially negative inflation rates. Thus low inflation is at best a stable factor, not a factor whose scope is likely to increase, encouraging further growth of the stock market.

The rise of public institutions promoting gambling appears unlikely to be reversed, unless some dramatic scandal or catastrophe turns public opinion against them. I have argued that the prominence of gambling institutions in our culture may encourage a speculative stance in financial markets. But what this means for the outlook for the market is highly uncertain, for the theoretical connection is admittedly weak.

Others among the factors I mentioned as supporting a high market valuation are quite likely to falter in the future. The effects of the post–World War II Baby Boom on the stock market are certain to become less pronounced over time. Barring an unforeseen event, such as the outbreak of a previously unknown disease that selectively kills the elderly, we know that there will be many more retired persons in 2030 than there are today. Thanks to improved medical technology, retirees will be living on in a state of increased dependency, and they will need to cash in their stock market investments to support themselves. Of course, as argued earlier, the ultimate meaning of this effect is clouded by uncertainty about fundamental economic growth and foreign demand for U.S. stocks. Still, the strong public perception that the Baby Boom supports the stock market will eventually fade.

It is sometimes thought that government reaction to the Baby Bust might be a reason to expect a boost in the stock market, instead of a fall. For example, President Clinton, in his 1999 State of the Union Address, proposed that over the next fifteen years $2.7 trillion of the projected federal surplus should be reserved for the Social Security Trust Fund and that about a quarter of that $2.7 trillion should be invested in the stock market. If a plan similar to this one is eventually adopted, it could represent a modest boost to the demand for stocks (compared to the $16 trillion value of the stock market) over the intermediate term. Of course, it is hard to say how much of this future demand for stocks has already been incorporated into market expectations and thus already reflected in share prices, and also to what extent government purchases of stocks for Social Security will be offset by declining individual purchases. It is also hard to know when such a boost would affect the market, and the government's policy would not prevent the ultimate decline in demand for stocks when the Boomers finally retire.

The sense of "victory" of capitalist economies that developed after some of our close competitors abroad began to falter after 1990 is not likely to persist indefinitely. No sports team comes out on top season after season. New symbolic losses here or gains there are to be expected as foreign economies make necessary course corrections.

What then is the rough scorecard for the likely future of the twelve precipitating factors in the opening years of the twenty-first century? Two (the Internet boom and the expansion of stock trading opportunities) will probably increase in strength, two (the Baby Boom and perceived victory over foreign economic rivals) will decrease, and the others will likely stay about the same. The conclusion is that no overall change in these twelve factors can be confidently predicted, and that, if constancy of the precipitating factors implies constancy of the market level, then returns will remain confined to the low dividend yield we now see for stocks.

Yet the absence of predictable change in the overall impact of these factors does not suggest that there will be no predictable change in the market. The market *level* got where it is substantially because of the *increased influence* of these precipitating factors in the past, with the support of the feedback mechanisms discussed in Chapter 3. Media publicity for the stock market (whose importance for market levels was argued in Chapter 4) was encouraged by the price increases due to these factors and by the newness of the factors themselves.

Without further growth in the precipitating factors in the opening decade or so of the twenty-first century, the market will have more and more trouble sustaining its present level. As time goes on, excitement for the market will likely fade. As time goes on, the culture of investing will likely fade. As time goes on, the sense that one is "playing with the house money" will likely fade. As time goes on, people will likely turn to other interests besides investing, and the attention to the "new era" theories discussed in Part II will likely fade. As time goes on, people's attention will likely switch to new psychological anchors for the market, and new conventional wisdom and new public attentions will develop (as discussed in Part III). All of these changes suggest a poor long-run outlook for the stock market.

### *Possible New Factors*

We should not dwell exclusively on the precipitating factors of the past. New precipitating factors, both supportive and destructive of market value, will no doubt develop, although it is difficult to anticipate what these will be. There is little public discussion of such possible new factors precisely because there is so little concrete to say about them now. In the public's imagination, future developments, at least as expressed in the media, seem largely confined to the realm of new technology, and then the coverage is generally upbeat.

Yet at a point in history where the U.S. economy has been relatively strong, it is useful to recall the kinds of things that could go wrong with economic growth and the growth of corporate earnings—things that have interrupted past spells of strong earnings growth and that could do so in the future.The kind of earnings growth the United States has seen since the recession of 1991 requires that all systems remain go, that there be no significant obstacles, and in this respect we have indeed been quite fortunate of late.

The list of factors that could potentially interrupt earnings growth is of course very long. We may list some of them, with no presumption that any of these is more or less likely at the present time: a decline in consumer demand, a dearth of new development opportunities, failures of major technological initiatives, heightened foreign competition, a resurgent labor movement, an oil crisis, a corporate tax increase, newly discovered problems with the longer-run consequences of downsizing and incentive-based compensation for employees, a decline in employee morale and productivity, a war (even one among foreign countries, which disrupts our own trade or destroys a stable environment for economic operations), a terrorist attack or even a new terrorist threat that hampers business activities, an industrial accident that suggests that certain technical processes are more dangerous than previously thought, heightened regulatory or antitrust activity, increased foreign tariffs or import quotas, a depression abroad, stricter environmental standards, class-action lawsuits against corporations, a suddenly erratic monetary policy, systemic problems due to a failure of major banks or financial institutions, a widespread computer system problem in the same vein as the once-predicted Y2K-related malfunctions or an unstoppable computer virus or communications satellite problems, large-scale weather problems, natural disasters, epidemics. . . . The list can never be complete. Indeed, some of the items on this list were virtually unknown a decade ago.

With so many possible causes, we are left now, as always, with the daunting problem of assessing not only their various probabilities—each of them by itself small and hard to quantify—but also the probabilities of several of them happening together, which would make the combined effect all the more serious. There are important reasons to think that various of these problems would tend to occur together, as one tends to precipitate others through its effects on society and the economy. Indeed, the recent Asian financial crisis was described in these terms, as due to the confluence of a number of independent factors: a drop in confidence among foreign investors in the Asian economies, an exchange rate crisis, a banking crisis, a stock market decline, and crises of revealed government corruption. These separate crises fed on each other; they were not independent factors in causing the ultimate financial meltdown.

### *Issues of Fairness and Resentment*

Many of the potential causes of earnings reversals listed earlier have ultimately to do with changes in morale, loyalty, and sense of fairness among the investing public. Currently, overt resentment by American citizens of their own corporations appears to be at a historic low. Businessmen are lionized, and labor unions are very weak by historical standards. But the growing unevenness of income distribution, and the increasingly frequent stories of fabulous wealth earned by the dealmakers, may turn U.S. public opinion away from its pro-business stance.

According to calculations by economist Ray Fair, if market expectations for earnings growth are realized, and if U.S. gross domestic product growth is 4% a year, then after-tax corporate profits as a fraction of gross domestic product will be over 12% in 2010, a value almost twice as high as it has been at any time since 1948.[4] It is hard to imagine that so high a fraction of gross domestic product going to corporate profits will be tolerated by the public without at least some resentment. It was such resentment of business that ended the "community of interest" boom after 1901 (see Chapter 5), by spurring vigorous antitrust legislation and regulation of corporations, and it was such resentment after 1929, in encouraging the growth of Socialist and Communist movements, that created an unusually uncertain and unstable atmosphere for the economy in the 1930s (see Chapter 5).

Resentment by foreigners toward the United States is another potential limiting factor for U.S. earnings growth. American dominance in high-technology is highly visible around the world. In recent years, numerous stories of American enterprise successes have been flaunted in the faces of people outside the United States. For example, the Internet is a symbol for much that is new and exciting today in technology, and it is U.S. software companies that seem to dominate it, from Web browsers to search engines to online providers. All over the world the name of an American company, Microsoft, appears on computer screens whenever people start up Windows to access the Internet. Does this not leave people in other countries with a sense of exclusion from this technology?

Something may seem fundamentally unfair about the United States' high-tech hegemony. How did Microsoft attain such overwhelming dominance? Whether true or not, the company is often described as cutthroat and grasping. Why is the Internet dominated by the United States? The World Wide Web was after all a European invention, developed in its initial form by a British and a Belgian scientist, working in a Swiss laboratory. We do not see their names when we start up our computers.

Resentment against the United States and its strong free enterprise system has moral overtones too; people in many other countries that are not quite as strong economically wonder if their relative lack of economic success might not be due to their greater concern as societies and as individuals with equity, fairness, and human values. If such a moral basis for resentment gains solid ground in public thinking, it could lead to heightened efforts to compete with or exclude American corporations.

Demonstrating another aspect of its high-tech dominance, the United States deployed its superior military technology in Kosovo in 1999, as it had in the Persian Gulf in 1991. It showed an ability and willingness to use its technology to kill large numbers of people with impunity, since it faced virtually no losses of its own. China's outrage against the United States after the accidental bombing of its embassy in Belgrade is illustrative of foreign reaction.

In the Asian financial crisis, it was the United States that was described as presenting a model for the faltering Asian economies to follow. The economists who were sent to offer advice were often U.S. trained. Although the basic intent was constructive, these actions too had some negative symbolic value.

Increased resentment against U.S. corporations both domestically and abroad could result in increases in the probability of occurrence of certain of the events listed earlier as threats to earnings growth. Resentment is not a word in most financial economists' vocabulary, but it has been a powerful force in history.

### *Sharing the Limits to Growth*

As the world develops, the level of atmosphere-polluting emissions will also grow. The level of concern with the adverse effects of these emissions has been such that the 1997 Kyoto Protocol proposed that thirty-eight industrially advanced countries of the world cut emissions of carbon dioxide and other greenhouse gases by an average of 5.2% of 1990 levels during the period from 2008 to 2012.

Economists have estimated that full implementation of the Kyoto Protocol without modification could result in an economic cost with a present value of $1.5 trillion, borne mainly by wealthy countries.[5] But the pain that would be caused by international efforts to control emissions could be greater still. By some accounts, the reductions proposed by the Kyoto Protocol are not nearly enough to deal with the problems of greenhouse gas emissions. In 1995 the United Nations Intergovernmental Panel on Climate Change called for greenhouse emissions to be cut immediately by 50–70%. But instead the level of emissions has continued to grow rapidly, with most of the increase coming from the developing countries.

It is impossible to predict the ultimate cost to individuals and corporations of efforts to reduce emissions or to deal with other global limits to growth. However, considering the inevitable conflicts as less-developed countries try to follow the path of developed countries, thus multiplying environmental problems, the kind of enormous earnings growth in the future that would justify recent stock market levels seems less likely.

These considerations of international resentment of the success of wealthy economies and of the limits to growth only reinforce our supposition that the current outlook for the stock market is not favorable.

### *What Should Investors Do Now?*

If over some interval in the first decade or so of the twenty-first century the U.S. stock market is going to follow an uneven course down, as well it might—back, let us say, to its levels in the mid-1990s or even lower—then individuals, foundations, college endowments, and other beneficiaries of the market are going to find themselves poorer, in the aggregate by trillions of dollars. The real losses could be comparable to the total destruction of all the schools in the country, or all the farms in the country, or possibly even all the homes in the country.[6]

One could say that such a fall would really be harmless, since nothing is physically destroyed by a fall in stock market values; it is only a change on paper and in our minds. One could say that if the market were to fall by half it would only bring us back to where we were a few years ago in terms of market value. But there is the problem that the loss will not be borne equally. Some who rode the market up to new prosperity will have lightened up on their stock holdings and will keep their gains; others will have recently entered the market and will take only the losses. Thus a substantial fall in the market would leave some people really poor while leaving others very rich.

We can imagine the effects on the lives of those people who had become too dependent on stocks as investments, and too optimistic regarding the performance of those investments in the future. People who have put away only a modest amount in the stock market for their children's college education may find that their savings are inadequate, that the real value of the portfolio has fallen far short of the increased cost of a college education. The children may have to take out substantial student loans and get unrewarding part-time jobs to pay for their college education. Or they may decide to choose a shorter career route, forgoing the dream of a career in medicine, law, or other professions. They may decide not to go to college at all.

Others, a little older, may find that their careers or ambitions are thwarted. With fewer economic resources at their disposal, the need to maintain an income level and fulfill everyday obligations will consume time and energy they had hoped to devote to individual fulfillment.

People who have saved virtually nothing for their retirement because of their faith in the stock market investments in their pension plans may find that the plans, along with Social Security, simply do not provide them with a very comfortable standard of living in their retirement. The "amazing power" of compound returns that has become such an article of faith among so many people does not apply if the returns are not there in the first place. Thus those with little savings will have to fend for themselves in a world with many more dependent elderly relative to the young.

They may have to live very simply—and that may mean sitting at home.

Colleges and foundations with endowments heavily invested in stocks may find that their ability to pursue their missions has suddenly been curtailed. Consider, as an example, the Ford Foundation, which published an influential report in 1969, near the peak of the stock market, that strongly suggested that educational endowments should be invested more in stocks to take advantage of their high returns. The foundation took its own advice on investing. After the 1974 stock market crash, it lost so much in the stock market that its endowment fell from $4.1 billion to $1.7 billion. The foundation cut its annual grants from $177 million in 1973 to $76 million in 1979. Although it continued to support antipoverty programs, the foundation sharply curtailed grants to universities for research, to scholarly exchange programs, and to the arts. The University of Rochester, which had been praised in the 1969 report for its aggressive stance to the stock market, took a similar hit; it lost over half its endowment between 1973 and 1974.[7] The same or worse could happen today to foundations and universities that have invested too large a share of their portfolios in the stock market.

So what should investors do now? The natural first step may be, depending on current holdings and specific circumstances, to reduce holdings of U.S. stocks. Certainly, the commonsense notion that one should not be overly dependent on any one investment is as true as ever now. One should at the very least diversify thoroughly.

But there is fundamental difficulty with advising individuals and institutions to get out of the stock market. If such advice were suddenly taken by large numbers, it would cause an immediate drop in the level of the market. In fact, we cannot *all* get out of the market. We can only sell our shares to someone else. Somebody must be left holding the outstanding shares. As a group, those unfortunate people who bought in at a market high have already made their mistake, and we cannot correct it for them as a group after the fact.

So an important action that all investors can take now is to decrease their reliance on the stock market in their *ongoing* economic decisions. Individuals should consider increasing their savings rates. Foundations and colleges should consider reducing the payout rate from their endowments.

The optimism represented by the high stock market has coincided with a much lower personal savings rate in the United States—in fact a personal savings rate of around zero. Most saving in the United States today is corporate (in the form of retained earnings) and governmental (in the form of the federal surplus), forms of saving whose beneficiaries are not distributed equally over the population.

It is reasonable to suppose that the stock market at some point in the first decade of the twenty-first century will decline in value by an amount on the order of one year's national income. The amount of additional personal saving that must be done to offset this decline is quite large. For example, if we are to offset by additional saving such a decline in ten years' time, without the advantages of supposedly high rates of return and high compounding, then we will have to be saving on the order of an additional 10% of our pretax incomes each year.

For the same reason, colleges and foundations with endowment funds invested in the market should consider, when possible, substantially lowering their payout rates. This conclusion stands in sharp contrast to some recent recommendations about endowment payout rates. For example, the National Network of Grantmakers, an organization of progressive foundations, issued a report in 1999 urging all foundations to increase their payout from the 5% of assets mandated by U.S. law to 6%.[8] Universities, whose endowments are growing rapidly thanks to the strong stock market and associated alumni giving, are being urged to increase their spending. For endowments heavily exposed to stock market risks, these recommendations are pointing in the wrong direction.

### *Retirement Plans*

The growth since the bottom of the market in 1982 of employer-sponsored defined contribution pension plans (in which the company makes contributions to an investment fund that is owned by the employee), in contrast to older defined benefit plans (in which the company guarantees specified pension benefits to the employee upon retirement), has marked a shift away from a notion of shared responsibility for the elderly toward a feeling that each person is responsible for his or her own welfare. These 401(k) and similar plans are designed to give ordinary people economic security in retirement by encouraging them to mimic the portfolio strategies long pursued by the wealthy. But little attention is usually paid to the fact that the wealthy, because of the overall level of their assets, have less reason to worry about losing substantial amounts in a market decline.

The shift toward defined contribution pension plans has in many respects been a good thing, since the older defined benefit plans were usually not indexed to inflation (an odd and hard-to-explain lapse in public judgment, and one that does not inspire confidence that people are better off letting institutional experts manage their investments for them).[9] People who retired and lived a long time under defined benefit plans often saw a substantial part of the real value of their pensions eroded away by inflation.

But even though the switch to defined contribution plans eliminated this problem, something was lost in the transition, namely a sense of group responsibility for the standard of living of pensioners. Properly designed defined benefit plans are risk-managing institutions for pensioners, and as such would offer risk-reducing advantages, which are particularly important for lower-income pensioners. Now participants in pension plans are told, in effect, choose your investments (for the pension contributions) and take your chances. As we have seen, they are typically given a large number of choices, including many varieties of stock market investments, and thus (as discussed in Chapter 2) there is a not-so-subtle nudge in the direction of investing heavily in the stock market.

Plans that offer the choice of investment in the government's inflation-indexed bonds are a rarity, despite the fact that these bonds have recently been yielding about 4% a year and are riskless. These bonds would be an obvious choice for people planning for retirement, a far better option today than the stock market. Their advantages would be particularly significant for low-income people. And yet there is little leadership on the part of employers or government to encourage them to shift their retirement funds into the bonds or to make it possible to include them in their 401(k) plans. The current institutional structure does not encourage employers to exert leadership through their plans, only to provide the standard options that other plans offer, always involving the stock market.

Furthermore the plan investments that participants choose are not well diversified. In the early 1990s, most 401(k) balances were invested in guaranteed investment contracts (GICs), fixed-income investments offered by insurance companies, not indexed to inflation. The reputation of GICs was tarnished by a couple of defaults in the early 1990s, which revealed that they were not really guaranteed. These coincided with a barrage of publicity suggesting that experts agreed that people did not put enough into the stock market. Since then, the trend in participant allocations has been sharply away from GICs, in favor of the stock market. According to the latest Investment Company Institute/Employee Benefits Research Institute study, more than two-thirds of 401(k) pension plan balances were in the stock market in 1996.[10] Even among participants nearing retirement, participants in their sixties, most of the plan balances were in the stock market. If the trend toward favoring the stock market for 401(k) investments has continued since 1996, the fraction of plan balances in the market today will be even higher. Many participants no doubt put virtually all of their pension funds into the stock market.[11]

Because so large a proportion of 401(k) investments is in the stock market, a sharp market decline would have important consequences for many retirees. A decline of the stock market to less than half its recent value is not improbable. Given the meagerness of most Social Security benefits, and given that most retirees have little more than their pension plan, their house, and their Social Security benefits, these declines would indeed be noticed.[12]

And yet there is a curious lack of public concern about this risk. Few are raising alarms about it. If anything, concerns are expressed that some plan participants are not putting enough into the stock market, and are thereby missing out on obviously good investments because of an excess of conservatism.

Managers of 401(k) plans generally do not offer advice to employees about how they should make their allocations. Until a Labor Department ruling in 1996, it was in fact legally difficult for the plans to offer any advice because of potential liability concerns.[13] Now plans will sometimes warn participants of the importance of diversification, but as we have seen these warnings are weak and have little effect. The general stance of public policy has been to respect completely participants' own choices, as if people have their own good reasons for putting so much into the stock market, or as if their judgments are related to purely personal matters rather than popular-culture myths about surefire profit opportunities in stocks.

The current policy of providing a menu of choices for participants without any strongly worded advice to diversify invites serious errors. But the current attitude toward the market puts pension plans under pressure to provide people with what they want and not to act paternally. Ultimately it is government policy that has fostered this situation, by encouraging defined contribution pension plans rather than encouraging the improvement, through indexation, of defined benefit pension plans.

Authorities who are responsible for pension plans (in the businesses that sponsor them or in the plans themselves) should come out much more strongly against putting all or almost all of one's plan balance into the stock market. They should instead recommend greater diversification and suggest that a substantial fraction of balances be put into safe investments, such as inflation-indexed government bonds. They should make available inflation-indexed retirement annuities and urge retirees to take their retirement income in this form. It may even be a good move, particularly for lower-income workers, for corporate pension plans to move back toward defined benefit plans, if these plans are appropriately indexed and vested. The indexation could be in terms of the Consumer Price Index, per capita national income, or a mixture of the two.[14] In the future, as a greater variety of risk management contracts become available, advice should be given to employees to take advantage of them.

## *Social Security*

As of this writing, a number of proposals have been advanced to invest at least a portion of the Social Security Trust Fund in the stock market. Having marveled at the high returns in the market, Americans are wondering why they have earned so much lower a return on their contributions to Social Security than they could have earned in a defined contribution pension plan, and why they have not been allowed to invest their contributions in the stock market. If the government were to implement fully such proposals, it would compromise another important national risk-sharing institution.

We may regard the Social Security system as the government's partial assumption of the intrafamily risk sharing of long ago. Young people have long felt a sense of obligation to care for their aging parents, in return for the care they received as children. Thus middle-aged people often found themselves caring simultaneously for their elderly parents as well as their children. Since the precise obligations were dictated by morals and feelings of love rather than legal bonds, this old family system encouraged some effective intergenerational risk sharing. One divided up one's attentions between one's dependent children and elderly parents as one perceived their relative needs and one's own needs, not by some contract formula. If the elderly were more in need of care, sicker, or more dependent, or lived longer, they received proportionally greater share of family resources, and the converse also applied. In this way, risks were shared across generations.

The problem with the family as an economic risk-sharing institution is that it is unreliable. Members may die young or become incapacitated or irresponsible at the age when they should be doing the work for others. Social Security was created to alleviate such problems by replacing individual "contracts" among family members with contractual obligations between generations at large.

In the United States (as in the systems of many other countries), Social Security is primarily a pay-as-you-go system: the contributions made by working people are not invested in any real assets but are given immediately to those retirees who need the money now. In this way, Social Security mimics the traditional family system, which also did not rely on any investments. Indeed, the traditional family system did not rely on investments to prepare for old age because in most times and places there were few reliable investments to use to save over decade-long intervals. Now, with the exaggerated public confidence in the market, we seem to think that there are such investments—in stocks. In fact, we are closer to the old situation than is widely realized. Stocks are not safe. Although individuals in the United States and some other countries can invest in inflation-indexed bonds, which are completely safe investments, these indexed bonds are not investments for society as a whole, since their net value is zero. The indexed government bonds are made safe only by the fact that taxpayers guarantee their payments. There is no safe investment for the country as a whole because there are so many things that can go wrong with an economy. If the economy takes a bad turn and national income declines, then the working population will see their tax rates go up to pay for the fixed Social Security benefits guaranteed to retirees, and thus they will experience an amplified effect of the economic decline. It does not make sense to protect one segment of the population from any economic setback by concentrating the effects of the setback on another segment.

The creation of Social Security in the United States in the 1930s is often described as having provided a windfall to the first generation of benefit recipients, who received much more in benefits than could be justified by the contributions they themselves had made. But there has been no clear windfall to them, since one must also take account of the decline in obligations that was felt within families to care for them, when families saw that they were being taken care of by the government. The first generation's "windfall gain" was probably offset by reduced levels of care from their children. Their children were paying into Social Security instead of putting time and effort into caring for their parents. In this way, the Social Security system merely took charge of part of the care young people had been giving to their parents, without changing its substance, and with the advantage of greater uniformity and reliability.

Offsetting this advantage of Social Security, however, is the loss of the sense of balance between the needs of the generations. These are now dealt with in a formulaic manner, argued about in abstract terms in Congress without the immediate evidence of relative needs that is so visible within the family. There is limited ability for national debate to come to grips with the relative needs and abilities of the generations, and so the family continues to function as the premier intergenerational risk-management institution.

It would be a serious mistake to adopt the policy, proposed by some, of replacing the current Social Security system with a defined contribution plan for retirement, investing plan balances in the stock market, or even a plan that would give individuals a choice of investment categories. Such a plan would replace the current societal commitments to the elderly with a hope that financial markets will do as well as in the past. Adopting such a plan at a time when the market is at a record high relative to fundamentals would be an error of historic proportions. Fortunately most serious proposals have called for only modest investments of the Social Security Trust Fund in the stock market.[15]

Reform of Social Security should take the form not of investing the trust fund in the stock market but of making the system more responsive to economic risks, so that the system promotes better risk sharing among economic groups within our population. Contribution rates and benefit rates should vary over time depending on the relative needs of workers and retirees. Both contributions and benefits should be indexed, but not primarily to the Consumer Price Index, rather to per capita national income. We must reform the Social Security system in the direction of making it more like a system that would seem just and humane were it to be implemented within a family—a system that shares risk and that does not leave anyone bearing an inordinate share of the economic burden.[16]

### *Monetary Policy and Speculative Bubbles*

There have been occasions on which tightened monetary policy was associated with the bursting of stock market bubbles. For example, on February 14, 1929, the Federal Reserve raised the rediscount rate from 5% to 6% for the ostensible purpose of checking speculation. In the early 1930s, the Fed continued the tight monetary policy and saw the initial stock market downturn evolve into the deepest stock market decline ever, and a recession into the most serious U.S. depression ever.

In Japan, at the peak of the Japanese stock market between May 1989 and August 1990, the Bank of Japan raised the discount rate from 2.5% to 6%, ostensibly to stabilize financial markets (which were thought to have become overpriced because of easy monetary policy) and also to stabilize the yen. It is hard to dismiss the possibility that this action by the bank played some role in the stock market crash and severe recession that followed.[17]

Although the precise causal links are hard to disentangle even in these dramatic episodes, one thing we do know about interest rate policy is that it affects the entire economy in fundamental ways, and that it is not focused exclusively on the speculative bubble it might be used to correct. It is whole-body irradiation, not a surgical laser. Moreover, the genesis of a speculative bubble, such as the one we are in now, is a long, slow process, involving gradual changes in people's thinking. Small changes in interest rates will not have any predictable effect on such thinking; big changes might, but only because they have the potential to exert a devastating impact on the economy as a whole.

The Great Depression of the 1930s was in fact substantially due to monetary authorities' trying to stabilize speculative markets through interest rate policies, although the markets they were focusing most on were not the stock markets but the markets for their own currencies. Countries attempted to preserve the fixed exchange rate system, represented by the gold standard, against attacks. The countries that gave up earliest and abandoned their efforts to defend their currencies were the ones to emerge from the depression the soonest.[18]

A small, but symbolic, increase in interest rates by monetary authorities at a time when markets are perceived by them to be overpriced may be a useful step, if the increase is accompanied by a public statement that it is intended to restrain speculation. But authorities should not generally try to burst a bubble through aggressive tightening of monetary policy.

### *The Stabilizing Authority of Opinion Leaders*

A time-honored way of restraining speculation in financial markets is for intellectual and moral leaders to try to call the attention of the public to over- and underpricing errors when they occur. This approach has been used repeatedly in the history of our financial markets, albeit with a degree of success that is hard to judge.

During the 1907 stock market crash, which coincided with a banking panic in October, national financial leaders made public statements expressing their confidence in the markets and stating that they would risk their own wealth in them. John D. Rockefeller said, "Personally, I have absolute faith in the future of the value of our securities and the soundness of underlying conditions." He and J. P. Morgan set up a bankers' pool to lend money to support the banks. On Black Thursday, October 24, 1929, five of the country's most influential bankers met with Morgan and issued a statement that they believed "the foundations of the market to be sound."[19] Although they did not announce specific plans to buy stocks, their statement was interpreted as suggesting they would. This attempt at stabilizing the market was not successful. The stock market crash of October 28–29, 1929, occurred just a few days later.

In each of the three major market peaks identified here that follow the founding of the Federal Reserve—that is, the peaks of the late 1920s, the mid-1960s, and the 1990s—the head of the Federal Reserve System issued warnings that the stock market was overpriced. The 1929 interest rate increase, discussed earlier, was announced as being directed against speculation. The 1966 peak of the U.S. stock market coincided roughly with a statement by Federal Reserve Chairman William McChesney Martin in 1965 that he found "disquieting similarities" between the economy then and the economy during the 1920s prelude to the Great Depression. He listed, as one of the similarities, the spreading conviction among the public that "a new economic era" had begun.[20] A statement warning against stock market excesses by a Federal Reserve chairman was not made again until Alan Greenspan's "irrational exuberance" speech in December 1996, that is, until the beginning of the next period of very high market levels. It appears that Fed chairmen reserve public statements about market pricing for periods of extreme mispricing. There is no way to judge the success of such rare statements in calming the markets, and we do not know how volatile they would have been otherwise.

The trouble with such exercises of moral authority is that, although views that the market is either very overpriced or very underpriced may become commonplace among the experts, they are never universally held. The leaders who make such statements find themselves doing so based on personal opinion: an intuitive judgment about the state of market fundamentals and psychology, a judgment that is so hard to prove that they probably feel that it takes an act of courage to make such a statement in the first place.

There probably is a role for such actions by opinion leaders, but it is only a minor one. If they are genuinely disinterested in their pronouncements and are perceived as true moral leaders, their pronouncements may have a small stabilizing effect on the market.

## *Dealing with Bubbles by Interrupting or Discouraging Trade*

Another method for reducing market volatility has been to shut down markets in times of rapid price change. The "circuit breakers" adopted by the stock exchanges are examples of this approach. Under the New York Stock Exchange's Rule 80B, whenever the Dow Jones Industrial Average drops by 10% (recently this would have corresponded to an absolute drop of 1,100 points) from the previous daily close before 2 P.M., the market is to be shut down for one hour; by 20% (2,250 points) before 1 P.M., for two hours; and by 30% (3,350 points) at any time of day, for the rest of the day. Such market closings might have the effect of giving investors a cooling-off period, to allow them to find time for reflection, and thereby stemming panic. But it is not clear that these relatively short closings do very much to restrain one-day price changes. After all, the two biggest stock market crashes in history, the crashes of October 1929 and October 1987, occurred on Mondays, after the price declines of the previous trading day had been interrupted by an entire weekend.

Another example of a deliberate restraint of trade to prevent bubbles is the uptick rule for short sales. The Securities and Exchange Commission has long required of exchanges that short sales be allowed only on an uptick, that is, only if the preceding trade was on an increasing price.

Yet these various policies of closing the market, for a matter of seconds, minutes, hours, or days, do not directly address the longer-term price movements—movements that take place over years—that represent the really big stock price shifts. It is plausible that by concealing a large short-term price change from the public eye we can head off public overreaction to that price change, and so prevent a longer-term price trend from developing in response to the vivid memory of a really large one-day change. Dramatic one-day changes are attention grabbers, are given tremendous hype by the media, and are remembered long afterward, especially if they set some kind of record. On the other hand, we really have very little information about the effects of a policy of closing markets for short periods of time on longer-term price changes. What if a really large price change is corrected soon after *by the market itself,* as was the October 1987 price change? Perhaps the public's experience of seeing a crash followed by a correction would have a more stabilizing effect than the experience of having a potential crash concealed from it by a market closing.

Longer cooling-off periods have been attempted; in fact the New York Stock Exchange was closed for three months in 1914.[21] However, because this long market closing is thus far unique in U.S. history, no significant lessons can be drawn from the experience.

Other proposals have been advanced to slow the pace of trade by discouraging frequent trading, that is, to "throw sand in the wheels" of speculative markets. James Tobin, a colleague of mine at Yale University, has proposed that the speculative price movements in the market for foreign currencies be restrained by levying a transaction tax on them.[22] This proposal was extended to stocks and to corporate and government bonds by Lawrence and Victoria Summers, although Lawrence Summers has not advocated this idea since assuming his current post as U.S. treasury secretary.[23] Securities transaction taxes are not a new concept, and they have been used in this country as well as many others, although they have not usually resulted from any clearly articulated theory of restraining speculation.

The idea of such transaction taxes, as expressed by Tobin, is that they will discourage short-run speculators in favor of investors concerned with long-run fundamentals. Although he recognizes that a transaction tax penalizes trades based on fundamentals as well as those for speculative reasons, Tobin believes that the tax would more often discourage the latter, since many speculators seem to be interested in very-short-run transactions.

Tobin might be right that speculators will be rather more inhibited by such a tax than long-term investors, since speculators appear, based on survey data on their expectations, to extrapolate past price changes primarily for short intervals. Jeffrey Frankel has found such evidence from survey data on speculators in foreign exchange markets.[24] I have found from my survey data that institutional investors in the stock market tend slightly more often to have bubble expectations, in essence expecting an increase and then a decrease in stock prices, when short-run (six-month) price increases have recently been high.[25] But such a tendency for short-run expectations to reinforce recent short-run price changes is actually fairly weak, and we cannot be sure that it will continue in the future, since speculators' theories about markets are likely to change with time.

It is not clear whether the transaction tax would indeed encourage long-term investors over short-term speculators. We should recognize that some speculative trading is done infrequently, while some trading based on information about fundamentals is done frequently. Real estate markets, which are subject to much higher transaction costs than stock markets, nevertheless seem to be vulnerable to speculative bubbles and crashes. Moreover, it has been found that countries that impose higher transaction costs do not have lower stock market volatility.[26] On balance, although I feel that there might be some merit in Tobin-style transaction taxes for reducing speculative volatility, I have not found the case strong enough to recommend any such action.

### *Dealing with Bubbles by Expanding or Encouraging Trade*

In the interest of longer-run economic stability, it may be that the best stabilizing influence on markets is to broaden them to allow as many people to trade as often as possible, and to broaden the scope of things traded on markets. This of course is just the opposite of the proposals discussed in the previous section.

Given that speculative bubbles are heavily influenced by word-of-mouth effects, by locally perceived values and information, and by patriotic feeling, foreign investors are less likely to go along with a bubble than are local investors, and they may even trade in a way that would tend to offset it. For example, in 1989, when the Japanese Nikkei index was at its peak, our questionnaire surveys found that the average Japanese institutional investor expected a 9.5% increase in the Nikkei in the following year, while U.S. institutional investors expected a 7.7% decrease in the Nikkei. Something about living in Japan encouraged very different feelings about the market. Had U.S. investors, or other foreign investors, been more prominent in Japanese markets all along, the Japanese stock market overpricing might never have happened.[27] Thus, more generally, broadening of markets by encouraging global participation in them should often have the effect of averaging over these disparate expectations and producing more stable market prices.

We should not assume that any policy that stabilizes markets from day to day is a good policy. Sudden price changes are probably not as bad, in terms of their impact on economic welfare, as long-term continuation of mispricing or, even worse, as the development of a speculative bubble that results in a worse crash in the future.

Given that speculative bubbles tend to occur, their eventual bursting may indeed be on balance a good thing. The Asian financial crisis of 1997–98, sparked by the withdrawal of world investors from Asian markets, may be viewed not as a crisis in the long-term sense but as a sanity check that prevented what might have turned out to be a more disastrous speculative bubble from ever developing. To the extent that this crisis encouraged Asian peoples to rethink their businesses and their economies in light of the criticism they received from abroad, the crisis may have been helpful for the countries.

The expansion of markets can, if done correctly, add salience to information about fundamentals, that is, encourage public attention to long-run fundamentals and deflect attention away from short-run speculation. Michael Brennan has proposed that new markets should be set up for "S&P 500 Strips," that is, a market for the future annual total dividends of the aggregate S&P 500 firms for each year in the future up to some distant horizon. There would thus be, for example, in the year 2005 a market for the 2006 aggregate S&P dividends, another market for the 2007 aggregate S&P dividends, yet another market for the 2008 aggregate S&P dividends, and in fact markets for all subsequent aggregate dividends up to the horizon, say twenty years, and then a market for the terminal index value (say, in 2025). Brennan argues that such markets would "provide an incentive for analysts to concentrate on forecasting those fundamentals [future dividends] . . . rather than to concentrate on simply forecasting the level of the market itself. In addition, since the level of the market index must be consistent with the prices of the future dividend flows, the relation between these will serve to reveal the implicit assumptions the market is making in arriving at its valuation. These assumptions will then be the focus of attention and debate."[28] Note that Brennan's proposal is fundamentally different from that of Tobin; Brennan is proposing shifting public attention to fundamentals rather than to longer-run holdings.

New institutions or markets should also be created that would make it easier for individuals to get out of their exposure to the stock market. The institutions we have—such as short sales, stock index futures, and put options—are not particularly user-friendly, and most investors do not avail themselves of these. Many investors today feel themselves locked into their stock holdings because of the capital-gains-tax consequences of selling and their inability to find other ways of reducing their exposure.

In my previous book, *Macro Markets: Creating Institutions for Managing Society's Largest Economic Risks,* I have argued that we should greatly expand the number and variety of markets, to allow trading of major risks that are untradable today. The proposed major international markets I call macro markets would include markets for long-term claims on national incomes for each of the major countries of the world; markets for long-term claims on the incomes of specific occupational groups; and markets for currently illiquid assets, such as single-family homes.[29] There are a number of ways to create macro markets, including using perpetual futures or the macro securities that Allan Weiss and I developed.[30] If such markets are created, people can take short positions in them corresponding to their own incomes, to protect themselves against fluctuations in the value of their own personal sources of income, and can invest in a truly diversified portfolio around the world. These markets could indeed be vastly larger than any existing market and far more numerous in the risks they allow to be offset. Moreover, retail institutions such as home equity insurance or pension plan options that correlate negatively with labor income or home values will help people make use of such risk management tools.[31]

I believe that creating such new markets may have, besides their obvious benefits of creating new risk management opportunities, a salutary effect on speculative excesses by broadening the scope of market participation. The creation of such markets would help us discover the prices of many assets that are totally unknown today. For example, no one today knows what the U.S. economy, the Japanese economy, or any other economy is worth, nor does anyone know what a medical career or a law career is worth, since there are no markets for them. There appear to be unseen speculative bubbles in the unobserved prices, as people in countries go through waves of optimism or pessimism for their own economies, and as people individually make career choices based on current fashions. These changes encourage excessive investment of real and human capital in some times and places and inadequate investment in others. Creating markets for claims on income flows will open up the markets to the generally sobering influence of the rest of the world.

Creating the macro markets would result in a fundamental shift of attention away from the relatively minor risks to the profits of the public firms that are traded in the stock markets of today to the risks to our livelihoods. Although one would expect that there will still be occasional speculative bubbles in the macro markets, the diversity of investment opportunities and the attention focused on fundamental risks by these markets around the world ought to be generally stabilizing to our economies and our lives.

## *Altering Conventional Wisdom about Diversification and Hedging*

In order to encourage proper risk management, especially once important new markets are in place, the advice given by public authorities should stress more genuine diversification. I argued in this book that people are ultimately highly influenced by the perceived wisdom of experts—the "they say that . . ." authorities—and they will not carry out investment diversification well unless experts encourage them to do so.

While financial experts today are typically extolling diversification, they do not stress what genuine diversification really means. Many people still think that they are diversified if they hold stock in a good number of companies in the U.S. stock market or any U.S. equity mutual fund. They must invest more broadly than that, and in fact to achieve true diversification they must also pay attention to other existing risks.

People have to be encouraged by experts to understand that true diversification largely means offsetting the risks that they are already locked into.[32] This means investing in assets that help insure their labor incomes, in assets that tend to rise in value when their labor income declines, or at least that do not tend to move in the same direction. This objective can be achieved efficiently after macro markets have been created by taking short positions in claims on income aggregates, or it can be achieved less effectively today by taking positions in existing assets that are found to correlate negatively (or at least less positively) with specific labor incomes.[33] It also means investing in assets that help insure the equity in their single-family homes, in assets that tend to rise in value when their home value declines. This can be achieved most directly by taking out home equity insurance policies or short positions in a single-family-home futures market, or it can be achieved less effectively today by making investments that tend to move opposite to one's local city property values.[34] Since labor income and home equity account for the great bulk of most people's wealth, offsetting the risks to these is the critical function of risk management.

Making such risk-offsetting investments is called *hedging,* a time-honored practice in business risk management. But hedging is foreign to most people's thinking. Few nonprofessionals could even define the term today. Discussion of how investment returns correlate with incomes or with home prices is almost totally absent from public discourse on investments.

It is difficult to change this mindset, since the public has so much invested in the conventional wisdom today, and in the notion that one can amass great wealth through stock market investments. The personal investment media typically feature the opinions of celebrity sources who are apparently already rich and who subtly suggest that their advice might make one rich too. It would be inconsistent with this fantasy to start talking about the mundane task of defending the value of the assets one already has. Those in the media and the investment community often do not want to risk disturbing the get-rich fantasy, which they have learned to exploit to their own advantage. But attitudes can be changed if public opinion leaders take it upon themselves to stress the changes in thinking that must be made. Once it becomes a "they say that . . ." item, people will routinely take proper steps to hedge their existing wealth, much as they routinely buy homeowners insurance today.

### Policy toward Speculative Volatility

The problems posed for policy makers by the tendency for speculative markets to show occasional bubbles are deep ones. They will have to take full account of our evolving understanding of the nature of these bubbles when formulating measures to deal with the problems they cause. Unfortunately, the nature of the bubbles is sufficiently complex and changing that we can never expect to document the particular role of any given policy in bringing about our objective of long-term economic welfare.

Policies that interfere with markets by shutting them down or limiting them, although under some very specific circumstances apparently useful, probably should not be high on our list of solutions to the problems caused by speculative bubbles. Speculative markets perform critical resource-allocation functions (a point I have taken for granted and have not focused on in this book), and any interference with markets to tame bubbles interferes with these functions as well.

Ultimately, in a free society, we cannot protect people from all the consequences of their own errors. We cannot protect people completely without denying them the possibility of achieving their own fulfillment. We cannot completely protect society from the effects of waves of irrational exuberance or irrational pessimism—emotional reactions that are themselves part of the human condition.

Policies to deal with speculative volatility are a little like policies to deal with political instability. We worry that a political party appealing to baser instincts or rash judgments will gain control. But we do not deal with this risk by shutting down certain political parties in times of unrest or by taxing their activities. Instead, we rely on the complete freedom of all political parties to express themselves, and we expect that common sense will ultimately prevail among voters. This good outcome is achieved by designing, and continually improving, rules for campaigns and elections.

By analogy, most of the thrust of our national policies to deal with speculative bubbles should take the form of facilitating more free trade, as well as greater opportunities for people to take positions in more and freer markets. A good outcome can be achieved by designing better forms of social insurance and creating better financial institutions to allow the real risks to be managed more effectively. The most important thing to keep in mind as we are experiencing a speculative bubble in the stock market today is that we should not let it distract us from such important tasks.

# *Notes*

### *Chapter One The Stock Market Level in Historical Perspective*

1. Home price data are courtesy Case Shiller Weiss, Inc.

2. The price, dividend, and earnings series are from the same sources as described in Chapter 26 of my earlier book (*Market Volatility* [Cambridge, Mass.: MIT Press, 1989]), although now I use monthly data, rather than annual data. Monthly dividend and earnings data are computed from the S&P four-quarter totals for the quarter since 1926, with linear interpolation to monthly figures. Dividend and earnings data before 1926 are from Cowles and associates (*Common Stock Indexes*, 2nd ed. [Bloomington, Ind.: Principia Press, 1939]), interpolated from annual data. Stock price data are monthly averages of daily closing prices through January 2000, the last month available as this book goes to press. The CPI-U (Consumer Price Index—All Urban Consumers) published by the U.S. Bureau of Labor Statistics begins in 1913; for years before 1913 I spliced to the CPI Warren and Pearson's price index, by multiplying it by the ratio of the indexes in January 1913. December 1999 and January 2000 values for the CPI-U are extrapolated. See George F. Warren and Frank A. Pearson, *Gold and Prices* (New York: John Wiley and Sons, 1935). Data are from their Table 1, pp. 11–14. For the plots, I have multiplied the inflation-corrected series by a constant so that their value in January 2000 equals their nominal value, i.e., so that all prices are effectively in January 2000 dollars.

In my older work on stock prices (much of it done jointly with John Campbell), I had used the Producer Price Index (PPI), All Commodities, rather than the

CPI, to deflate. In the past, there was not much difference between the PPI and the CPI, except for short-run oscillations, but since the mid-1980s the levels of the series have diverged substantially. Unless otherwise noted, any statistics reported in this book for the U.S. stock market are from the data set described in this endnote. The data used here (as well as Chapter 26 from *Market Volatility*) are currently available on my Web site: http://www.econ.yale.edu/~shiller.

3. Some have urged that I use a log or ratio scale for the plot, so that the apparent price growth at the end is not "misleading." I do not believe that plotting levels is in any way misleading. There is no sense of any unusual behavior at the end of the earnings series that is plotted in the same way.

4. It should be abundantly clear that some smoothing is necessary: consider the possibility of zero earnings in a given year. Earnings per share adjusted to the S&P Composite Index have always been strictly greater than zero in every year since the inception of the index in 1871, but they have come close to zero, and they could of course pass below zero in the future. Total after-tax corporate profits were actually negative in the national income accounts for 1931 and 1932. When earnings are zero, the price-earnings ratio would be *infinite* in that year, suggesting that there is no upper bound on the price of the aggregate stock market.

5. Scholars have pointed out that since there was no year zero, each new century begins on January 1 of a year ending in 1. In 1900, people were more respectful of such scholarship, and waited a year to celebrate. A celebration of the third millennium, in contrast, happened at the start of 2000.

6. There had been a very slow and gradual growth of price relative to earnings for thirty years (real earnings grew at the rate of 2.3% a year from July 1871 to July 1900, while prices grew at a slightly faster rate of 3.4% a year).

7. These are geometric average real returns using the S&P Composite Index and the Producer Price Index (since the Consumer Price Index begins in 1913) to convert to real values.

8. See also Ibbotson Associates, *Stocks, Bonds, Bills and Inflation: 1999 Yearbook, Market Results for 1926–1998* (Chicago: Ibbotson Associates, 1999), Tables 2-8 through 2-11, pp. 45–51. When comparing the returns shown here with returns given for similar intervals since 1926 in their book, it must be borne in mind that theirs are for calendar years only, and therefore do not generally catch the peaks or troughs of the market.

9. See John Y. Campbell and Robert J. Shiller, "Valuation Ratios and the Long-Run Stock Market Outlook," *Journal of Portfolio Management*, 24 (1998): 11–26.

10. See Campbell and Shiller, "Valuation Ratios," and my earlier compilation, in *Market Volatility*, of some of our studies.

11. In addition to this long-run tendency toward reversal of trends, there is a shorter-run weak tendency toward momentum, for stock prices to continue

moving in the same direction. See John Y. Campbell, Andrew Lo, and Craig Mackinlay, *The Econometrics of Financial Markets* (Princeton, N.J.: Princeton University Press, 1997); Narasimhan Jegadeesh and Sheridan Titman, "Returns to Buying Winners and Selling Losers: Implications for Stock Market Efficiency," *Journal of Finance,* 48 (1993): 65–91; and Bruce N. Lehmann, "Fads, Martingales, and Market Efficiency," *Quarterly Journal of Economics,* 60 (1990): 1–28.

12. It was shown long ago that dividends tend to behave over time like a long moving average of earnings. See John Lintner, "The Distribution of Incomes of Corporations among Dividends, Retained Earnings and Taxes," *American Economic Review,* 46 (1956): 97–113.

## *Chapter Two Precipitating Factors: The Internet, the Baby Boom, and Other Events*

1. A number of studies of international data have provided evidence that countries with more highly developed financial markets show higher economic growth or allocate resources more efficiently. See Robert G. King and Ross Levine, "Finance and Growth: Schumpeter May Be Right," *Quarterly Journal of Economics,* 108 (1993): 717–37; Rafael LaPorta, Florencio Lopez-de-Silanes, and Andrei Shleifer, "Corporate Ownership around the World," *Journal of Finance,* 54 (1999): 471–518; and Jeffrey Wurgler, "Financial Markets and the Allocation of Capital," unpublished paper, Yale University, 1999.

2. One study finds that individual investors tend to be less heavily invested in stocks during business cycle troughs, when expected returns tend to be high, while institutional investors tend to do the opposite, and hence to work in the direction of stabilizing the market. See Randolph Cohen, "Asset Allocation Decisions of Individuals and Institutions," unpublished paper, Harvard Business School, 1999. A Merrill Lynch survey shows that professional fund managers outside the United States have been generally selling U.S. stocks during bull markets since 1994, but there is no such clear pattern for U.S. fund managers; see Trevor Greetham, Owain Evans, and Charles I. Clough, Jr., "Fund Manager Survey: November 1999" (London: Merrill Lynch & Co., Global Securities Research and Economics Group, 1999).

3. Some simple economic growth models suggest that a sudden technological advance will have no effect on stock prices; for such models see Robert Barro and Xavier Sala-i-Martin, *Economic Growth* (New York: McGraw-Hill, 1995); Olivier Blanchard and Stanley Fischer, *Lectures on Macroeconomics* (Cambridge, Mass.: MIT Press, 1989); or David Romer, *Advanced Macroeconomics* (New York: McGraw-Hill, 1996). For example, the theoretical effect of a sudden technological advance might be to spur investment in new capital, which will compete away any extra profits that the technological advance might generate for existing capital.

4. On November 1, 1999, Microsoft and Intel were added to the Dow Jones Industrial Average.

5. Survey by Roper-Starch Worldwide, cited in Karlyn Bowman, "A Reaffirmation of Self-Reliance? A New Ethic of Self-Sufficiency?" *The Public Perspective,* February-March 1996, pp. 5–8. The plausibility of changes in materialistic values over time is enhanced by evidence of differences in such values across cultures. See Güliz Ger and Russell W. Belk, "Cross-Cultural Differences in Materialism," *Journal of Economic Psychology,* 17 (1996): 55–77.

6. Data from U.S. Bureau of Labor Statistics, Current Population Survey.

7. See J. Nellie Liang and Steven A. Sharpe, "Share Repurchases and Employee Stock Options and Their Implications for S&P 500 Share Retirements and Expected Returns," unpublished paper, Board of Governors of the Federal Reserve System, Washington, D.C., 1999.

8. Ibid. Historical data confirm that dividend payouts tend to be reduced after executive incentive option plans are adopted; see Richard A. Lambert, W. Lanen, and D. Larker, "Executive Stock Option Plans and Corporate Dividend Policy," *Journal of Finance and Quantitative Analysis,* 24 (1985): 409–25.

9. Share repurchases may also have become more popular in recent years because firms with higher earnings do not wish to commit themselves to higher dividends (which investors would then expect to see continued) and because investors are increasingly aware of the tax advantages of share repurchases over dividends. Managers also seem to vary their share repurchases from year to year so as to repurchase when high aggregate stock market returns are coming; therefore the high level of repurchases in recent years might conceivably be explained in terms of managers' anticipating the bull market. For evidence on share repurchases and subsequent returns, see William R. Nelson, "Three Essays on the Ability of the Change in Shares Outstanding to Predict Stock Returns," unpublished Ph.D. dissertation, Yale University, 1999; and Malcolm Baker and Jeffrey Wurgler, "The Equity Share in New Issues and Aggregate Stock Market Return," unpublished paper, Harvard University, 1999.

10. See Joel E. Cohen, "A Global Garden for the Twenty-First Century," *The Key Reporter,* Spring 1998, p. 1.

11. See World Bank, *Averting the Old Age Crisis* (New York: Oxford University Press, 1994).

12. Gurdip S. Bakshi and Zhiwu Chen ("Baby Boom, Population Aging and Capital Markets," *Journal of Business,* 67 [1994]: 165–202) found a substantial correlation between the average age of the U.S. population over age 20 and the real S&P Index, 1950–92. However, Robin Brooks ("Asset Market and Savings Effects of Demographic Transitions," unpublished Ph.D. dissertation, Yale University, 1998) showed that their result was sensitive to the cutoff age (20), and when he

extended their analysis to seven other countries, he found that the fit was poorer. Bakshi and Chen are probably on the right track, but the evidence for a relation between the Baby Boom and the level of the stock market is weak.

13. Economists have argued that given the increase in the stock market recently, savings rates are in fact surprisingly high; see William G. Gale and John Sabelhaus, "Perspectives on the Household Saving Rate," *Brookings Papers on Economic Activity*, 1 (1999): 181–224.

14. See Ronald Inglehart, "Aggregate Stability and Individual-Level Flux in Mass Belief Systems," *American Political Science Review*, 79(1) (1985): 97–116.

15. Richard Parker, "The Media Knowledge and Reporting of Financial Issues," presentation at the Brookings-Wharton Conference on Financial Services, Brookings Institution, Washington, D.C., October 22, 1998.

16. Data courtesy Mitchell Zacks of Zacks Investment Research. According to a *Business Week* article, the change is even more dramatic: in mid-1983, fully 26.8% were sells, 24.5% were buys, and 48.7% were holds. See Jeffrey Laderman, "Wall Street's Spin Game," *Business Week*, October 5, 1998, p. 148.

17. See Hsiou-Wei Lin and Maureen F. McNichols, "Underwriting Relationships, Analysts' Earnings Forecasts and Investment Recommendations," *Journal of Accounting and Economics*, 25(1) (1998): 101–27.

18. See James Grant, "Talking Up the Market," *Financial Times*, July 19, 1999, p. 12. Nevertheless, the analysts' recommendations are still useful if we take account of this bias. Kent Womack ("Do Brokerage Analysts' Recommendations Have Investment Value?" *Journal of Finance*, 51[1] [1996]: 137–67) shows that when analysts' recommendations are switched from hold to buy, the stock does tend to do well afterward, indicating that analysts do have some ability to predict the stocks' returns. When recommendations are switched from hold to sell, the event is even more accurately predictive (of poorer return). Womack interprets this asymmetric effect as indicating that because analysts are reluctant to issue sell recommendations, they do so only when there is a very good reason.

19. See Steven Sharpe, "Stock Prices, Expected Returns and Inflation," unpublished paper, Federal Reserve Board, Washington, D.C., 1999, Figure 1.2. Earnings forecasts are from I/B/E/S and are aggregated from forecasts for individual firms to forecasts of the S&P 500. Sharpe's results do not give any clear evidence that the bias in earnings forecasts has increased since 1979.

20. Public perception of such a downward bias has encouraged the proliferation of "whisper numbers" on the Internet: earnings forecasts with no attributed sources.

21. The tax shelter was written into the Internal Revenue Act of 1978 under Section 401(k), but its applicability to company pension plans was not then clear. R. Theodore Benna, executive vice-president of the Johnson Companies, an

employee benefits consulting firm, tested the IRS by creating the first 401(k) plan in 1981. The IRS announced in February 1982 that the tax benefits of such plans would be allowed.

22. See New York Stock Exchange, *The Public Speaks to the Exchange Community* (New York, 1955).

23. Shlomo Benartzi and Richard H. Thaler, "Naive Diversification Strategies in Defined Contribution Plans," unpublished paper, University of Chicago, 1998.

24. Investment Company Institute, *Mutual Fund Fact Book* (Washington, D.C., 1999), http://www.ici.org.

25. See Hugh Bullock, *The Story of Investment Companies* (New York: Columbia University Press, 1959).

26. See Rudolph Weissman, *The Investment Company and the Investor* (New York: Harper and Brothers, 1951), p. 144.

27. Indeed, the flow of investment dollars into mutual funds seems to bear an important relation to market performance, as mutual fund inflows show an immediate and substantial reaction when the stock market goes up. See Vincent A. Warther, "Aggregate Mutual Fund Flows and Security Returns," *Journal of Financial Economics,* 39 (1995): 209–35; and William Goetzmann and Massimo Massa, "Index Fund Investors," unpublished paper, Yale University, 1999.

28. See my article "Why Do People Dislike Inflation?" in Christina D. Romer and David H. Romer (eds.), *Reducing Inflation: Motivation and Strategy* (Chicago: University of Chicago Press and National Bureau of Economic Research, 1997), pp. 13–65.

29. See Franco Modigliani and Richard A. Cohn, "Inflation, Rational Valuation, and the Market," *Financial Analysts' Journal,* 35 (1979): 22–44; see also Robert J. Shiller and Andrea Beltratti, "Stock Prices and Bond Yields: Can Their Comovements Be Explained in Terms of Present Value Models?" *Journal of Monetary Economics,* 30 (1992): 25–46.

30. Jay R. Ritter and Richard S. Warr ("The Decline of Inflation and the Bull Market of 1982–1997," unpublished paper, University of Florida, Gainesville, 1999) have shown that market misvaluation of individual firms is related both to the level of inflation and to the degree of firm leverage, thus offering evidence in support of the Modigliani-Cohn theory.

31. Public misunderstandings of inflation are described in Eldar Shafir, Peter Diamond, and Amos Tversky, "Money Illusion," *Quarterly Journal of Economics,* 112(2) (1997): 341–74; and Robert J. Shiller, "Public Resistance to Indexation: A Puzzle," *Brookings Papers on Economic Activity,* 1 (1997): 159–211.

32. *New York Stock Exchange Fact Book* (New York, 1998), http://www.nyse.com. Data on shares traded show an even more dramatic increase, but this increase is substantially due to inflation and the increase in the market value, which

together encourage splits and therefore an increase in the total number of shares outstanding.

33. See Gretchen Morgenson, "Investing's Longtime Best Bet Is Being Trampled by the Bulls," *New York Times,* January 15, 2000, p. 1.

34. U.S. Securities and Exchange Commission, "Special Study: On-Line Brokerage: Keeping Apace of Cyberspace," 1999, http://www.sec.gov/pdf/cybrtrnd.pdf.

35. See Kenneth R. French and Richard Roll, "Stock Return Variances: The Arrival of Information and the Reaction of Traders," *Journal of Financial Economics,* 17 (1986): 5–26; see also Richard Roll, "Orange Juice and Weather," *American Economic Review,* 74 (1984): 861–80.

36. See Shlomo Benartzi and Richard H. Thaler, "Myopic Loss Aversion and the Equity Premium Puzzle," *Quarterly Journal of Economics,* 110(1) (1995): 73–92.

37. Data are from the National Gambling Impact Study Commission, *Final Report*, Washington D.C., 1999, http://www.ngisc.gov/reports/exsum_1-7.pdf.

38. See also William N. Thompson, *Legalized Gambling: A Reference Handbook* (Santa Barbara, Calif.: ABC-CLIO, 1994), pp. 52–53.

39. Quantitative evidence on gambling behavior is hard to come by for the 1920s. I counted the number of articles about gambling in the *Reader's Guide to Periodical Literature* and reported the percentage of all articles on the subject, as follows (where I and II denote the first and second halves of the year 1938, respectively):

| | |
|---|---|
| 1919–21 | 0% |
| 1922–24 | 0.004% |
| 1925–28 | 0.021% |
| 1929–32 | 0.035% |
| 1933–35 | 0.006% |
| 1936–38-I | 0.003% |
| 1938-II–42 | 0.008% |

These numbers do strongly suggest a sudden and temporary surge in public interest in gambling between 1925 and 1932, but of course they do not convey anything qualitatively about the nature of changed public attitudes toward gambling. For a history of gambling and its relation to speculation, see James Grant, *The Trouble with Prosperity: A Contrarian Tale of Boom, Bust, and Speculation* (New York: John Wiley and Sons, 1996).

40. The Internet boom, the decline of foreign economic rivals, cultural changes tending to lionize business success, expanded media reporting of financial news, analysts' increasingly optimistic forecasts, the decline of inflation, and the expansion of the volume of stock market trades are all factors in Europe, though often not as strongly felt as in the United States. Although Europe had less of a

post–World War II Baby Boom than the United States, it did have a pronounced Baby Bust after the mid-1960s. Europe does not appear to show the same increase in gambling opportunities evident in the United States. Nevertheless, even though not all of the precipitating factors are operative in Europe, the strong cultural connections between the United States and Europe, and the effects of U.S. investors' demand for European stocks, should cause a substantial contagion effect.

### *Chapter Three Amplification Mechanisms: Naturally Occurring Ponzi Processes*

1. I have been conducting various surveys of investors since the mid-1980s, most notably regular surveys starting in 1989 of institutional investors in both the United States and (with the collaboration of Fumiko Kon-Ya and Yoshiro Tsutsui) Japan. I have surveyed individual investors only intermittently, and I had not thought to ask these questions until 1996. See Robert J. Shiller, "Measuring Bubble Expectations and Investor Confidence," *Journal of Psychology and Markets,* 1(1) (2000): 49–60. Wealthy individuals were surveyed, rather than a random sample of the entire population, because wealthy people have more investments and are more influential in the markets.

2. The sample size is large enough that the standard error on the 96% is only ±2%; standard errors of percentages reported in this section are all less than ±5%. Of course, it is conceivable that the results are unreliable for reasons other than sample size; for example, those who chose to answer the questionnaire might be more likely than others to feel confident about the stock market. On the other hand, those who answer the questionnaire are more likely to be the kind of active investors who influence markets, and so the respondents may be more representative of the investors who are behind the stock market boom than would be a truly random group of wealthy respondents.

3. I have seen evidence of investor overconfidence in real estate markets as well. In a 1988 questionnaire survey of new home buyers in California that I undertook with Karl Case during a housing price boom there, we asked home buyers in Anaheim (a city near Los Angeles) whether they thought that the housing prices in their city would go up or down in the next several years; 98% thought that prices would go up. When asked whether buying a house today entails risk, 63% answered that there was "little or no risk." See Karl E. Case, Jr., and Robert J. Shiller, "The Behavior of Home Buyers in Boom and Post-Boom Markets," *New England Economic Review,* November-December 1988, pp. 29–46. As a matter of fact, housing prices in the Los Angeles area experienced a major bust starting two years after the survey, and now, even after some recovery, prices are still 20% lower in real (inflation-corrected) terms than they were at the time of the survey in 1988 (data from Case Shiller Weiss, Inc.). A 20% decline in real value is approximately

equal to the entire down payment of a typical home buyer. Buying a house then was hardly the riskless investment that most interviewees thought it was.

4. I did not ask on the questionnaire whether they thought the market would surely go down, but available data on expectations show that most do not think so today.

5. I have asked the same question of institutional investors every six months since 1989. There is an upward trend in the percentage of those who predict an increase, but the uptrend has been less dramatic than for individual investors. See Shiller, "Measuring Bubble Expectations and Investor Confidence." In that paper I also discuss other measures of investor confidence and construct an index of investor confidence. The index shows no clear trend among institutional investors since 1989.

6. Frederick Lewis Allen, *Only Yesterday* (New York: Harper and Brothers, 1931), p. 309.

7. David Elias, *Dow 40,000: Strategies for Profiting from the Greatest Bull Market in History* (New York: McGraw-Hill, 1999), p. 8.

8. Dwight R. Lee and Richard B. MacKenzie, "How to (Really) Get Rich in America," *USA Weekend*, August 13–15, 1999, p. 6.

9. Samuel Crowther, "Everybody Ought to Be Rich: An Interview with John J. Raskob," *Ladies Home Journal*, August 1929, pp. 9, 36.

10. Bodo Schäfer, *Der Weg zur finanziellen Freiheit: In sieben Jahren die erste Million* (Frankfurt: Campus Verlag, 1999); Bernd Niquet, *Keine Angst vorm nächsten Crash: Warum Aktien als Langfristanlage unschlagbar sind* (Frankfurt: Campus Verlag, 1999).

11. Robert McGough, "Was Investor Survey a Rush to Judgment?" *Wall Street Journal*, October 27, 1997, p. C23.

12. See David E. Bell, "Regret in Decision Making Under Uncertainty," *Operations Research*, 30(5) (1982): 961–81; and Graham Loomes and Robert Sugden, "Regret Theory: An Alternative Theory of Rational Choice under Uncertainty," *The Economic Journal*, 92 (1982): 805–24.

13. See Richard H. Thaler and Eric J. Johnson, "Gambling with the House Money and Trying to Break Even: The Effect of Prior Outcomes on Risky Choice," *Management Science*, 36 (1990): 643–60.

14. John Kenneth Galbraith, *The Great Crash: 1929*, 2nd ed. (Boston: Houghton Mifflin, 1961), p. 79.

15. Data from the National Association of Investors Corporation Web site, http://www.better-investing.org/member/history.html.

16. See Meir Statman and Steven Thorley, "Overconfidence, Disposition, and Trading Volume," unpublished paper, Santa Clara University, 1999.

17. Brad M. Barber and Terrance Odean, "Online Investors: Do the Slow Die First?" unpublished paper, University of California at Davis, 1999.

18. A psychological theory rationale for such feedback is offered by Nicholas Barberis, Andrei Shleifer, and Robert Vishny, "A Model of Investor Sentiment," *Journal of Financial Economics,* 49 (1998): 307–43.

19. See John Y. Campbell and John H. Cochrane, "By Force of Habit: A Consumption-Based Explanation of Aggregate Stock Market Behavior," *Journal of Political Economy,* 107(2) (1999): 205–51.

20. See Robert J. Shiller, "Market Volatility and Investor Behavior," *American Economic Review,* 80 (1990): 58–62; and Shiller, *Market Volatility,* pp. 376–77.

21. Some economic theorists claim that negative bubbles cannot occur, since prices have a floor at zero; therefore investors know that price cannot fall forever, and they should figure out that a negative bubble cannot even get started. But what they mean to say is that bubbles cannot occur when everyone is rational and calculating—and when everyone assumes that everyone else is rational and calculating.

22. The literature on applications of chaos theory to economics usually does not stress the kind of price feedback model discussed here, but it may nonetheless offer some insights into the sources of complexity in financial markets. See Michael Boldrin and Michael Woodford, "Equilibrium Models Displaying Endogenous Fluctuations and Chaos: A Survey," *Journal of Monetary Economics,* 25(2) (1990): 189–222, for a survey of this literature. See also Benoit Mandelbrot, *Fractals and Scaling in Finance: Discontinuity, Concentration, Risk* (New York: Springer-Verlag, 1997); and Brian Arthur, John H. Holland, Blake LeBaron, Richard Palmer, and Paul Tayler, "Asset Pricing under Endogenous Expectations in an Artificial Stock Market," in W. B. Arthur, S. Durlauf, and D. Lane (eds.), *The Economy as an Evolving Complex System II* (Reading, Mass.: Addison-Wesley, 1997). Another related literature sets up experimental markets in which people trade in an environment that is designed so that there is no news or other confounding factors. In these controlled circumstances there tend to be extraneous "bubble" price movements; see Vernon L. Smith, Gary L. Suchanek, and Arlington W. Williams, "Bubbles, Crashes and Endogenous Expectations in Experimental Spot Asset Markets," *Econometrica,* 56 (1988): 1119–51.

23. Lauren R. Rublin, "Party On! America's Portfolio Managers Grow More Bullish on Stocks and Interest Rates," *Barrons,* May 3, 1999, pp. 31–38.

24. See Joseph Bulgatz, *Ponzi Schemes, Invaders from Mars, and Other Extraordinary Popular Delusions, and the Madness of Crowds* (New York: Harmony, 1992), p. 13.

25. Mike Hinman, "World Plus Pleas: Guilty, Guilty," *Anchorage Daily News,* July 1, 1998, p. 1F; and Bill Richards, "Highflying Ponzi Scheme Angers and Awes Alaskans," *Wall Street Journal,* August 13, 1998, p. B1.

26. John Templeman, "Pyramids Rock Albania," *Business Week,* February 10, 1997, p. 59.

27. Kerin Hope, "Pyramid Finance Schemes," *Financial Times,* February 19, 1997, p. 3; and Jane Perlez, "Albania Calls an Emergency as Chaos Rises," *New York Times,* March 3, 1997, p. A1.

28. Jane Perlez, "Albanians, Cash-Poor, Scheming to Get Rich," *New York Times,* October 27, 1996, p. A9.

29. This willingness to believe may be related to the human tendency for overconfidence discussed in Chapter 7; see also Steven Pressman, "On Financial Frauds and Their Causes: Investor Overconfidence," *American Journal of Economics and Sociology,* 57 (1998): 405–21.

30. The term *no-Ponzi condition* has entered the vocabulary of theoretical finance; however, it refers not to feedback loops but instead to an assumption in their models that investors cannot go deeper and deeper into debt forever.

### *Chapter Four The News Media*

1. No doubt there were speculative price movements before there were newspapers, but I have found no pre-newspaper accounts of widespread public attention to speculative price movements that are described by contemporaries as wild and inexplicable or as due solely to investors' exuberance.

The first regularly published newspapers appeared in the early 1600s. Once publishers discovered how to generate public interest, increase circulation, and make a profit, papers sprung up rapidly in many European cities.

We might date the beginning of the mass media somewhat earlier, to the invention of printing itself, when publication became no longer dependent on patrons. Innumerable pamphlets, broadsides, and religious and political tracts were printed during the 1500s. Historian of printing David Zaret (*Origins of Democratic Culture: Printing, Petitions, and the Public Sphere in Early-Modern England* [Princeton, N.J.: Princeton University Press, 1999], p. 136) notes that "printing put commerce squarely at the center of textual production. Unlike that of scribal production, the economics of text production increasingly involved calculation, risk taking, and other market behaviors in which printers oriented production to vague estimations of popular demand for printed texts." The advent of printing brought with it an increased incentive for literacy; by the 1600s many if not most urban people in Europe could read.

Histories of speculative manias, such as Charles P. Kindlberger, *Manias, Panics and Crashes: A History of Financial Crises,* 2nd ed. (London: Macmillan, 1989) give no examples of speculative bubbles before the 1600s, and my polling of local historians provided none either. However, I cannot claim to have researched their history exhaustively.

Indeed there are probably some stories that *could* be regarded as an exception to my generalization about the coincidence of the first manias and the first newspapers, although other interpretations are also possible. Yale historian Paul Freedman offered me the example of pepper as a possible exception: its price in the spice trade seems at times to have been surprisingly high, and in the 1500s it was very volatile. There are ancient and medieval examples of grain prices soaring at times of famine. Land price movements were also remarked in history. For example, in a letter to Nepos around A.D. 95, Pliny the Younger writes, "Have you heard that the price of land has gone up, particularly in the neighborhood of Rome? The reason for the sudden increase in price has given rise to a good deal of discussion." (Pliny the Younger, *Letters and Panegyrics,* trans. Betty Radice [Cambridge, Mass.: Harvard University Press, 1969], Book 6, No. 19, pp. 437–38.) By saying that there was much discussion, he is suggesting word-of-mouth effects, but he really does not tell a mania story.

2. The tulip mania, a speculative bubble in the price of tulips in Holland in the 1630s, will be discussed in Chapter 9.

There were Dutch newspapers by 1618, and Holland, in contrast to other countries at the time, allowed the printing of domestic news, not just foreign news. On these pioneering Dutch newspapers, see Robert W. Desmond, *The Information Process: World News Reporting to the Twentieth Century* (Iowa City: University of Iowa Press, 1978).

The primary surviving source of information about the tulip mania is a pamphlet published in Holland during its peak. The anonymous 1637 document, in the form of a dialogue between two men, gives detailed news of the speculation as it was then unfolding. Numerous other pamphlets about the mania, published just after its end, also survive; see Peter Garber, *Famous First Bubbles: The Fundamentals of Early Manias* (Cambridge, Mass.: MIT Press, 2000). These surviving pamphlets confirm the existence of well-developed print media capable of disseminating information about the tulip mania as it happened.

3. Transcript 3143, MacNeil/Lehrer NewsHour, WNET/Thirteen, New York, October 14, 1987, p. 10.

4. Victor Niederhoffer, "The Analysis of World News Events and Stock Prices," *Journal of Business,* 44(2) (1971): 205; see also David Cutler, James Poterba, and Lawrence Summers, "What Moves Stock Prices?" *Journal of Portfolio Management,* 15(3) (1989): 4–12.

5. Robert J. Shiller and William J. Feltus, "Fear of a Crash Caused the Crash," *New York Times,* October 29, 1989, Section 3, p. 3, col. 1.

6. Cutler, Poterba, and Summers, "What Moves Stock Prices?" p. 10.

7. That is, there is none unless one counts as substantial President Dwight Eisenhower's heart attack on September 26, 1955.

8. "The Tokyo Earthquake: Not 'If' but 'When,'" *Tokyo Business Today,* April 1995, p. 8.

9. David Santry, "The Long-Shot Choice of a Gambling Guru," *Business Week,* May 12, 1980, p. 112; "The Prophet of Profits," *Time,* September 15, 1980, p. 69.

10. Professors Gur Huberman and Tomer Regev of Columbia University wrote a case study of the soaring price of an individual company's stock in response to a newspaper story that, while compellingly written, actually revealed no news. The share price of EntreMed rose from 12 to 85 from the close of the market the day before to its opening on the day of a front-page *New York Times* story that described the potential of the company's drugs to cure cancer. They document that every fact in the story had already been published five months earlier. (See Gur Huberman and Tomer Regev, "Speculating on a Cure for Cancer: A Non-Event that Made Stock Prices Soar," unpublished manuscript, Columbia University Graduate School of Business, 1999.) It is plausible—although the authors do not document this—that many of the buyers of EntreMed shares on that day knew there was no news in the story, but merely bought thinking that a story that was so well written and featured so prominently would boost the share price.

11. (New Orleans) *Times-Picayune,* October 29, 1929, p. 1, col. 8; *New York Times,* October 29, 1929, p. 1; *Wall Street Journal,* October 29, 1929, p. 1, col. 2.

12. Jude Wanniski, *The Way the World Works,* 2nd ed. (New York: Simon and Schuster, 1983), Chapter 7.

13. Allan H. Meltzer, "Monetary and Other Explanations of the Start of the Great Depression," *Journal of Monetary Economics,* 2 (1976): 460.

14. Rudiger Dornbusch and Stanley Fischer, "The Open Economy: Implications for Monetary and Fiscal Policy," in Robert J. Gordon (ed.), *The American Business Cycle: Continuity and Change* (Chicago: National Bureau of Economic Research and University of Chicago Press, 1986), pp. 459–501.

15. *New York Times,* October 28, 1929, p. 1.

16. *Wall Street Journal,* October 28, 1929, p. 1.

17. O. A. Mather, *Chicago Tribune,* October 27, 1929, p. A1; *New York Times,* October 25, 1929, p. 1, col. 8; Guaranty survey quoted in *New York Times,* October 28, 1929, p. 37, col. 3.

18. The mailing list for individual investors was a list of high-income active investors (active as indicated by such characteristics as subscriptions to investment publications and maintaining accounts with stock brokers) purchased from W. S. Ponton, Inc. The list for institutional investors was compiled from a random sample from the investment managers section of *The Money Market Directory of Pension Funds and Their Investment Managers.* A total of 3,000 questionnaires were sent out during the week of October 19: 2,000 to the individual investors and 1,000 to the institutional investors. There were no follow-up mailings or reminders. I received 605 completed responses from individual investors

and 284 completed responses from institutional investors. See Shiller, *Market Volatility*, pp. 379–402, for the analysis of the results that I wrote in November 1987.

19. Of course, since the questionnaire was filled out *after* the crash, part of this reported concern with overpricing may have been due to hindsight bias. Indeed we cannot completely trust even the self-categorization, into buyers versus sellers on October 19, that respondents made on the questionnaire. The anonymity of the questionnaires, the plea for truthfulness, and the stated purpose of the questionnaire as a tool for scientific research on the crash should all have helped to provide us with more nearly objective answers, but of course no survey results can be trusted completely.

20. Presidential Task Force on Market Mechanisms, *Report of the Presidential Task Force on Market Mechanisms (Brady Commission Report)* (Washington, D.C.: U.S. Government Printing Office, 1988), p. v.

21. Mark L. Mitchell and Jeffrey M. Netter ("Triggering the 1987 Stock Market Crash: Antitakeover Provisions in the Proposed House Ways and Means Tax Bill," *Journal of Financial Economics*, 24 [1989]: 37–68) argue that the news did have an immediate impact on some stocks. It is possible that this news served as a trigger for the crash, as the Brady Commission concludes, by generating initial price decreases, even if the news had been largely forgotten by the day of the crash.

22. Hayne Leland, "Who Should Buy Portfolio Insurance," *Journal of Finance*, 35 (1980): 582.

23. See Robert J. Shiller, "Portfolio Insurance and Other Investor Fashions as Factors in the 1987 Stock Market Crash," in *NBER Macroeconomics Annual* (Cambridge, Mass.: National Bureau of Economic Research, 1988), pp. 287–95.

24. "Repeating the 1920s? Some Parallels but Some Contrasts," *Wall Street Journal*, October 19, 1987, p. 15. This plot was in a box measuring some five inches by ten inches, associated with a story on the same page by Cynthia Crossen, "Market Slide Has Analysts Eating Crow; Justification of Summer Rally Questioned."

### *Chapter Five New Era Economic Thinking*

1. Dean Foust, "Alan Greenspan's Brave New World," *Business Week*, July 14, 1997, pp. 44–50.

2. Aaron Zitner, "Shhhh, Listen: Could That Be the Ghosts of '29?," and Peter Gosselin, "Dow at 10,000: Don't Laugh Yet," *Boston Globe*, June 22, 1997, p. E1; Paul Krugman, "How Fast Can the U.S. Economy Grow?" *Harvard Business Review*, 75 (1997): 123–29.

3. A Nexis search on *new era economics* produced forty-eight stories, all of which included the words *stock market*.

4. See George Katona, *Psychological Economics* (New York: Elsevier, 1975).

5. Alexander Dana Noyes, *Forty Years of American Finance* (New York: G. P. Putnam's Sons, 1909), pp. 300–301.

6. *Boston Post,* January 1, 1901, p. 3.

7. Thomas Fleming, *Around the Pan with Uncle Hank: His Trip through the Pan-American Exposition* (New York: Nutshell, 1901), p. 50.

8. "A Booming Stock Market: Strength of the Underlying Conditions," *New York Daily Tribune,* April 6, 1901, p. 3.

9. A. A. Housman, "Reasons for Confidence," *New York Times,* May 26, 1901, p. v.

10. Allen, *Only Yesterday,* p. 315.

11. Tracy J. Sutliff, "Revival in All Industries Exceeds Most Sanguine Hopes," *New York Herald Tribune,* January 2, 1925, p. 1.

12. John Moody, "The New Era in Wall Street," *Atlantic Monthly,* August 1928, p. 260.

13. Charles Amos Dice, *New Levels in the Stock Market* (New York: McGraw-Hill, 1929), pp. 75–183.

14. Irving Fisher, *The Stock Market Crash—And After* (New York: Macmillan, 1930), pp. 101–74.

15. Craig B. Hazelwood, "Buying Power Termed Basis for Prosperity," *New York Herald Tribune,* January 2, 1929, p. 31.

16. Quoted in *Commercial and Financial Chronicle,* March 9, 1929, p. 1444.

17. "Is 'New Era' Really Here?" *U.S. News and World Report,* May 20, 1955, p. 21.

18. "The Stock Market: Onward and Upward?" *Newsweek,* December 12, 1955, p. 59.

19. "The U.S. Prosperity Today," *Time,* November 28, 1955, p. 15.

20. "The Stock Market: Onward and Upward?" p. 59.

21. "Why Businessmen Are Optimistic," *U.S. News and World Report,* December 23, 1955, p. 18.

22. "Is 'New Era' Really Here?" p. 21.

23. "The New America," *Newsweek,* December 12, 1955, p. 58.

24. "Investors Bet on a Kennedy-Sparked Upturn," *Business Week,* February 4, 1961, p. 84; Dean S. Ammer, "Entering the New Economy," *Harvard Business Review* (1967), pp. 3–4.

25. "Investors Bet on a Kennedy-Sparked Upturn," p. 84; "The Bull Market," *Business Week,* March 18, 1961, p. 142.

26. "Battling Toward 900," *Business Week,* January 23, 1965, p. 26; "Year of the White Chips?" *Newsweek,* February 1, 1965, p. 57; "On Toward 1000," *Time,* January 14, 1966, p. 78.

27. E. S. Browning and Danielle Sessa, "Stocks Pass 10,000 before Slipping Back," *Wall Street Journal,* March 17, 1999, p. C1.

28. This is a geometric average real return on the S&P Composite Index.

29. Michael Mandel, "The Triumph of the New Economy," *Business Week,* December 30, 1996, pp. 68–70.

30. See Michael Bruno and William Easterly, "Inflation Crises and Long-Run Growth," *Journal of Monetary Economics,* 41(1) (1998): 2–26. There are of course complicated issues of timing to consider: a stock market might move down on news that inflation is likely to be higher in the future and then move up again gradually as consumer prices increase. Careful thought about such timing issues is too technical for most public discourse, and therefore the issue will most likely never be resolved in the popular mind (or, for that matter, definitively by economists).

31. Roger Bootle, *The Death of Inflation: Surviving and Thriving in the Zero Era* (London: Nicholas Brealey, 1998), pp. 27, 31.

32. Steven Weber, "The End of the Business Cycle?" *Foreign Affairs,* 76(4) (1997): 65–82.

33. "When the Shoeshine Boys Talk Stocks," *Fortune,* April 15, 1996, p. 99; *U.S. News and World Report,* July 14, 1997, p. 57; *Forbes,* May 18, 1998, p. 325; *Fortune,* June 22, 1998, p. 197.

34. Albert W. Atwood, "Vanished Millions: The Aftermath of a Great Bull Market," *Saturday Evening Post,* September 1921, p. 51.

35. Christina Romer, "The Great Crash and the Onset of the Great Depression," *Quarterly Journal of Economics,* 105 (1990): 597–624.

36. Oscar Lange, "Is the American Economy Contracting?" *American Economic Review,* 29(3) (1939): 503.

37. See Harvey Klehr, *The Heyday of American Communism: The Depression Decade* (New York: Basic Books, 1984).

38. Okun quoted in *Time,* January 14, 1974, p. 61; Burns quoted in *U.S. News and World Report,* June 10, 1974, p. 20.

39. See Bruno and Easterly, "Inflation Crises."

## Chapter Six New Eras and Bubbles around the World

1. The data for thirty of the countries are from the International Monetary Fund, International Financial Statistics. The countries for which data start in January 1957 are Austria, Belgium, Canada, France, Germany, Finland, India, Italy, Japan, the Netherlands, Norway, the Philippines, South Africa, the United States, and Venezuela. The remaining countries from this data source and their starting dates are as follows: Brazil, August 1991; Chile, November 1978; Colombia, October 1963; Denmark, February 1969; Israel, November 1982; Jamaica, July 1969; Korea, January 1978; Luxembourg, January 1980; Mexico, July 1985; Pakistan, July 1960; Peru, September 1989; Portugal, January 1988; Spain, January 1961; Sweden, January 1976; and the United Kingdom, December 1957. The data for the

other six countries are taken from Datastream, and their starting dates are as follows: Australia, March 1973; Hong Kong, July 1974; Indonesia, January 1996; Singapore, February 1986; Taiwan, January 1986; and Thailand, January 1984.

For each country, the monthly stock price index was divided by the consumer price index for the same month to produce a real stock price index. Changes in the real stock price index reported are largest month-to-month changes in the real indexes over the intervals shown, excluding intervals that occurred within three years of each other. Periods of consumer price index inflation greater than 4% a month were excluded, since in times of high inflation inaccuracies of timing or calculation of the consumer price index could cause spurious jumps in stock price indexes.

The tables also show, at the far right, the percentage change in the real stock price index for the period of the same length (twelve months or five years) starting in the month at which the period shown in the table ends. Thus, for example, reading from Table 6.1, we see that the Philippine stock market rose 683.4% in real, inflation-corrected terms from December 1985 to December 1986, and rose another 28.4% from December 1986 to December 1987. For another example, reading from Table 6.4, we see that the Spanish stock market fell 86.6% in real, inflation-corrected terms from December 1974 to December 1979 and then rose 0.1% from December 1979 to December 1984.

2. Note from the rightmost column of Table 6.2 that Korea has had a stock price increase in 1999 that would have placed it again in Table 6.1 had 1999 fallen within our sample for Table 6.1.

3. "Casino Times: After 280% Increase This Year, Taiwan's Stock Market May Be Poised for a Plunge," *Asian Wall Street Journal Weekly,* October 12, 1987.

4. "Obsessed with Numbers, the Taiwanese Are Forsaking Work, Health and Sanity," *Asian Wall Street Journal Weekly,* September 14, 1987.

5. James Brooke, "Venezuela Isn't Exactly Wild for Another Boom," *New York Times,* September 2, 1990, p. IV.3.

6. Eugene Robinson, "As Venezuela Restructures, Even Gas Prices Must Rise," *Toronto Star,* May 21, 1990, p. C6.

7. "Bonanza for Bombay?" *Far Eastern Economic Review,* May 28, 1992, p. 48.

8. *La Repubblica,* quoted by Ruth Graber, "Milan Stock Market Has Gone to the Bulls," *Toronto Star,* May 25, 1986, p. F1.

9. Alan Friedman, "Milan's Bulls Run Wild: Italy's Stock Market Boom," *Financial Times,* March 25, 1986, p. I.25.

10. David Marsh, "The New Appetite for Enterprise: The French Bourse," *Financial Times,* July 4, 1984, p. I.14.

11. Even though the French bull market has been extraordinary, enthusiasm for the stock market does not seem to have invaded French culture as it has the American way of life. See J. Mo, "Despite Exceptional Performance, the Stock Market Does Not Attract the French," *Le Monde,* November 25, 1999, electronic edition.

12. Werner De Bondt and Richard H. Thaler, "Does the Stock Market Overreact?" *Journal of Finance,* 40(3) (1985): 793–805. See Campbell et al., *The Econometrics of Financial Markets,* pp. 27–82, 253–89, for a survey of literature on serial correlation of returns.

13. To judge whether a large price increase (or decrease) portends future increases or decreases, it is tempting to try to use the results shown in the tables alone. One notes, for example, from Table 6.3 that of the twenty episodes whose large price increases occurred long enough ago that we can observe the subsequent five-year price change, thirteen (65%) of the subsequent price changes were down, and the average real price change, averaging over all episodes shown in Table 6.3, was –10%. One notes, too, from Table 6.4, that of the twenty-one episodes whose large price decreases occurred long enough ago that we can observe the subsequent five-year real price change, sixteen (76%) were positive, and the average price increase, averaging over all the episodes shown in Table 6.4, was 130%.

However, there is a problem in interpreting these results as evidence that the markets can be predicted, since we used data subsequent to the five-year intervals shown in the tables to identify the five-year intervals as the largest. To find evidence that markets can be predicted, we must use some method of identifying periods of large price increase that allows these periods to be identified just as they happen. The results shown in the text here use the data that underlie the tables but instead are based on identifying all intervals of the length shown that would make the table. (Let us refer to all such real price changes as *large* changes.) Then, for each large-change interval, we identify a subsequent interval of the same length, which starts in the month that the large-change interval ended. For each country, we computed the average subsequent real price change by averaging over the subsequent price intervals for the country—either intervals subsequent to large-price-increase intervals or intervals subsequent to large-price-decrease intervals. We then report (separately for intervals subsequent to increases and subsequent to decreases) the fraction of countries for which this average is positive, and we report the average over the countries of the country-average real price change.

For example, in Table 6.3, the smallest five-year price increase that makes the table is 230.9% (for Hong Kong, row 25 of the table). For each country for which data made it possible to do so, we identified all sixty-month large-price-increase intervals (sixty-month intervals whose real price increase was 230.9% or more, many of these intervals overlapping with each other), and for each of these intervals we computed the percentage real price change for the subsequent sixty-month interval. We then averaged these percentage real price changes for all of the subsequent intervals for the country, to produce for that country the average subsequent real price change.

The average value reported in the text, the average of these averages over all countries, is the average return one would have received if one had invested equal amounts in all countries after the periods of price change. It should be noted that the differences observed in these averages between intervals subsequent to large price increases and intervals subsequent to large price decreases still do not by themselves positively prove that there is a profit opportunity in investing in countries whose market prices have gone down or in shorting stocks in countries whose market prices have gone up. There are still other issues, concerning possible differences across countries and over time in riskiness, in market returns, or in dividend yields. Furthermore, even though the difference between the five-year subsequent real price changes is highly statistically significant, there is also the issue of a possible bias in my decision to select five-year price intervals to study. These issues are not addressed by the analysis here, and most could not be completely settled with any degree of further analysis of such data. Rigorous and incontrovertible proof that profit opportunities exist has always been elusive in financial research, and it is not so much any one study, but rather the weight of the evidence from years of careful research on market inefficiencies within the finance profession, that inspires confidence that markets are not fully efficient. See Chapter 9 for a further discussion of these issues.

### *Chapter Seven Psychological Anchors for the Market*

1. For a more comprehensive recent survey of the role of psychology in finance, see Hersh Shefrin, *Beyond Greed and Fear: Understanding Behavioral Finance and the Psychology of Investing* (Boston: Harvard Business School Press, 2000); or Andrei Shleifer, *Inefficient Markets: An Introduction to Behavioral Finance* (Oxford: Oxford University Press, 2000).

2. See Amos Tversky and Daniel Kahneman, "Judgment under Uncertainty: Heuristics and Biases," *Science,* 185 (1974): 1124–31.

3. See Robert J. Shiller, "Comovements in Stock Prices and Comovements in Dividends," *Journal of Finance,* 44 (1989): 719–29.

4. See Steven L. Heston and K. Geert Rouwenhorst, "Does Industrial Structure Explain the Benefits of International Diversification?" *Journal of Financial Economics,* 36 (1994): 3–27; John M. Griffin and G. Andrew Karolyi, "Another Look at the Role of Industrial Structure of Markets for International Diversification Strategies," *Journal of Financial Economics,* 50 (1998): 351–73; and Kenneth Froot and Emil Dabora, "How Are Stock Prices Affected by the Location of Trade?" Working Paper W6572 (Cambridge, Mass.: National Bureau of Economic Research, May 1998). Investor attention also appears to be attracted to countries with a common language, as anchoring theory would suggest; see Mark Grinblatt and Matti Keloharju, "Distance Bias, Language Bias, and Investor Sophistication: Results from

Finland," unpublished working paper, University of California at Los Angeles, 1999.

5. See James D. Petersen and Cheng-Ho Hsieh, "Do Common Risk Factors in the Returns on Stocks and Bonds Explain Returns on REITs?" *Real Estate Economics,* 25 (1997): 321–45.

6. Nancy Pennington and Reid Hastie, "Reasoning in Explanation-Based Decision Making," *Cognition,* 49 (1993): 123–63.

7. See D. W. Bolen and W. H. Boyd, "Gambling and the Gambler: A Review of Preliminary Findings," *Archives of General Psychiatry,* 18(5) (1968): 617–29. Gambling provides stimulation and excitement, and people who are attracted to games of risk tend to be people who have a stronger inclination toward sensation seeking; see Marvin Zuckerman, Elizabeth Kolin, Leah Price, and Ina Zoob, "Development of a Sensation-Seeking Scale," *Journal of Consulting Psychology,* 28(6) (1964): 477–82; William F. Straub, "Sensation Seeking among High- and Low-Risk Male Athletes," *Journal of Sports Psychology,* 4(3) (1982): 243–53; and Helen Gilchrist, Robert Povey, Adrian Dickenson, and Rachel Povey, "The Sensation-Seeking Scale: Its Use in a Study of People Choosing Adventure Holidays," *Personality and Individual Differences,* 19(4) (1995): 513–16.

8. See Gideon Keren, "The Rationality of Gambling: Gamblers' Conceptions of Probability, Chance and Luck," in George Wright and Peter Ayton (eds.), *Subjective Probability* (Chichester, England: John Wiley and Sons, 1994), pp. 485–99.

9. See Shlomo Benartzi, "Why Do Employees Invest Their Retirement Savings in Company Stock?" unpublished paper, Anderson School, University of California at Los Angeles, 1999. Benartzi finds that employee investment in company stock is strongly influenced by the return on the company stock over the past ten years. He shows that it is extremely rare for companies to offer discount incentives for employees to buy company stocks, that employees freely make choices to invest in company stock, and that employee decisions to invest in company stock do not reflect superior employee information about the company, since the level of purchases does not predict returns on the stock in the future.

10. Eldar Shafir, Itamar Simonson, and Amos Tversky, "Reason-Based Choice," *Cognition,* 49 (1993): 11–36.

11. Thomas J. Stanley and William D. Danko, *The Millionaire Next Door: The Surprising Secrets of America's Wealthy* (New York: Pocket Books, 1996).

12. Baruch Fischhof, Paul Slovic, and Sarah Lichtenstein, "Knowing with Uncertainty: The Appropriateness of Extreme Confidence," *Journal of Experimental Psychology: Human Perception and Performance,* 3 (1977): 522–64.

13. See G. Gigerenzer, "How to Make Cognitive Illusion Disappear: Beyond 'Heuristic and Biases,'" *European Review of Social Psychology,* 2 (1991): 83–115.

14. See Gordon W. Pitz, "Subjective Probability Distributions for Imperfectly Known Quantities," in Lee W. Gregg (ed.), *Knowledge and Cognition* (Potomac, Md.: Lawrence Erlbaum Associates, 1975), pp. 29–41.

15. See Allan Collins, Eleanor Warnock, Nelleke Acello, and Mark L. Miller, "Reasoning from Incomplete Knowledge," in Daniel G. Bobrow and Allan Collins (eds.), *Representation and Understanding: Studies in Cognitive Science* (New York: Academic Press, 1975), pp. 383–415.

16. See Dagmar Strahlberg and Anne Maass, "Hindsight Bias: Impaired Memory or Biased Reconstruction," *European Review of Social Psychology*, 8 (1998): 105–32.

17. See E. J. Langer, "The Illusion of Control," *Journal of Personality and Social Psychology*, 32 (1975): 311–28; see also G. A. Quattrone and Amos Tversky, "Causal versus Diagnostic Contingencies: On Self-Deception and the Voter's Delusion," *Journal of Personality and Social Psychology*, 46(2) (1984): 237–48.

18. Tversky and Kahneman, "Judgment under Uncertainty."

19. See Nicholas Barberis, Andrei Shleifer, and Robert Vishny, "A Model of Investor Sentiment," *Journal of Financial Economics*, 49 (1998): 307–43. For further theoretical discussions about overconfidence and the stock market, see also Nicholas Barberis, Ming Huang, and Tano Santos, "Prospect Theory and Asset Prices," unpublished paper, University of Chicago, 1999; Kent Daniel, David Hirshleifer, and Avanidhar Subrahmanyam, "Investor Psychology and Security Market Over- and Underreaction," *Journal of Finance*, 53(6) (1998): 1839–86; and Harrison Hong and Jeremy Stein, "A Unified Theory of Underreaction, Momentum Trading, and Overreaction in Asset Markets," working paper, Massachusetts Institute of Technology, Sloan School of Management, 1998.

20. Such ideas are formalized by Paul Milgrom and Nancy Stokey, "Information, Trade, and Common Knowledge," *Econometrica*, 49 (1982): 219–22; and John Geanakoplos, "Common Knowledge," *Journal of Economic Perspectives*, 6(4) (1992): 53–82.

21. Eldar Shafir and Amos Tversky, "Thinking through Uncertainty: Nonconsequential Reasoning and Choice," *Cognitive Psychology*, 24 (1992): 449–74.

## *Chapter Eight Herd Behavior and Epidemics*

1. Solomon Asch, *Social Psychology* (Englewood Cliffs, N.J.: Prentice Hall, 1952), pp. 450–501.

2. Morton Deutsch and Harold B. Gerard, "A Study of Normative and Informational Social Influences upon Individual Judgment," *Journal of Abnormal and Social Psychology*, 51 (1955): 629–36.

3. Stanley Milgram, *Obedience to Authority* (New York: Harper and Row, 1974), pp. 13–54.

4. Milgram noted that subjects believed that the experimenter was an expert who knew more than they did. When he tried a variation of the experiment in which the experimenter was clearly not an expert, he found a much-diminished tendency for subjects to administer the shocks (ibid., pp. 89–112). Nevertheless Milgram, like Asch, did not seem to be aware of an information-based interpretation for his results. He thought that they revealed an "instinct for obedience" that had developed from a general evolutionary principle of the "survival of value hierarchy" (ibid., pp. 123–25).

5. See S. D. Bikhchandani, David Hirshleifer, and Ivo Welch, "A Theory of Fashion, Social Custom and Cultural Change," *Journal of Political Economy,* 81 (1992): 637–54; and Abhijit V. Banerjee, "A Simple Model of Herd Behavior," *Quarterly Journal of Economics,* 107(3) (1992): 797–817.

6. See Christopher Avery and Peter Zemsky, "Multidimensional Uncertainty and Herd Behavior in Financial Markets," *American Economic Review,* 88(4) (1998): 724–48; and In Ho Lee, "Market Crashes and Informational Avalanches," *The Review of Economic Studies,* 65(4) (1998): 741–60.

7. The respondents were drawn from a random sample of high-income individuals in the United States by Survey Sampling, Inc. We coded their answers into ten categories. The percentages of 131 respondents in each category were as follows: (1) friend or relative (13%), (2) worked for company (21%), (3) someone involved with company (3%), (4) broker (33%), (5) spinoff of successful company (2%), (6) IPO–publicity (2%), (7) periodicals–newspapers (6%), (8) customer of company (2%), (9) stock was inherited or a gift (2%), (10) performance of similar company (0%). The remaining answers could not be placed into categories. See Robert J. Shiller and John Pound, "Survey Evidence on the Diffusion of Interest and Information among Investors," *Journal of Economic Behavior and Organization,* 12 (1989): 47–66. If we repeated this study today, we would of course have to include television (which now has extensive business reporting) and the Internet on the list. In *Psychological Economics,* the psychologist-economist George Katona presented evidence that a process of repeated human interaction is needed to promote the kind of "social learning" that spurs people to take action. Robin Barlow and his colleagues found evidence similar to ours, that individual investors usually make decisions after conversations with others; see Robin Barlow, Harvey E. Brazer, and James N. Morgan, *Economic Behavior of the Affluent* (Washington, D.C.: Brookings Institution, 1966).

8. Amy Feldman and Bill Egbert, "Mess of an Invest: Little People in Big Trouble with 1.3 Million Scam," *New York Daily News,* May 27, 1999, p. 5.

9. See A. A. L. Reid, "Comparing Telephone with Face-to-Face Contact," in Ithiel de Sola Poole (ed.), *The Social Impact of the Telephone* (Cambridge, Mass.: MIT Press, 1977), pp. 386–414.

10. Regarding securities fraud in the 1920s and contemporary legislation to limit it, see Emmanuel Stein, *Government and the Investor* (New York: Farrar and Reinhart, 1941).

11. International Data Corporation, "Press Release: New Technologies Make for Better Viewing Experience," http://www.idc.com/Data/Personal/content/PS082399PR.htm, 1999.

12. See Norman T. Bailey, *The Mathematical Theory of Epidemics* (London: C. Griffin, 1957).

13. The logistic curve is $P = 1/(1 + e^{-rt})$, where $P$ is the proportion of the population infected, $r$ is the infection rate per unit of time, and $t$ is time. This expression is a solution to the differential equation $dP/P = r(1 - P)dt$, and $(1 - P)$ is the proportion of the population that is susceptible to infection.

14. Alan Kirman, "Ants, Rationality and Recruitment," *Quarterly Journal of Economics,* 108(1) (1993): 137–56.

15. See David J. Bartholomew, *Stochastic Models for Social Processes* (New York: John Wiley and Sons, 1967).

16. See Tom Burnam, *More Misinformation* (Philadelphia: Lippincott and Crowell, 1980), pp. 20–21.

17. John Kenneth Galbraith laid to rest the suicide myth. The New York suicide rate did, however, rise during the 1930s with the advent of the Great Depression. See Galbraith, *The Great Crash: 1929,* pp. 132–37.

18. The sample sizes were 30 (control) and 40 (experimental); see Shiller and Pound, "Survey Evidence," p. 54.

19. See N. R. F. Maier, "Reasoning in Humans. II. The Solution of a Problem and Its Appearance in Consciousness," *Journal of Comparative Psychology,* 12 (1931): 181–94; see also Robert E. Nisbett and Timothy DeCamp Wilson, "Telling More Than We Can Know: Verbal Reports on Mental Processes," *Psychological Review,* 84(3) (1977): 231–59.

### *Chapter Nine Efficient Markets, Random Walks, and Bubbles*

1. See Eugene Fama, "Efficient Capital Markets: A Review of Empirical Work," *Journal of Finance,* 25 (1970): 383–417.

2. George Gibson, *The Stock Markets of London, Paris and New York* (New York: G. P. Putnam's Sons, 1889), p. 11.

3. Joseph Stagg Lawrence, *Wall Street and Washington* (Princeton, N.J.: Princeton University Press, 1929), p. 179.

4. There does seem to be an advantage to following professional analysts' advice—if one disregards the trading costs associated with following the frequent changes in their opinions. See Womack, "Brokerage Analysts' Recommendations"; and Brad Barber, Reuven Lehavy, Maureen McNichols, and Brett Trueman, "Can

Investors Profit from the Prophets? Consensus Analyst Recommendations and Stock Returns," unpublished paper, University of California at Davis, 1998. The latter argue that, despite transaction costs, "consensus recommendations remain valuable to investors who are otherwise considering buying or selling" (p. 25).

5. Judith Chevalier and Glenn Ellison, "Are Some Mutual Fund Managers Better Than Others? Cross-Sectional Patterns in Behavior and Performance," *Journal of Finance,* 54(3) (1999): 875–99.

6. Andrew Edgecliffe, "eToys Surges after Listing," *Financial Times,* May 21, 1999, p. 29.

7. Although the term *Nifty Fifty* was used earlier, the exact date when the "Nifty Fifty" list was clearly and authoritatively identified appears to be 1977, with the *Forbes* article. However, the article defines the list as the stocks with the highest price-earnings ratio in 1972, whereas Siegel uses 1970 as the starting date for his analysis.

8. Jeremy J. Siegel, *Stocks for the Long Run,* 2nd ed. (New York: McGraw-Hill, 1998), pp. 105–14.

9. Charles Mackay, *Memoirs of Extraordinary Popular Delusions and the Madness of Crowds* (London: Bentley, 1841), p. 142.

10. Peter Garber, *Famous First Bubbles: The Fundamentals of Early Manias* (Cambridge, Mass.: MIT Press, 2000).

11. Siegel, *Stocks for the Long Run,* p. 107.

12. See Jeremy J. Siegel, "Are Internet Stocks Overvalued? Are They Ever," *Wall Street Journal,* April 19, 1999, p. 22. This article appears to have caused a mini-crash in Internet stocks the day it appeared: the NASDAQ, which is heavy on high-tech stocks, dropped 5.6% that day, representing its third largest percentage drop in ten years.

13. Peter Garber, "Tulipmania," *Journal of Political Economy,* 97(3) (1989): 557.

14. Sanjoy Basu, "The Investment Performance of Common Stocks Relative to Their Price-Earnings Ratios: A Test of the Efficient Markets," *Journal of Finance,* 32(3) (1977): 663–82; Eugene Fama and Kenneth French, "The Cross Section of Expected Stock Returns," *Journal of Finance,* 47 (1992): 427–66. Firms' managers also seem to know when their shares are relatively overpriced by the market and tend to issue new equity less often then. Thus firms' equity financing is a negative signal of future returns; see Malcolm Baker and Jeffrey Wurgler, "The Equity Share in New Issues and Aggregate Stock Returns," unpublished paper, Harvard University, 1999.

15. Werner De Bondt and Richard H. Thaler, "Does the Stock Market Overreact?" *Journal of Finance,* 40(3) (1985): 793–805; see also James Poterba and Lawrence Summers, "Mean Reversion in Stock Prices: Evidence and Implications," *Journal of Financial Economics,* 22 (1988): 26–59.

16. Jay R. Ritter, "The Long-Run Performance of Initial Public Offerings," *Journal of Finance*, 46(1) (1991): 3–27.

17. The advertisement quoting Lynch appeared in numerous places, for example in *Mutual Funds*, September 1999, p. 37. The ad says that the data are for the S&P 500 Index, but it does not give the sample period. By searching for the interval of greatest earnings growth, and making no correction for inflation, I can roughly replicate the quoted results. To maximize earnings growth, one chooses a start date right after World War II, when earnings were still depressed by the war, and also at the bottom of the recession in October 1945. Lagging four-quarter-total S&P earnings went up 48-fold from the second quarter of 1946 to the third quarter of 1997. Between June 1946 and April 1998, the S&P 500 went up 60-fold. Lynch's basic result is therefore more or less confirmed for these intervals. But if one chooses other intervals the results look very different. Between the fourth quarter of 1947 and the fourth quarter of 1998, earnings went up only 23-fold, while between December 1947 and April 1999 the S&P 500 went up 83-fold. These slightly different sample periods give a very different impression than that created by the ad: these results show price growing far more than earnings.

Over the period from 1946 to 1997, the producer-price index went up sevenfold, and so in fact real earnings increased only sevenfold in this period. A sevenfold earnings increase is a growth rate of real earnings of about 4% a year. Between the fourth quarter of 1947 and the fourth quarter of 1998, the growth rate of real earnings was only 3% per year. The growth of inflation-corrected earnings over this entire interval has not been impressive: no more than the current rate of interest on inflation-indexed government bonds. But the ad—by choosing sample creatively, by reporting changes over very long time intervals, and by not making an inflation correction—fosters the false impression that enormous price increases are warranted by enormous earnings increases.

18. Robert Barsky and J. Bradford De Long, "Why Have Stock Prices Fluctuated?" *Quarterly Journal of Economics*, 108 (1993): 291–311.

19. Kenneth Froot and Maurice Obstfeld, "Intrinsic Bubbles: The Case of Stock Prices," *American Economic Review*, 81 (1991): 1189–1214. The fit of their "warranted price" to actual price is not much better than the fit of dividends themselves to actual price, except that their model, by making stock prices more responsive to dividends when dividends are higher, makes warranted price correspond more closely to actual price after 1950.

20. A nice review of all these anomalies is found in Siegel, *Stocks for the Long Run*, pp. 254, 259, 91–104, 264–66.

21. The inconstancy of anomalies reported in studies of market efficiency is also due to the varying econometric methodologies employed in the different studies; see Tim Loughran and Jay R. Ritter, "Uniformly Least Powerful Tests of

Market Efficiency," unpublished paper, University of Notre Dame, 1999 (forthcoming in *Journal of Financial Economics* [2000]).

22. Merton Miller, "Behavioral Rationality in Finance: The Case of Dividends," in Robin M. Hogarth and Melvin W. Reder (eds.), *Rational Choice: The Contrast between Economics and Psychology* (Chicago: University of Chicago Press, 1986), p. 283.

23. Robert J. Shiller, "Do Stock Prices Move Too Much to Be Justified by Subsequent Movements in Dividends?" *American Economic Review,* 71(3) (1981): 421–36; Stephen LeRoy and Richard Porter, "Stock Price Volatility: A Test Based on Implied Variance Bounds," *Econometrica,* 49 (1981): 97–113. See also Sanford J. Grossman and Robert J. Shiller, "The Determinants of the Variability of Stock Market Prices," *American Economic Review,* 71 (1981): 222–27.

24. To compute the dividend present value for any given month, one sums over each subsequent month the present discounted value for the given month of the real dividends paid in that subsequent month. The present discounted value in the given month of a real dividend paid in a subsequent month is the real dividend divided by $(1+r)^t$, where $r$ is the monthly real discount rate and $t$ is the number of months between the given month and the subsequent month. The dividend present value in Figure 9.1 was drawn with a constant discount rate $r$ equal to the historical geometric average real monthly return on the market from January 1871 to June 1999, or 0.6% a month. The assumption that $r$ is constant through time corresponds to an efficient markets assumption that expected returns on the market are constant through time, that there are no good or bad times to enter the stock market in terms of predictable returns. Some more sophisticated versions of the efficient markets hypothesis allow $r$ to vary over time, but these versions imply that the returns on the stock market are forecastable. The simple present value computed here is relevant to the most popular, and most important, version of the efficient markets model.

Of course, we do not know now what dividends will be after the latest year for which data are available. To compute the dividend present value, I assumed that real dividends will grow from 1.25 times their December 1999 value at their historical average growth rate from January 1871 to December 1999, which is 0.1% per month. The 1.25 factor makes a rough correction for the fact that dividend payout rates have, in recent years, been about 80% of their historical average payout rate (dividends as a fraction of ten-year moving average earnings). The need to make an assumption about real dividend growth after December 1999 means that the more recent values of the dividend present value shown in the figure are unreliable as indicators of actual dividend present value. However, the numbers given for the dividend present value a couple of decades or more before 2000 are most likely fairly accurate, since for these years the subsequent years after 2000 are heavily discounted in the present value calculations. Even the dividend present value shown in the Figure 9.1 for 2000 is quite possibly fairly accurate, if one accepts that growth possibilities for future dividends are different from those of the past only to the extent that dividend payout is lower.

The series shown in my 1981 article were detrended.

25. It must be stressed that efficient markets theory does not mean that the stock price curve must be more smooth than the dividend present value curve, only that it must be—in a sense that must be carefully defined—less volatile overall. I took great pains to explain this point in my first article on excess volatility; see Robert J. Shiller, "The Volatility of Long-Term Interest Rates and Expectations Models of the Term Structure," *Journal of Political Economy*, 87 (1979): 1062–88. But some critics, overlooking this explanation, thought they were raising a fresh and original idea when they later pointed it out again; see, notably, Allan Kleidon, "Variance Bounds Tests and Stock Price Valuation Models," *Journal of Political Economy*, 94 (1986): 953–1001. No definitive conclusions can be drawn about efficient markets just by looking at this figure. Nonetheless the figure is, I believe, quite informative about the lack of big-picture evidence for efficient markets in aggregate U.S. stock market data. Looking at this figure can help disabuse us of some possibly erroneous notions about the nature of the evidence for market efficiency.

26. Their argument had to do with firms' setting dividends in response to price, and thereby achieving a certain sort of nonstationarity in dividends; see Terry A. Marsh and Robert C. Merton, "Dividend Variability and Variance Bounds Tests for the Rationality of Stock Market Prices," *American Economic Review*, 76(3) (1986): 483–98. In my reply, I argued that although their model was technically correct, it was hardly relevant to actual U.S. experience over the last century; see Robert J. Shiller, "The Marsh-Merton Model of Managers' Smoothing of Dividends," *American Economic Review*, 76(3) (1986): 499–503. The entire debate is now moot, since econometric work testing for excess volatility no longer relies on assumed stationarity for dividends; see, for example, John Y. Campbell and John Ammer, "What Moves Stock and Bond Markets? A Variance Decomposition for Long-Term Asset Returns," *Journal of Finance*, 48(1) (1993): 3–38.

27. Campbell and I developed a co-integrated log-linear vector-autoregressive model that was capable of representing various forms of the efficient markets model. See John Y. Campbell and Robert J. Shiller, "The Dividend-Price Ratio and Expectations of Future Dividends and Discount Factors," *Review of Financial Studies*, 1 (1988): 195–228; Shiller, *Market Volatility*; and Campbell et al., *Econometrics of Financial Markets*, pp. 253–337.

28. See Campbell and Shiller, "The Dividend-Price Ratio."

29. See Campbell and Ammer, "What Moves Stock and Bond Markets?"

30. See Shiller, *Market Volatility*, pp. 197–214.

31. Concern has been expressed recently that measured dividends in the 1990s may understate cash flow from the firm to investors. Kevin Cole, Jean Helwege, and David Laster ("Stock Market Valuation Indicators: Is This Time Different?" *Financial Analysts Journal,* 52 [1996]: 56–64) estimate that considering share repurchase as a form of dividend would raise dividend-price ratios in the mid-1990s by about 80 basis points. This adjustment would still leave dividend-price ratios on the S&P Composite far below their record historic lows until now. Liang and Sharpe, "Share Repurchases and Employee Stock Options," point out that the Cole et al. assumption that share issues occur at market prices is inaccurate because many issues come about in response to the exercise of employee stock options. Consideration of the fact that issues are made below market price might be interpreted as suggesting lowering the terminal value for the dividend present value below the amount shown in Figure 9.1.

## *Chapter Ten Investor Learning—And Unlearning*

1. Economists have long puzzled over why the equity premium has been so high historically. How, they wonder, can it be that over the years people haven't invested more in stocks, given that stocks so outperform other investments? See Raj Mehra and Edward C. Prescott, "The Equity Premium Puzzle," *Journal of Monetary Economics,* 15 (1988): 145–61. According to the learning theory discussed in this chapter, the equity premium puzzle is supposed to be a thing of the past—people have finally wised up.

2. Edgar Lawrence Smith, *Common Stocks as Long-Term Investments* (New York: Macmillan, 1924).

3. Kenneth S. Van Strum, *Investing in Purchasing Power* (Boston: Barrons, 1925).

4. Fisher, *Stock Market Crash,* pp. 202, 99. It is puzzling that he includes the phrase "during a period of dollar depreciation," since he emphasizes elsewhere in the book that the 1920s were a period of exceptionally stable prices. Perhaps he meant to say "even during a period of dollar depreciation" and may have been referring to one of the periods in the 1920s when there was slight inflation. He cannot be referring to the exchange rate of the dollar, since we were then on the gold standard.

5. Dice, *New Levels in the Stock Market,* p. 126.

6. Franklin L. Dame, "Public Interest in Business Is Found Growing," *New York Herald Tribune,* January 2, 1929, p. 30.

7. Siegel, *Stocks for the Long Run,* p. 15.

8. See Ibbotson Associates, *Stocks, Bonds, Bills and Inflation,* Table 2-9, p. 46, or consult the data on my Web site, http://www.econ.yale.edu/~shiller.

9. According to data shown in Ibbotson Associates, *Stocks, Bonds, Bills and Inflation,* Table 2-11, p. 50, there has been no twenty-year period since 1926 when stocks underperformed short-term interest rates. They do not show data on the 1901–21

time period. My data, from my book *Market Volatility* (updated by using the Consumer Price Index to measure inflation after 1913), actually show a slight underperformance of stocks versus short-term interest rates for 1966–86 as well as 1901–21, and the difference in results between my data and Ibbotson's for 1966–86 can be attributed to a difference in the short-term interest rate (commercial paper versus Treasury bills) and slight differences in timing.

10. See Philippe Jorion and William N. Goetzmann, "Global Stock Markets in the Twentieth Century," *Journal of Finance*, 54(3) (1999): 953–80, and also Stephen J. Brown, William N. Goetzmann, and Stephen A. Ross, "Survival," *Journal of Finance*, 50(3) (1995): 853–73. Jeremy Siegel points out that with financial returns the median is generally much lower than the mean, and the mean appreciation rate over all these countries is not so low.

11. James K. Glassman and Kevin A. Hassett, "Are Stocks Overvalued? Not a Chance," *Wall Street Journal*, March 30, 1998, p. 18, and "Stock Prices Are Still Far Too Low," March 17, 1999, p. 26; the quote is from the 1999 article.

12. James K. Glassman and Kevin Hassett, *Dow 36,000: The New Strategy for Profiting from the Coming Rise in the Stock Market* (New York: Times Business/Random House, 1999), p. 140.

13. See, for example, William Goetzmann and Roger Ibbotson, "Do Winners Repeat? Patterns in Mutual Fund Performance," *Journal of Portfolio Management*, 20 (1994): 9–17; Edwin J. Elton, Martin Gruber, and Christopher R. Blake, "Survivorship Bias and Mutual Fund Performance," *Review of Financial Studies*, 9(4) (1996): 1097–120; and "The Persistence of Risk-Adjusted Mutual Fund Performance," *Journal of Business*, 69 (1996): 133–37.

14. To the extent that mutual funds make better diversification possible for individual investors, they lower the riskiness of stocks, and therefore the proliferation of mutual funds may lower the risk premium that investors require. John Heaton and Deborah Lucas conclude that increased diversification "goes at least half way towards justifying the current high price dividend ratio in the United States." Heaton and Lucas raise a valid and potentially significant issue; nevertheless their theory is a little unsatisfying, as it depicts individuals as completely rational at all times but does not explain why people did not invest that much in mutual funds until recently. See John Heaton and Deborah Lucas, "Stock Prices and Fundamentals," unpublished paper, Northwestern University, 1999.

### Chapter Eleven Speculative Volatility in a Free Society

1. One might expect to see some offset of the low dividend yield to the extent that share repurchases are substituting for dividends (recall the discussion in Chapter 2). But with annual net share repurchases on the order of 1% of shares, dividend yields are still very low even after accounting for repurchases.

2. "Internet Users Now Exceed 100 Million," *New York Times*, November 11, 1999, p. C8.

3. See Forrester Research, "Net Investing Goes Mainstream," http://www.forrester.com/ER/Research/Report/Analysis/0,1338,5876,FF.html, 1999.

4. See Ray C. Fair, "How Much Is the Stock Market Overvalued?" unpublished paper, Cowles Foundation, Yale University, 1999.

5. See William D. Nordhaus and Joseph G. Boyer, "Requiem for Kyoto: An Economic Analysis of the Kyoto Protocol," Cowles Foundation Discussion Paper 1201 (New Haven, Conn.: Yale University, November 1998).

6. Data on values of housing over time can be inferred for each state from home price indexes, home ownership rates, numbers of households, and census median prices on benchmark dates. The inferred national value can then be compared with stock market capitalization. See Karl E. Case and Robert J. Shiller, "The Stock Market, the Housing Market, and Consumer Spending," paper presented at the American Economic Association–American Real Estate and Urban Economics Association meetings, Boston, January 9, 2000.

7. Advisory Committee on Endowment Management, *Managing Educational Endowments: Report to the Ford Foundation* (Barker Report) (New York: Ford Foundation, 1969); Kathleen Teltsch, "Streamlining the Ford Foundation," *New York Times*, October 10, 1982, p. 41. The impact of the 1973–74 stock market crash on the endowments of Harvard, Rochester, and Yale is discussed in Andrew Tobias, "The Billion-Dollar Harvard-Yale Game," *Esquire*, December 19, 1978, pp. 77–85. This article appears to be the source of the oft-repeated story that Yale responded to the 1969 Ford Foundation report by investing its endowment heavily in the stock market just before the 1973–74 crash and then suffered greatly. But if one reads the Tobias story carefully one sees that his own data do not support such a conclusion. In fact, although it suffered in the 1973–74 crash, Yale did not increase its level of investment in the stock market after the Ford Foundation report, and the exposure of the Yale endowment to stock market risk was actually reduced just before the 1973–74 crash.

8. Christine Triano, *Private Foundations and Public Charities: Is It Time to Increase Payout?* National Network of Grantmakers, 1999, http://www.nng.org/html/ourprograms/campaign/payoutppr_table.html#fulltext.

9. I have tried to understand the failure of the public to be very interested in indexing their contracts. The reason appears to be tied up with money illusion, a tendency to see the currency as the ultimate indicator of value (see Chapter 2), and with a failure to appreciate the risks of price level change, along with a mistrust of formulas and price indexes; see Robert J. Shiller, "Public Resistance to Indexation: A Puzzle," *Brookings Papers on Economic Activity*, 1 (1997): 159–211.

10. See Jack VanDerhei, Russell Galer, Carol Quick, and John Rea, "401(k) Plan Asset Allocation, Account Balances, and Loan Activity," *Perspective* (Investment

Company Institute, Washington, D.C.), 5(1) (1999): 2. Results are based on a sample that covers 6.6 million active participants.

11. According to the ICI/EBRI study (VanDerhei et al., "401(k) Plan Asset Allocation"), 24.5% of the participants in the 1996 sample had 80% or more of their plan balances invested in equity funds. This figure underestimates their exposure to the stock market, since the category of equity funds excludes investments in their own company's stock and exposure to the stock market from balanced funds. According to a TIAA-CREF study of its own participants' premium allocations, the percentage of participants who allocate 100% to equities has risen almost monotonically from 1986 to 1996, from 3.3% of participants in 1986 to 22.2% in 1996. More recently, according to data provided to me by John Ameriks, the percent allocating 100% to equities has risen to 28.8% as of June 1999. See John Ameriks, Francis P. King, and Mark Warshawsky, "Premium Allocations and Accumulations in TIAA-CREF—Trends in Participant Choices among Asset Classes and Investment Accounts," *TIAA-CREF Research Dialogues,* 51 (1997): 2.

12. For an analysis of the assets of retirees, see Alan L. Gustman and Thomas L. Steinmeier, "Effects of Pensions on Savings: Analysis with Data from the Health and Retirement Survey," *Carnegie Rochester Conference Series on Public Policy,* 50 (1999): 271–324.

13. See U.S. Department of Labor, Pension and Welfare Benefits Administration, "Participant Investment Education: Final Rule," 29 CFR Part 2509, Interpretive Bulletin 96-1, *Federal Register,* 61(113) (1996): 29,585–90, http://www.dol.gov/dol/pwba/public/regs/fedreg/final/96_14093.htm.

14. See Robert J. Shiller, "Social Security and Institutions for Intergenerational, Intragenerational and International Risk Sharing," *Carnegie Rochester Conference Series on Public Policy,* 50 (1999): 165–204.

15. There is of course also the issue, if we were to switch to a defined contribution Social Security plan, of who would pay for the existing obligations to the currently retired; see John Geanakoplos, Olivia S. Mitchell, and Stephen P. Zeldes, "Social Security Money's Worth," in Olivia S. Mitchell, Robert J. Myers, and Howard Young (eds.), *Prospects for Social Security Reform* (Philadelphia: University of Pennsylvania Press, 1999), pp. 79–151.

16. See Shiller, "Social Security and Institutions."

17. These events are described in Yukio Noguchi, *Baburu no Keizaigaku (Bubble Economics)* (Tokyo: Nihon Keizai Shimbun Sha, 1992). To suppose that the bubble would not have burst even without the monetary policy is also reasonable, and there were changes in speculative expectations that suggest other origins of the Japanese stock market decline; see Robert J. Shiller, Fumiko Kon-Ya, and Yoshiro Tsutsui, "Why Did the Nikkei Crash? Expanding the Scope of Expectations Data Collection," *Review of Economics and Statistics,* 78(1) (1996): 156–64.

18. See Barry Eichengreen, *Golden Fetters: The Gold Standard and the Great Depression: 1919–1939* (New York: Oxford University Press, 1992), Table 12.1, p. 351.

19. "Courtelyou puts in $25,000,000," *New York Times*, October 24, 1907, p. 1; "Worst Stock Crash Stemmed by Banks, *New York Times*, October 25, 1929, p. 1.

20. "Will History Repeat the '29 Crash?" *Newsweek*, June 14, 1965, p. 78.

21. The closing came in response to closings of the European stock exchanges at the outbreak of World War I and panic selling by Europeans on the exchange. The New York Stock Exchange was the only major stock market still open at the end of July 1914, the only place where stocks could still be converted into cash, and that was thought to be an untenable situation. There might well have been a world stock market crash of record proportions at that time, but we will never know, since it was forestalled by the market closings.

22. See James Tobin, "The New Economics One Decade Older," in *The Eliot Janeway Lectures on Historical Economics in Honor of Joseph Schumpeter* (Princeton, N.J.: Princeton University Press, 1974); James Tobin, "A Proposal for International Monetary Reform," *Eastern Economic Journal*, 4 (1978): 153–59; and Barry Eichengreen, James Tobin, and Charles Wyplosz, "Two Cases for Sand in the Wheels of International Finance," *Economic Journal*, 105 (1995): 162–72. Mahbub ul Haq, Inge Kaul, and Isabelle Grunberg have edited a volume (*The Tobin Tax: Coping with Financial Volatility* [New York: Oxford University Press, 1996]) of papers commenting on the Tobin proposal.

23. Lawrence H. Summers and Victoria P. Summers, "When Financial Markets Work Too Well: A Cautious Case for a Securities Transactions Tax," *Journal of Financial Services Research*, 3(2–3) (1988): 163–88.

24. See Jeffrey Frankel, *On Exchange Rates* (Cambridge, Mass.: MIT Press, 1993) and "How Well Do Foreign Exchange Markets Work: Might a Tobin Tax Help?" in ul Haq et al., *The Tobin Tax*, pp. 41–81.

25. See Shiller, "Measuring Bubble Expectations."

26. See Richard Roll, "Price Volatility, International Market Links, and Their Implication for Regulatory Policies," *Journal of Financial Services Research*, 2(2–3) (1989): 211–46.

27. See Shiller et al., "Why Did the Nikkei Crash?"

28. Michael Brennan, "Stripping the S&P 500," *Financial Analysts' Journal*, 54(1) (1998): 14.

29. Robert Shiller, *Macro Markets: Creating Institutions for Managing Society's Largest Economic Risks* (Oxford: Oxford University Press, 1993). I have been working with my colleague Allan Weiss and others at my firm, Case Shiller Weiss, Inc., to develop certain of these new markets. See Karl E. Case, Robert J. Shiller, and Allan N. Weiss, "Index-Based Futures and Options Trading in Real Estate," *Journal of Portfolio Management*, 19(2) (1993): 83–92; Robert J. Shiller and Allan N.

Weiss, "Home Equity Insurance," *Journal of Real Estate Finance and Economics,* 19 (1999): 21–47; and Robert J. Shiller and Allan N. Weiss, "Moral Hazard in Home Equity Conversion," forthcoming in *Real Estate Economics* (2000).

30. Shiller, *Macro Markets,* pp. 42–46. For a description of the macro securities (proxy assets) system that Allan Weiss and I devised, see our patent 5,987,435 (Proxy Asset Data Processor) at http://www.uspto.gov/patft/. Macro Securities LLC, a subsidiary of Case Shiller Weiss, Inc., is developing these securities.

31. Stefano Athanasoulis and I have proposed creating first a market for a long-term claim on the combined national incomes of all the nations of the world ("The Significance of the Market Portfolio," forthcoming in *Review of Financial Studies* [2000]). By investing in it, one would have a totally diversified portfolio, the so-called true "market portfolio" that finance theorists only dream about. Younger working people and people who are less risk averse may short this market, and elderly people who are no longer working can take long positions, thereby living off a completely diversified portfolio in their retirement.

32. See Marianne Baxter and Urban Jermann, "The International Diversification Puzzle Is Worse Than You Think," *American Economic Review,* 87 (1997): 170–80.

33. Athanasoulis and I show, using a theoretical finance model calibrated with real data, that proper management of national income risks alone can have large effects on economic welfare. See Stefano Athanasoulis and Robert J. Shiller, "World Income Components: Discovering and Implementing Risk Sharing Opportunities," unpublished paper, Yale University, 1999.

34. See Shiller and Weiss, "Home Equity Insurance."

# *References*

Advisory Committee on Endowment Management. *Managing Educational Endowments: Report to the Ford Foundation* (Barker Report). New York: Ford Foundation, 1969.

Allen, Frederick Lewis. *Only Yesterday.* New York: Harper and Brothers, 1931.

Ameriks, John, Francis P. King, and Mark Warshawsky. "Premium Allocations and Accumulations in TIAA-CREF—Trends in Participant Choices among Asset Classes and Investment Accounts." *TIAA-CREF Research Dialogues,* 51 (July 1997).

Ammer, Dean S. "Entering the New Economy," *Harvard Business Review,* September-October 1967, pp. 3–4.

Arthur, Brian, John H. Holland, Blake LeBaron, Richard Palmer, and Paul Tayler. "Asset Pricing under Endogenous Expectations in an Artificial Stock Market," in W. B. Arthur, S. Durlauf, and D. Lane (eds.), *The Economy as an Evolving Complex System II.* Reading, Mass.: Addison-Wesley, 1997.

Asch, Solomon. *Social Psychology.* Englewood Cliffs, N.J.: Prentice Hall, 1952.

Athanasoulis, Stefano, and Robert J. Shiller. "World Income Components: Discovering and Implementing Risk Sharing Opportunities." Unpublished paper, Yale University, 1999.

———. "The Significance of the Market Portfolio." *Review of Financial Studies,* forthcoming, 2000.

Avery, Christopher, and Peter Zemsky. "Multidimensional Uncertainty and Herd Behavior in Financial Markets." *American Economic Review,* 88(4) (1998): 724–48.

Bailey, Norman T. *The Mathematical Theory of Epidemics.* London: C. Griffin, 1957.

Baker, Malcolm, and Jeffrey Wurgler. "The Equity Share in New Issues and Aggregate Stock Market Return." Unpublished paper, Harvard University, 1999.

Bakshi, Gurdip S., and Zhiwu Chen. "Baby Boom, Population Aging and Capital Markets." *Journal of Business,* 67 (1994): 165–202.

Banerjee, Abhijit V. "A Simple Model of Herd Behavior." *Quarterly Journal of Economics,* 107(3) (1992): 797–817.

Barber, Brad M., and Terrance Odean. "Online Investors: Do the Slow Die First?" Unpublished paper, University of California at Davis, 1999.

Barberis, Nicholas, Ming Huang, and Tano Santos. "Prospect Theory and Asset Prices." Unpublished paper, University of Chicago, 1999.

Barberis, Nicholas, Andrei Shleifer, and Robert Vishny. "A Model of Investor Sentiment." *Journal of Financial Economics,* 49 (1998): 307–43.

Barlow, Robin, Harvey E. Brazer, and James N. Morgan. *Economic Behavior of the Affluent.* Washington, D.C.: Brookings, 1966.

Barro, Robert, and Xavier Sala-i-Martin. *Economic Growth.* New York: McGraw-Hill, 1995.

Barsky, Robert, and J. Bradford De Long. "Why Have Stock Prices Fluctuated?" *Quarterly Journal of Economics,* 108 (1993): 291–311.

Bartholomew, David J. *Stochastic Models for Social Processes.* New York: John Wiley and Sons, 1967.

Basu, Sanjoy. "The Investment Performance of Common Stocks Relative to Their Price-Earnings Ratios: A Test of the Efficient Markets." *Journal of Finance,* 32(3) (1977): 663–82.

Batra, Ravi. *The Great Depression of 1990: Why It's Got to Happen, How to Protect Yourself,* rev. ed. New York: Simon & Schuster, 1987.

Baxter, Marianne, and Urban Jermann. "The International Diversification Puzzle Is Worse Than You Think," *American Economic Review,* 87 (1997): 177–80.

Bell, David E. "Regret in Decision Making under Uncertainty." *Operations Research,* 30(5) (1982): 961–81.

Benartzi, Shlomo. "Why Do Employees Invest Their Retirement Savings in Company Stock?" Unpublished paper, Anderson School, University of California, Los Angeles, 1999.

Benartzi, Shlomo, and Richard H. Thaler. "Myopic Loss Aversion and the Equity Premium Puzzle." *Quarterly Journal of Economics,* 110(1) (1995): 73–92.

———. "Naive Diversification Strategies in Defined Contribution Plans." Unpublished paper, University of Chicago, 1998.

Bikhchandani, S. D., David Hirshleifer, and Ivo Welch. "A Theory of Fashion, Social Custom and Cultural Change." *Journal of Political Economy*, 81 (1992): 637–54.

Blanchard, Olivier, and Stanley Fischer. *Lectures on Macroeconomics*. Cambridge, Mass.: MIT Press, 1989.

Boldrin, Michael, and Michael Woodford. "Equilibrium Models Displaying Endogenous Fluctuations and Chaos: A Survey." *Journal of Monetary Economics*, 25(2) (1990): 189–222.

Bolen, D. W., and W. H. Boyd. "Gambling and the Gambler: A Review of Preliminary Findings." *Archives of General Psychiatry*, 18(5) (1968): 617–29.

Bootle, Roger. *The Death of Inflation: Surviving and Thriving in the Zero Era*. London: Nicholas Brealey, 1998.

Bowman, Karlyn. "A Reaffirmation of Self-Reliance? A New Ethic of Self-Sufficiency?" *The Public Perspective*, February-March 1996, pp. 5–8.

Brennan, Michael. "Stripping the S&P 500." *Financial Analysts' Journal*, 54(1) (1998): 12–22.

Brooks, Robin. "Asset Market and Savings Effects of Demographic Transitions." Unpublished Ph.D. dissertation, Yale University, 1998.

Brown, Stephen J., William Goetzmann, and Stephen Ross. "Survival." *Journal of Finance*, 50 (1995): 583–73.

Bruno, Michael, and William Easterly. "Inflation Crises and Long-Run Growth." *Journal of Monetary Economics*, 41(1) (1998): 2–26.

Bulgatz, Joseph. *Ponzi Schemes, Invaders from Mars, and Other Extraordinary Popular Delusions, and the Madness of Crowds*. New York: Harmony, 1992.

Bullock, Hugh. *The Story of Investment Companies*. New York: Columbia University Press, 1959.

Burnam, Tom. *More Misinformation*. Philadelphia: Lippincott and Crowell, 1980.

Campbell, John Y., and John Ammer. "What Moves Stock and Bond Markets? A Variance Decomposition for Long-Term Asset Returns." *Journal of Finance*, 48(1) (1993): 3–38.

Campbell, John Y., and John H. Cochrane. "By Force of Habit: A Consumption-Based Explanation of Aggregate Stock Market Behavior." *Journal of Political Economy*, 107(2) (1999): 205–51.

Campbell, John Y., Andrew Lo, and Craig Mackinlay. *The Econometrics of Financial Markets*. Princeton, N.J.: Princeton University Press, 1997.

Campbell, John Y., and Robert J. Shiller. "The Dividend-Price Ratio and Expectations of Future Dividends and Discount Factors." *Review of Financial Studies*, 1 (1988): 195–228.

———. "Valuation Ratios and the Long-Run Stock Market Outlook." *Journal of Portfolio Management*, 24 (1998): 11–26.

Case, Karl E., Jr., and Robert J. Shiller. "The Behavior of Home Buyers in Boom and Post-Boom Markets." *New England Economic Review,* November-December 1988, pp. 29–46.

Case, Karl E., Robert J. Shiller, and Allan N. Weiss. "Index-Based Futures and Options Trading in Real Estate." *Journal of Portfolio Management,* 19(2) (1993): 83–92.

Chevalier, Judith, and Glenn Ellison. "Are Some Mutual Fund Managers Better Than Others? Cross-Sectional Patterns in Behavior and Performance." *Journal of Finance,* 54(3) (1999): 875–99.

Cohen, Randolph. "Asset Allocation Decisions of Individuals and Institutions." Unpublished paper, Harvard Business School, 1999.

Cole, Kevin, Jean Helwege, and David Laster. "Stock Market Valuation Indicators: Is This Time Different?" *Financial Analysts Journal,* 52 (1996): 56–64.

Collins, Allan, Eleanor Warnock, Nelleke Acello, and Mark L. Miller. "Reasoning from Incomplete Knowledge," in Daniel G. Bobrow and Allan Collins (eds.), *Representation and Understanding: Studies in Cognitive Science.* New York: Academic Press, 1975, pp. 383–415.

Cowles, Alfred III, and associates. *Common Stock Indexes,* 2nd ed. Bloomington, Ind.: Principia Press, 1939.

Cutler, David, James Poterba, and Lawrence Summers. "What Moves Stock Prices?" *Journal of Portfolio Management,* 15(3) (1989): 4–12.

Daniel, Kent, David Hirshleifer, and Avanidhar Subrahmanyam. "Investor Psychology and Security Market Over- and Underreaction." *Journal of Finance,* 53(6) (1998): 1839–86.

De Bondt, Werner, and Richard H. Thaler. "Does the Stock Market Overreact?" *Journal of Finance,* 40(3) (1985): 793–805.

Dent, Harry S. *The Great Boom Ahead: Your Comprehensive Guide to Personal and Business Profit in the New Era of Prosperity.* New York: Hyperion, 1993.

———. *The Roaring 2000s: Building the Wealth & Lifestyle You Desire in the Greatest Boom in History.* New York: Simon & Schuster, 1998.

———. *The Roaring 2000s Investor: Strategies for the Life You Want.* New York: Simon & Schuster, 1999.

Desmond, Robert W. *The Information Process: World News Reporting to the Twentieth Century.* Iowa City: University of Iowa Press, 1978.

Deutsch, Morton, and Harold B. Gerard. "A Study of Normative and Informational Social Influences upon Individual Judgment." *Journal of Abnormal and Social Psychology,* 51 (1955): 629–36.

Dice, Charles Amos. *New Levels in the Stock Market.* New York: McGraw-Hill, 1929.

Diggins, John Patrick. *The Proud Decades: America in War and in Peace 1941–1960.* New York: W. W. Norton, 1988.

Dornbusch, Rudiger, and Stanley Fischer. "The Open Economy: Implications for Monetary and Fiscal Policy," in Robert J. Gordon (ed.), *The American Business Cycle: Continuity and Change.* Chicago: National Bureau of Economic Research and University of Chicago Press, 1986, pp. 459–501.

Eichengreen, Barry. *Golden Fetters: The Gold Standard and the Great Depression: 1919–1939.* New York: Oxford University Press, 1992.

Eichengreen, Barry, James Tobin, and Charles Wyplosz. "Two Cases for Sand in the Wheels of International Finance." *Economic Journal,* 105 (1995): 162–72.

Elias, David. *Dow 40,000: Strategies for Profiting from the Greatest Bull Market in History.* New York: McGraw-Hill, 1999.

Elton, Edwin J., Martin Gruber, and Christopher R. Blake. "Survivorship Bias and Mutual Fund Performance." *Review of Financial Studies,* 9(4) (1996): 1097–1120.

———. "The Persistence of Risk-Adjusted Mutual Fund Performance," *Journal of Business,* 69 (1996): 133–37.

Fair, Ray C. "How Much Is the Stock Market Overvalued?" Unpublished paper, Cowles Foundation, Yale University, 1999.

Fama, Eugene. "Efficient Capital Markets: A Review of Theory and Empirical Work." *Journal of Finance,* 25 (1970): 383–417.

Fama, Eugene, and Kenneth French. "The Cross Section of Expected Stock Returns." *Journal of Finance,* 47 (1992): 427–66.

Fischhof, Baruch, Paul Slovic, and Sarah Lichtenstein. "Knowing with Uncertainty: The Appropriateness of Extreme Confidence." *Journal of Experimental Psychology: Human Perception and Performance,* 3 (1977): 522–64.

Fisher, Irving. *The Stock Market Crash—And After.* New York: Macmillan, 1930.

Fleming, Thomas. *Around the Pan with Uncle Hank: His Trip through the Pan-American Exposition.* New York: Nutshell, 1901.

Foot, David K., and Daniel Stoffman. *Boom, Bust & Echo: How to Profit from the Coming Demographic Shift.* Toronto: McFarlane, Walter & Ross, 1996.

Frankel, Jeffrey. *On Exchange Rates.* Cambridge, Mass.: MIT Press, 1993.

———. "How Well Do Foreign Exchange Markets Work: Might a Tobin Tax Help?" in Mahbub ul Haq, Inge Kaul, and Isabelle Grunberg (eds.), *The Tobin Tax: Coping with Financial Volatility.* New York: Oxford University Press, 1996, pp. 41–81.

French, Kenneth R., and Richard Roll. "Stock Return Variances: The Arrival of Information and the Reaction of Traders." *Journal of Financial Economics,* 17 (1986): 5–26.

Froot, Kenneth, and Emil Dabora. "How Are Stock Prices Affected by the Location of Trade?" Working Paper W6572. Cambridge, Mass.: National Bureau of Economic Research, May 1998.

Froot, Kenneth, and Maurice Obstfeld. "Intrinsic Bubbles: The Case of Stock Prices." *American Economic Review,* 81 (1991): 1189–1214.

Galbraith, John Kenneth. *The Great Crash: 1929,* 2nd ed. Boston: Houghton Mifflin, 1961.

Gale, William G., and John Sabelhaus. "Perspectives on the Household Saving Rate." *Brookings Papers on Economic Activity,* 1 (1999): 181–224.

Garber, Peter. "Tulipmania." *Journal of Political Economy,* 97(3) (1989): 535–60.

———. *Famous First Bubbles: The Fundamentals of Early Manias.* Cambridge, Mass.: MIT Press, 2000.

Geanakoplos, John. "Common Knowledge." *Journal of Economic Perspectives,* 6(4) (1992): 53–82.

Geanakoplos, John, Olivia S. Mitchell, and Stephen P. Zeldes. "Social Security Money's Worth," in Olivia S. Mitchell, Robert J. Myers, and Howard Young (eds.), *Prospects for Social Security Reform.* Philadelphia: University of Pennsylvania Press, 1999, pp. 79–151.

Ger, Güliz, and Russell W. Belk. "Cross-Cultural Differences in Materialism." *Journal of Economic Psychology,* 17 (1996): 55–77.

Gibson, George. *The Stock Markets of London, Paris and New York.* New York: G. P. Putnam's Sons, 1889.

Gigerenzer, G. "How to Make Cognitive Illusion Disappear: Beyond 'Heuristic and Biases.'" *European Review of Social Psychology,* 2 (1991): 83–115.

Gilchrist, Helen, Robert Povey, Adrian Dickenson, and Rachel Povey. "The Sensation-Seeking Scale: Its Use in a Study of People Choosing Adventure Holidays." *Personality and Individual Differences,* 19(4) (1995): 513–16.

Glassman, James K., and Kevin A. Hassett. *Dow 36,000: The New Strategy for Profiting from the Coming Rise in the Stock Market.* New York: Times Business/Random House, 1999.

Goetzmann, William, and Roger Ibbotson. "Do Winners Repeat? Patterns in Mutual Fund Performance." *Journal of Portfolio Management,* 20 (1994): 9–17.

Goetzmann, William, and Massimo Massa. "Index Fund Investors." Unpublished paper, Yale University, 1999.

Graham, Benjamin, and David Dodd. *Securities Analysis.* New York: McGraw-Hill, 1934.

Grant, James. *The Trouble with Prosperity: A Contrarian Tale of Boom, Bust, and Speculation.* New York: John Wiley and Sons, 1996.

Greetham, Trevor, Owain Evans, and Charles I. Clough, Jr. "Fund Manager Survey: November 1999." London: Merrill Lynch & Co., Global Securities Research and Economics Group, 1999.

Griffin, John M., and G. Andrew Karolyi. "Another Look at the Role of Industrial Structure of Markets for International Diversification Strategies." *Journal of Financial Economics,* 50 (1998): 351–73.

Grinblatt, Mark, and Matti Keloharju. "Distance Bias, Language Bias, and Investor Sophistication: Results from Finland." Unpublished working paper, University of California at Los Angeles, 1999.

Grossman, Sanford J., and Robert J. Shiller. "The Determinants of the Variability of Stock Market Prices." *American Economic Review,* 71 (1981): 222–27.

Gustman, Alan L., and Thomas L. Steinmeier, "Effects of Pensions on Savings: Analysis with Data from the Health and Retirement Survey," *Carnegie Rochester Conference Series on Public Policy,* 50 (1999): 271–324.

Heaton, John, and Deborah Lucas. "Stock Prices and Fundamentals." Unpublished paper, Northwestern University, 1999.

Heston, Steven L., and K. Geert Rouwenhorst. "Does Industrial Structure Explain the Benefits of International Diversification?" *Journal of Financial Economics,* 36 (1994): 3–27.

Hong, Harrison, and Jeremy Stein. "A Unified Theory of Underreaction, Momentum Trading, and Overreaction in Asset Markets." Working paper, Massachusetts Institute of Technology, Sloan School of Management, 1998.

Huberman, Gur, and Tomer Regev. "Speculating on a Cure for Cancer: A Non-Event that Made Stock Prices Soar." Unpublished manuscript, Columbia University Graduate School of Business, 1999.

Ibbotson Associates. *Stocks, Bonds, Bills and Inflation: 1999 Yearbook, Market Results for 1926–1998.* Chicago: Ibbotson Associates, 1999.

Inglehart, Ronald. "Aggregate Stability and Individual-Level Flux in Mass Belief Systems." *American Political Science Review,* 79(1) (1985): 97–116.

International Monetary Fund. *International Financial Statistics.* Washington, D.C., 1999.

Investment Company Institute. *Mutual Fund Fact Book.* Washington, D.C., 1999.

Jegadeesh, Narasimhan, and Sheridan Titman. "Returns to Buying Winners and Selling Losers: Implications for Stock Market Efficiency." *Journal of Finance,* 48 (1993): 65–91.

Jorion, Philippe, and William N. Goetzmann. "Global Stock Markets in the Twentieth Century." *Journal of Finance,* 54(3) (1999): 953–80.

Katona, George. *Psychological Economics.* New York: Elsevier, 1975.

Keren, Gideon. "The Rationality of Gambling: Gamblers' Conceptions of Probability, Chance and Luck," in George Wright and Peter Ayton (eds.), *Subjective Probability.* Chichester, England: John Wiley and Sons, 1994, pp. 485–99.

Kindlberger, Charles P. *Manias, Panics and Crashes: A History of Financial Crises,* 2nd ed. London: Macmillan, 1989.

King, Robert G., and Ross Levine. "Finance and Growth: Schumpeter May Be Right." *Quarterly Journal of Economics,* 108 (1993): 717–37.

Kirman, Alan. "Ants, Rationality and Recruitment." *Quarterly Journal of Economics,* 108(1) (1993): 137–56.

Klehr, Harvey. *The Heyday of American Communism: The Depression Decade.* New York: Basic Books, 1984.

Kleidon, Allan. "Variance Bounds Tests and Stock Price Valuation Models." *Journal of Political Economy,* 94 (1986): 953–1001.

Krugman, Paul. "How Fast Can the U.S. Economy Grow?" *Harvard Business Review,* 75 (1977): 123–29.

Lambert, Richard A., W. Lanen, and D. Larker. "Executive Stock Option Plans and Corporate Dividend Policy." *Journal of Finance and Quantitative Analysis,* 24 (1985): 409–25.

Lange, Oscar. "Is the American Economy Contracting?" *American Economic Review,* 29(3) (1939): 503–13.

Langer, E. J. "The Illusion of Control." *Journal of Personality and Social Psychology,* 32 (1975): 311–28.

LaPorta, Rafael, Florencio Lopez-de-Silanes, and Andrei Shleifer. "Corporate Ownership around the World." *Journal of Finance,* 54 (1999): 471–518.

Lawrence, Joseph Stagg. *Wall Street and Washington.* Princeton, N.J.: Princeton University Press, 1929.

Lee, In Ho. "Market Crashes and Informational Avalanches." *The Review of Economic Studies,* 65(4) (1998): 741–60.

Lehmann, Bruce N. "Fads, Martingales, and Market Efficiency." *Quarterly Journal of Economics,* 60 (1990): 1–28.

Leland, Hayne. "Who Should Buy Portfolio Insurance." *Journal of Finance,* 35 (1980): 581–94.

LeRoy, Stephen, and Richard Porter. "Stock Price Volatility: A Test Based on Implied Variance Bounds." *Econometrica,* 49 (1981): 97–113.

Liang, J. Nellie, and Steven A. Sharpe. "Share Repurchases and Employee Stock Options and Their Implications for S&P 500 Share Retirements and Expected Returns." Unpublished paper, Board of Governors of the Federal Reserve System, Washington, D.C., 1999.

Lin, Hsiou-Wei, and Maureen F. McNichols. "Underwriting Relationships, Analysts' Earnings Forecasts and Investment Recommendations." *Journal of Accounting and Economics,* 25(1) (1998): 101–27.

Lintner, John. "The Distribution of Incomes of Corporations among Dividends, Retained Earnings and Taxes," *American Economic Review,* 46 (1956): 97–113.

Loomes, Graham, and Robert Sugden. "Regret Theory: An Alternative Theory of Rational Choice under Uncertainty." *The Economic Journal,* 92 (1982): 805–24.

Loughran, Tim, and Jay R. Ritter. "Uniformly Least Powerful Tests of Market Efficiency." Unpublished paper, University of Notre Dame, 2000 (forthcoming in *Journal of Financial Economics*).

Mackay, Charles. *Memoirs of Extraordinary Popular Delusions and the Madness of Crowds.* London: Bentley, 1841.

Maier, N. R. F. "Reasoning in Humans. II. The Solution of a Problem and Its Appearance in Consciousness." *Journal of Comparative Psychology,* 12 (1931): 181–94.

Mandelbrot, Benoit. *Fractals and Scaling in Finance: Discontinuity, Concentration, Risk.* New York: Springer-Verlag, 1997.

Marsh, Terry A., and Robert C. Merton. "Dividend Variability and Variance Bounds Tests for the Rationality of Stock Market Prices." *American Economic Review,* 76(3) (1986): 483–98.

Mehra, Raj, and Edward C. Prescott. "The Equity Premium Puzzle." *Journal of Monetary Economics,* 15 (1988): 145–61.

Meltzer, Allan H. "Monetary and Other Explanations of the Start of the Great Depression." *Journal of Monetary Economics,* 2 (1976): 455–71.

Milgram, Stanley. *Obedience to Authority.* New York: Harper and Row, 1974.

Milgrom, Paul, and Nancy Stokey. "Information, Trade, and Common Knowledge." *Econometrica,* 49 (1982): 219–22.

Miller, Merton. "Behavioral Rationality in Finance: The Case of Dividends," in Robin M. Hogarth and Melvin W. Reder (eds.), *Rational Choice: The Contrast between Economics and Psychology.* Chicago: University of Chicago Press, 1986, 267–84.

Mitchell, Mark L., and Jeffrey M. Netter. "Triggering the 1987 Stock Market Crash: Antitakeover Provisions in the Proposed House Ways and Means Tax Bill." *Journal of Financial Economics,* 24 (1989): 37–68.

Modigliani, Franco, and Richard A. Cohn. "Inflation, Rational Valuation, and the Market." *Financial Analysts' Journal,* 35 (1979): 22–44. Reprinted in Simon Johnson, ed., *The Collected Papers of Franco Modigliani,* Vol. 5. Cambridge, Mass.: MIT Press, 1989.

Nelson, William R. "Three Essays on the Ability of the Change in Shares Outstanding to Predict Stock Returns." Unpublished Ph.D. dissertation, Yale University, 1999.

New York Stock Exchange. *The Public Speaks to the Exchange Community.* New York, 1955.

———. *New York Stock Exchange Fact Book.* New York, 1998.

Niederhoffer, Victor. "The Analysis of World News Events and Stock Prices." *Journal of Business,* 44(2) (1971): 193–219.

Niquet, Bernd. *Keine Angst vorm nächsten Crash: Warum Aktien als Langfristanlage unschlagbar sind.* Frankfurt: Campus Verlag, 1999.

Nisbett, Robert E., and Timothy DeCamp Wilson. "Telling More Than We Can Know: Verbal Reports on Mental Processes." *Psychological Review,* 84(3) (1977): 231–59.

Noguchi, Yukio. *Baburu no Keizaigaku* (*Bubble Economics*). Tokyo: Nihon Keizai Shimbun Sha, 1992.

Nordhaus, William D., and Joseph G. Boyer. "Requiem for Kyoto: An Economic Analysis of the Kyoto Protocol." Cowles Foundation Discussion Paper 1201. New Haven, Conn.: Yale University, November 1998.

Noyes, Alexander Dana. *Forty Years of American Finance.* New York: G. P. Putnam's Sons, 1909.

Orman, Suze. *The 9 Steps to Financial Freedom.* New York: Crown, 1997.

———. *The Courage to Be Rich: Creating a Life of Material and Spiritual Abundance.* Rutherford, N.J.: Putnam, 1999.

Pennington, Nancy, and Reid Hastie. "Reasoning in Explanation-Based Decision Making." *Cognition,* 49 (1993): 123–63.

Petersen, James D., and Cheng-Ho Hsieh. "Do Common Risk Factors in the Returns on Stocks and Bonds Explain Returns on REITs?" *Real Estate Economics,* 25 (1997): 321–45.

Pitz, Gordon W. "Subjective Probability Distributions for Imperfectly Known Quantities," in Lee W. Gregg (ed.), *Knowledge and Cognition.* Potomac, Md.: Lawrence Erlbaum Associates, 1975, pp. 29–41.

Pliny the Younger. *Letters and Panegyrics,* trans. Betty Radice. Cambridge, Mass.: Harvard University Press, 1969.

Poterba, James, and Lawrence Summers. "Mean Reversion in Stock Prices: Evidence and Implications." *Journal of Financial Economics,* 22 (1988): 26–59.

Presidential Task Force on Market Mechanisms. *Report of the Presidential Task Force on Market Mechanisms* (Brady Commission Report). Washington, D.C.: U.S. Government Printing Office, 1988.

Pressman, Steven. "On Financial Frauds and Their Causes: Investor Overconfidence," *American Journal of Economics and Sociology,* 57 (1998): 405–21.

Quattrone, G. A., and Amos Tversky. "Causal versus Diagnostic Contingencies: On Self-Deception and the Voter's Delusion." *Journal of Personality and Social Psychology,* 46(2) (1984): 237–48.

Reid, A. A. L. "Comparing Telephone with Face-to-Face Contact," in Ithiel de Sola Poole (ed.), *The Social Impact of the Telephone.* Cambridge, Mass.: MIT Press, 1977, pp. 386–414.

Ritter, Jay R. "The Long-Run Performance of Initial Public Offerings." *Journal of Finance,* 46(1) (1991): 3–27.

Ritter, Jay R., and Richard S. Warr. "The Decline of Inflation and the Bull Market of 1982–1997." Unpublished paper, University of Florida, Gainesville, 1999.

Roll, Richard. "Orange Juice and Weather." *American Economic Review,* 74 (1984): 861–80.

———. "Price Volatility, International Market Links, and Their Implication for Regulatory Policies." *Journal of Financial Services Research,* 2(2–3) (1989): 211–46.

Romer, Christina. "The Great Crash and the Onset of the Great Depression." *Quarterly Journal of Economics,* 105 (1990): 597–624.

Romer, David. *Advanced Macroeconomics.* New York: McGraw-Hill, 1996.

Schäfer, Bodo. *Der Weg zur finanziellen Freiheit: In sieben Jahren die erste Million.* Frankfurt: Campus Verlag, 1999.

Shafir, Eldar, Peter Diamond, and Amos Tversky. "Money Illusion." *Quarterly Journal of Economics,* 112(2) (1997): 341–74.

Shafir, Eldar, Itamar Simonson, and Amos Tversky. "Reason-Based Choice." *Cognition,* 49 (1993): 11–36.

Shafir, Eldar, and Amos Tversky. "Thinking through Uncertainty: Nonconsequential Reasoning and Choice." *Cognitive Psychology,* 24 (1992): 449–74.

Sharpe, Steven. "Stock Prices, Expected Returns and Inflation." Unpublished paper, Board of Governors of the Federal Reserve System, Washington, D.C., 1999.

Shefrin, Hersh. *Beyond Greed and Fear: Understanding Behavioral Finance and the Psychology of Investing.* Boston: Harvard Business School Press, 2000.

Shiller, Robert J. "The Volatility of Long-Term Interest Rates and Expectations Models of the Term Structure." *Journal of Political Economy,* 87 (1979): 1062–88.

———. "Do Stock Prices Move Too Much to Be Justified by Subsequent Movements in Dividends?" *American Economic Review,* 71(3) (1981): 421–36.

———. "The Marsh-Merton Model of Managers' Smoothing of Dividends." *American Economic Review,* 76(3) (1986): 499–503.

———. "Portfolio Insurance and Other Investor Fashions as Factors in the 1987 Stock Market Crash," in *NBER Macroeconomics Annual.* Cambridge, Mass.: National Bureau of Economic Research, 1988, pp. 287–95.

———. *Market Volatility.* Cambridge, Mass.: MIT Press, 1989.

———. "Comovements in Stock Prices and Comovements in Dividends." *Journal of Finance,* 44 (1989): 719–29.

———. "Market Volatility and Investor Behavior." *American Economic Review,* 80 (1990): 58–62.

———. *Macro Markets: Creating Institutions for Managing Society's Largest Economic Risks.* Oxford: Oxford University Press, 1993.

———. "Why Do People Dislike Inflation?" in Christina D. Romer and David H. Romer (eds.), *Reducing Inflation: Motivation and Strategy.* Chicago: University of Chicago Press and National Bureau of Economic Research, 1997, pp. 13–65.

———. "Public Resistance to Indexation: A Puzzle." *Brookings Papers on Economic Activity,* 1 (1997): 159–211.

———. "Social Security and Institutions for Intergenerational, Intragenerational and International Risk Sharing." *Carnegie Rochester Conference Series on Public Policy,* 50 (1999): 165–204.

———. "Measuring Bubble Expectations and Investor Confidence," *Journal of Psychology and Markets*, 1(1) (2000): 49–60.

Shiller, Robert J., and Andrea Beltratti. "Stock Prices and Bond Yields: Can Their Comovements Be Explained in Terms of Present Value Models?" *Journal of Monetary Economics*, 30 (1992): 25–46.

Shiller, Robert J., Fumiko Kon-Ya, and Yoshiro Tsutsui. "Why Did the Nikkei Crash? Expanding the Scope of Expectations Data Collection." *Review of Economics and Statistics*, 78(1) (1996): 156–64.

Shiller, Robert J., and John Pound. "Survey Evidence on the Diffusion of Interest and Information among Investors." *Journal of Economic Behavior and Organization*, 12 (1989): 47–66.

Shiller, Robert J., and Allan N. Weiss. "Home Equity Insurance." *Journal of Real Estate Finance and Economics*, 19 (1999): 21–47.

———. "Moral Hazard in Home Equity Conversion." *Real Estate Economics*, forthcoming, 2000.

Shleifer, Andrei. *Inefficient Markets: An Introduction to Behavioral Finance*. Oxford: Oxford University Press, 2000.

Siegel, Jeremy J. *Stocks for the Long Run*, 2nd ed. New York: McGraw-Hill, 1998.

Smith, Edgar Lawrence. *Common Stocks as Long-Term Investments*. New York: Macmillan, 1924.

Smith, Vernon L., Gary L. Suchanek, and Arlington W. Williams. "Bubbles, Crashes and Endogenous Expectations in Experimental Spot Asset Markets." *Econometrica*, 56 (1988): 1119–51.

Spillman, Lyn. "Enriching Exchange: Cultural Dimensions of Markets." *American Journal of Economics and Sociology*, 58(4) (1999): 1047–71.

Stanley, Thomas J., and William D. Danko. *The Millionaire Next Door: The Surprising Secrets of America's Wealthy*. New York: Pocket Books, 1996.

Statman, Meir, and Steven Thorley. "Overconfidence, Disposition, and Trading Volume." Unpublished paper, Santa Clara University, 1999.

Stein, Emmanuel. *Government and the Investor*. New York: Farrar and Reinhart, 1941.

Sterling, William P., and Stephen R. Waite. *Boomernomics: The Future of Your Money in the Upcoming Generational Warfare*. Westminster, Md.: Ballantine, 1998.

Strahlberg, Dagmar, and Anne Maass. "Hindsight Bias: Impaired Memory or Biased Reconstruction." *European Review of Social Psychology*, 8 (1998): 105–32.

Straub, William F. "Sensation Seeking among High- and Low-Risk Male Athletes." *Journal of Sports Psychology*, 4(3) (1982): 243–53.

Summers, Lawrence H., and Victoria P. Summers. "When Financial Markets Work Too Well: A Cautious Case for a Securities Transactions Tax." *Journal of Financial Services Research*, 3(2–3) (1988): 163–88.

Thaler, Richard H., and Eric J. Johnson. "Gambling with the House Money and Trying to Break Even: The Effect of Prior Outcomes on Risky Choice." *Management Science,* 36 (1990): 643–60.

Thompson, William N. *Legalized Gambling: A Reference Handbook.* Santa Barbara, Calif.: ABC-CLIO, 1994.

Tobias, Andrew. "The Billion-Dollar Harvard-Yale Game." *Esquire,* December 19, 1978, pp. 77–85.

Tobin, James. "The New Economics One Decade Older," in *The Eliot Janeway Lectures on Historical Economics in Honor of Joseph Schumpeter.* Princeton, N.J.: Princeton University Press, 1974.

———. "A Proposal for International Monetary Reform." *Eastern Economic Journal,* 4 (1978): 153–59.

Tversky, Amos, and Daniel Kahneman. "Judgment under Uncertainty: Heuristics and Biases." *Science,* 185 (1974): 1124–31.

Ul Haq, Mahbub, Inge Kaul, and Isabelle Grunberg (eds.). *The Tobin Tax: Coping with Financial Volatility.* New York: Oxford University Press, 1996.

VanDerhei, Jack, Russell Galer, Carol Quick, and John Rea. "401(k) Plan Asset Allocation, Account Balances, and Loan Activity." *Perspective* (Investment Company Institute, Washington, D.C.), 5(1) (1999): 1–14.

Van Strum, Kenneth S. *Investing in Purchasing Power.* Boston: Barrons, 1925.

Wanniski, Jude. *The Way the World Works,* 2nd ed. New York: Simon and Schuster, 1983.

Warren, George F., and Frank A. Pearson. *Gold and Prices.* New York: John Wiley and Sons, 1935.

Warther, Vincent A. "Aggregate Mutual Fund Flows and Security Returns." *Journal of Financial Economics,* 39 (1995): 209–35.

Weber, Steven. "The End of the Business Cycle?" *Foreign Affairs,* 76(4) (1997): 65–82.

Weiss, Allan N., and Robert J. Shiller. "Proxy Asset Data Processor." U.S. Patent 5,987,435, filed October 30, 1997. See http://www.uspto.gov/patft/.

Weissman, Rudolph. *The Investment Company and the Investor.* New York: Harper and Brothers, 1951.

Womack, Kent. "Do Brokerage Analysts' Recommendations Have Investment Value?" *Journal of Finance,* 51(1) (1996): 137–67.

World Bank. *Averting the Old Age Crisis.* New York: Oxford University Press, 1994.

Wurgler, Jeffrey. "Financial Markets and the Allocation of Capital." Unpublished paper, Yale University, 1999.

Zaret, David. *Origins of Democratic Culture: Printing, Petitions, and the Public Sphere in Early-Modern England.* Princeton, N.J.: Princeton University Press, 1999.

Zuckerman, Marvin, Elizabeth Kolin, Leah Price, and Ina Zoob. "Development of a Sensation-Seeking Scale." *Journal of Consulting Psychology,* 28(6) (1964): 477–82.

# *Index*

Page numbers for entries occurring in notes are followed by an *n* and those for entries occurring in tables, by a *t*.